"I think he has one of the best grips arour[...] tick and he is most sensitive about its rel[...] This exceedingly intelligent book shows th[...]
—[...]

"A series of personal essays that take the literature of Latin America and of American Hispanics as the raw material for a jaunt across the Western hemisphere.... Even a reader familiar with writers as diverse as Pablo Neruda and Sandra Cisneros will find fresh insights, and the newcomer is in for a rousing introduction." —*Newsday*

"Ilan Stavans explores the ever-present tensions between his native and adopted languages, attitudes and tastes.... His book is a compelling read for Americans of any ethnicity." —*Mother Jones*

"A landmark study that explores with defiance and originality the convoluted Latino identity and its ambiguous relationship in the United States ... written with both poetry and lucidity. A text to remember and to illuminate who we are, or who we will become." —Marjorie Agosin, Wellesley College

"Stavans brings to this thoughtful, probing, often lyrical analysis of history, culture, and identity of Latinos in the U.S. the perspective of his own experience of 'life in the hyphen.'... Stavans views each of his subjects—the ethnic groups that compose the U.S. Latino population, U.S. Latinos as a group, U.S. Anglo culture and politics, and the Americas as a region—as both insider and outsider.... A provocative, often enlightening analysis." —*Booklist*

"One of the best definitive books about the Latino condition written since Gloria Anzaldúa's *Borderlands* and Gustavo Perez Firmat's *Life on the Hyphen*. It is an important book, especially for those of us who teach Latino and multicultural literatures and need such a valuable and incisive tool.... Its author possesses a magnificent eye for the nuances of the culture and its language." —Virgil Suarez

THE
HISPANIC
CONDITION

◆ ◆ ◆

*Reflections on Culture
and Identity in America*

ILAN STAVANS

HarperPerennial
A Division of HarperCollinsPublishers

A hardcover edition of this book was published in 1995 by HarperCollins Publishers.

HarperCollins books may be purchased for educational, business, or sales promotional use. For information please write: Special Markets Department, HarperCollins Publishers, Inc., 10 East 53rd Street, New York, NY 10022.

First HarperPerennial edition published 1996.

Designed by Barbara DuPree Knowles, BDK Books, Inc.

The Library of Congress has catalogued the hardcover edition as follows:

Stavans, Ilan, 1961–
    The Hispanic condition : reflections on culture and identity in America / Ilan Stavans. — 1st ed.
       p. cm.
    Includes bibliographical references and index.
    ISBN 0-06-017005-0
    1. Hispanic Americans. I. Title.
E184.S75S75 1994
305.868'073—dc20   94-5070

ISBN 0-06-092693-7 (pbk.)

96 97 98 99 00 ❖/RRD 10 9 8 7 6 5 4 3 2

To Cass Canfield, Jr.

Contents

*I walk beneath your pens, and am not what I
truly am, but what you'd prefer to imagine me.*
—SOR JUANA INÉS DE LA CRUZ

*There is no cultural document that is not at
the same time a record of barbarism.*
—WALTER BENJAMIN

*Man is only half himself, the other half is his
expression.* —RALPH WALDO EMERSON

Acknowledgments

Since I came here from Mexico in 1985, I have been reading and writing about Hispanic culture in the United States. This book was completed in the period 1991–93, thanks to a generous grant from the National Endowment for the Humanities, which enabled me to pursue this and other projects. I am deeply thankful to the following editors for space to experiment and reflect: Art Winslow and Elsa Dixler at *The Nation*; Alvaro Vargas Llosa and Richard Bard in *The Miami Herald*; Miles Harvey, James Weinstein, Sheryl Larson, Joel Bleifuss, and David Futrelle at *In These Times*; Henry Louis Gates, Jr., Kwame Anthony Appiah, and Henry Finder at *Transition*; Catherine Oloffson at *The American Prospect*; Michael Kazin at *Tikkun*; Paul Baumann at *Commonweal*; Eva Hoffman and Alida Becker at the *New York Times Book Review*; Steve Moore at the *Review of Contemporary Fiction*; Laurence Goldstein at the *Michigan Quarterly Review*; Jules Chametzky, Mary Heath, and Paul Jenkins at the *Massachusetts Review*; James L. W. West III at *Review,* published by The University Press of Virginia; Jack Schwartz at New York *Newsday*; as well as Marylin and Tom Auer and Scott Vickers at *The Bloomsbury Review*. I also wish to acknowledge the help from the staff at Columbia University Butler Library, the New York Public Library, and my colleagues at Amherst College, especially Antonio Benítez-Rojo, James Maraniss, and Caryl Phillips. Thanks to Harold Augenbraum at The Mercantile Library of New York, for exciting years of friendship; to Liz T. Fowler, my literary agent; Tracy Behar, Christopher Sweet, José Yglesias, Edward Rivera, Oscar Hijuelos, Ed Vega, Cristina Garcia, and Jaime Manrique in New York; Ray González in San Antonio; Gustavo Pérez-Firmat at Durham, North Carolina; Judith Ortíz Cofer at Georgia; Rudolfo A. Anaya in Albuquerque; Rolando Hinojosa-Smith at the University of Texas-Austin; Gary Soto and Victor Perera at University of California-Berkeley; and Julia Alvarez at Middlebury College, Vermont. Marc Jaffe, Robert Grover, and Denise Fullbrook at Houghton Mifflin, and Alan A. Williams at Grove Weidenfeld, helped open up the path to my research. Cass Canfield, Jr., my dear friend and editor at HarperCollins, believed in this volume and pushed it to a successful fruition—thus the dedication. And last but never least, thanks to my beloved wife and most critical reader—Alison Stavchansky.

I gratefully acknowledge permission to reprint segments from the following works: Guillermo Gómez-Peña, *High Performances* 35 (1986): 34; *Romeo and Juliet* and *West Side Story,* introduction by Norris Houghton, notes by John Bettenbender (New York: Dell Publications, 1965), 162 and 184; Tato Laviera, *AmeR'can* (Houston: Arte Público Press, 1985); Francisco Alarcón's poem in Juan Flores's *Divided Borders: Essays on Puerto Rican Identity* (Houston: Arte Público Press, 1993), 182; José Martí's poem "Dos patrias" and Rubén Darío's "Lo fatal," in *Antología crítica de la poesía modernista hispanoamericana,* José Olivio Jiménez, ed. (Madrid: Hiperión, 1985); Abelardo Delgado, "Stupid America," from *Chicano: 25 Pieces of a Chicano Mind* (Denver: Barrio Publications, 1969); Jimmy Santiago Baca, *Immigrants in Our Own Land & Selected Early Poems* (New York: New Directions, 1990); "Corrido de Joaquín Murrieta," Philip Sonnechsen Collection, *Texas-Mexican Border Music,* vols. 2 and 3, Corridos 1–2 (Arhollie Records 1975); *I Am Joaquín/Yo Soy Joaquín,* by Rodolfo "Corky" González (New York: Bantam Books, 1972); Sor Juana Inés de La Cruz, *Obras Completas* (Mexico: Fondo de Cultura Económica, 1966); Judith Ortíz Cofer, *The Latin Deli: Prose & Poetry* (Athens, Ga.: University of Georgia Press, 1993); Ambrose Bierce, *The Devil's Dictionary* (New York: Dover Publications, 1978); Gustavo Pérez-Firmat, "Dedication," in *Bilingual Blues* (Tempe, Ariz.: Bilingual Press, 1994); Américo Peredes, *With His Pistol in His Hand: A Border Ballad and Its Hero* (Austin, Tex.: University of Texas Press, 1958); "Side 20" by Victor Hernández Cruz, *Tropicalizations* (New York: Reed, Cannon & Johnson, 1976); Felipe Alfau, *Sentimental Songs/La poesía cursi,* translated and with an introduction by Ilan Stavans (Naperville, Ill.: Dalkey Archive Press, 1992); Tino Villanueva, "Scene from the Movie *Giant*" (Curbstone Press, 1993). The quote by Fernando Ortíz, from Pérez-Firmat's *The Cuban Condition: Translation and Identity in Modern Cuban Culture* (London, Cambridge, and New York: Cambridge University Press, 1989). Segments in "Sanavabiche" originated in my foreword to *Growing Up Latino: Memoirs and Stories,* edited by Harold Augenbraum and Ilan Stavans (Boston and New York: Houghton Mifflin, 1993). Parts of the chapter on bilingualism were inspired by Gregory Rabassa's "No Two Snowflakes Are Alike: Translation as Metaphor," in *The Craft of Translation,* John Biguenet and Rainer Schulte, eds. (Chicago and London: University of Chicago Press, 1989).

I made substantial use of "The Contexts of Chicano Art and Culture" by Holly Barnet-Sánchez and Dana Leibsohn (*Cara: Chicano Arts,* Wright Art Gallery, University of California Press) as well as the obituaries of César Chávez (24 April 1993) and Mario Moreno (21 April 1993) in *Excelsior,* the *New York Times,* and the *Washington Post.* I also incorporated segments of my interviews with Antonio Benítez Rojo ("Carnival of Hyphens," *The Bloomsbury Review* 14, no. 5, Sept.-Oct. 1994) and my essay "Oscar Hijuelos" in the collection *Prontuario* (Joaquin Montiz, 1992). Finally, under the title "2061," the preface appeared in *The Literary Review* 38, no. 1.

Prologue

I had a pleasant dream in which I saw the future in our Americas. According to my abstruse calculations, it took place in the year 2061, more than a couple of centuries after the Treaty of Guadalupe Hidalgo. Made of disconnected halves, I found myself in bizarre, almost-unrecognizable locations—one looking like Santa Barbara, California, the other, a tropical setting, probably Havana. For inexplicable reasons, during the whole dream I longed for the ugly metropolitan landscapes of my Mexican childhood, which I was able to invoke in brief conversations with a waitress I saw at a college cafeteria.

Ultramodern architecture, without the slightest hint of baroque style, was in the background in the first location in my dream. A gigantic clock hung on top of a brick tower. While I sat on a glorious beach next to a majestic academic institution, a polite old lady, almost fluent in what sounded at first like my mother tongue, Spanish, and with what appeared to be an Arabic accent, came to me offering a rotten, yellowish pear. I politely rejected it. She asked me what had brought me to the place. I answered I had come to research the life and times of Oscar "Zeta" Acosta, a militant lawyer of the hippie generation who befriended Hunter S. Thompson and wrote a couple of autobiographical narratives, including *The Revolt of the Cockroach People*. His papers were in archives at the University of California at Santa Barbara. She smiled and began feeding dry bread to hungry seagulls. She assured me that no such place still existed. It had been relocated to the East Coast, somewhere in New England. I laughed, partly because I had trouble understanding her. She then reflected on historical events and discussed revolutions and gradual social changes.

Decades after the North American Free Trade Agreement among the United States, Canada, and Mexico, also known as Tratado de Libre Comercio, was signed in late 1993, she assured me, the region north of the Rio Grande, by then known as the Tiguex River (a name first used around 1540), had changed fundamentally. A high-speed highway had been built between Los Angeles, the capital of the Hispanic world and the metropolis with the most Mexicans, some 78 million, and Tenochtitlán, a name that substituted for the standard appellation: Mexico City. Poverty was still ubiquitous in numerous rural areas and urban ghettos, even after politicians' repeated attempts to abolish it. In fact, at the end of the previous millennium, Mexico had undergone a bloody civil war, which was led by unhappy Indian soldiers of Mayan descent, who belonged to the Ejército Zapatista de Liberación Nacional. The civil war had begun in the southern state of Chiapas and spread throughout the Yucatán peninsula and Veracruz. Inequality was no longer based on racial lines. White Anglos had slowly been alienated from society and now lived on the fringes, unequivocally resented. I remember my interlocutor reciting from memory a fin de siècle text by Guillermo Gómez-Peña, a cult Chicano figure during my own lifetime:

Mexico is sinking
California is on Fire
& we are all getting burned
aren't we?
But what if suddenly the continent turned upside down?
what if the U.S. was Mexico?
what if 200,000 Anglo-Saxicans
were to cross the border each month
to work as gardeners, waiters
3rd chair musicians, movie extras,
bouncers, baby sitters, chauffeurs,
syndicated cartoonists, feather-weight boxers, fruit-pickers, &
anonymous poets?
what if they were called waspanos,
waspitos, wasperos or waspbacks?
what if we were the top dogs?
what if literature was life, eh?
what if yo were you
& tú fueras I, Mister?

In my dream a new global culture had indeed emerged, one with Latino, French, Portuguese, and Anglo elements intermingled. Other nations, including Chile, Argentina, and Colombia, had joined the trade pact originally set forth in North America, and stranded diplomatic boundaries dividing North America had quickly vanished. No more Monroe doctrines, no more Good Neighbor policies; the Anglo-Saxon and Hispanic worlds had finally become one. With the fall of Communism in China, a monumental influx of industrious Asian immigrants settled first in Los Angeles, then in Tenochtitlán, and finally in Piedras Negras. Children of mixed marriages, part Asian and part Hispanic, had increased in considerable numbers. Even for those who constantly rejected change, ethnic and cultural purity were totally irretrievable. *Caliban's Utopia: or, Barbarism Reconsidered,* an epoch-making book published in 2021 by Dr. Alejandro Morales III, a theoretician at the University of Ciudad Juárez, claimed that a new race had been born: *la arroza de bronce*—the Bronze Race of the Rice People. My Arab interlocutor, referring to the volume as "prophetic," explained Morales's thesis. Based on José Vasconcelos's early-twentieth-century volume about *la raza cósmica,* a triumphant mix of European and Aztec roots, the volume argued that Asian Hispanics, as true superhumans, had been called to rule the entire globe. The author based his argument on the new function of the Rio Grande (which he called Río de Buenaventura del Norte): Once an artificial division, it had become "just another Mississippi River," a natural sight, a commercial avenue, a tourist spot. And, indeed, in 2020, after the War of Mannequins between Cuba and the United States, an agreement was signed by all governments in the region dismantling all North American borders to establish a single hybrid nation of nations, simply called the New World.

People originally thought Shakespeare's and Cervantes's tongues would share the status of "official language," but a strange phenomenon took place—Spanglish became an astonishing linguistic force. Television, radio, and the print media soon modified their communication codes to accommodate the new dialect, a sort of Yiddish: English with a phonetic Iberian spelling. A vast quantity of what sounded to me as unrecognized words circulated.

Suddenly, I was transported to the next scene in my dream—the cafeteria, still in Santa Barbara. I had finished eating and was sitting next to the fire, rereading a story by H. G. Wells (I forget which one). The Arab woman was seated next to a Filipino waitress, who reminded me of a woman I met at age eighteen and whom I loved deeply. After much quick talk that, once again, I had trouble understanding, the waitress, for some mysterious reason, mentioned Edna Ferber's *Giant*, set in Texas. I told her I had recently been recalling the scene in the book in which a handful of Mexicans are vilified at a bar. The conversation moved to another topic: my love for and hatred of Mexico. She also referred to Morales's *Caliban's Utopia* and handed me the copy she happened to be carrying in her purse. When I opened it, I realized its pages were totally virginal—blank.

During most of my dream's second half, I wandered through the labyrinthine historical streets in a downtown Caribbean capital. By then I was seventy-six years old and was walking with the help of a cane. Curiously, in spite of the balmy, temperate heat, a heavy snowstorm had fallen the night before. At some point, I met Henrick Larsen, a mature man who was ready to act as a *lazarillo,* guiding me around. His name was stamped in my mind because of its resemblance to a character by the Uruguayan writer Juan Carlos Onetti. "Years, Christmas, and the Fourth of July no longer exist; there are no watches or calendars. Time, with a capital T, has ceased to be counted. Our present is eternal," he said. As we walked, I had the impression of being on a film set. Street lamps were lighted, and buildings had been recreated to give the impression of accumulated decay. Even a passerby or two walked as if fixed by a movie camera. A tourist heaven, I thought. I soon realized I was witnessing the Hispanic future. The colonial vista surrounding me had been frozen, immobilized forever, turned into a magisterial museum. Henrick Larsen and I entered a print shop, where a few men were busy making engravings. One of the men, who had a big belly, looked like José Guadalupe Posada, the legendary south-of-the-Rio Grande lampooner during the 1910 Revolution of Pancho Villa and Emiliano Zapata. I approached him. He told me that his trade was the preservation of the collective memory through cartoons. He had a typical Cuban accent, but most of his words were unintelligible.

"He is the silent genius, a cornerstone personality of Olympian virtuosity," Larsen whispered in my ear.

"What?" I asked. I barely understood his message.

"He nurtures a desire and determination to record the collective history, to prove that our past is well documented, widely known, at least within ethnic circles, and administered as a stimulating and inspiring tradition for coming generations."

I still felt puzzled. His sentences had a Borgesian tone. Had I read these same words somewhere before?

"The last grain of sand in our hourglass has brought us a reminder. In a fashion similar to the way all the faithful are called to prayer in the East, we are called to render an account of our stewardship. The problem of the twenty-first century is the problem of miscegenation."

At that point I woke up, uneasy, bewildered, with Nietzsche's dictum in my mind: Only the past, neither the future nor the present, is a lie. What also crossed my mind was an unspecified scene from the film *Blade Runner*, based on a haunting novel by Philip K. Dick, that dealt with, as Kevin Star once wrote, the fusion of individual cultures into a demonic polyglotism that is ominous with unresolved hostilities. As I opened my eyes, I managed to see, lost in darkness, a copy of *Caliban's Utopia* on the bedroom table. I also thought I felt the hands of the gigantic clock on Santa Barbara's brick tower move behind me.

1

◆ ◆ ◆

Life in the Hyphen

What if *yo* were you and *tú fueras* I, Mister?

Born in 1885 in Jalisco, Mexico, the painter Martín Ramírez spent most of his life in a California madhouse, in a pavilion reserved for incurable patients. Since his death in 1960 he has become a symbol in Hispanic immigrant experience and is considered today a leading painter with a permanent place in Chicano visual art. As a young man, Ramírez worked first in the fields and then in a laundry; he later worked as a migrant railroad worker, relocating across the Rio Grande in search of a better life and to escape the dangers of the violent upheaval sweeping his native land. He lost the power to talk around 1915, at the age of thirty, and wandered for many years, until the Los Angeles police picked him up and sent him to Pershing Square, a shelter for the homeless. Diagnosed by doctors as a "deteriorated paranoid schizo-phrenic" and sent to the Dewitt Hospital, Ramírez never recovered his speech. But in 1945, some fifteen years before his death, he began to draw. Ramírez was fortunate to be discovered by a psychiatrist, Dr. Tarmo Pasto, of the University of California, Sacramento, who, as the legend claims, was visit-ing the hospital one day with a few pupils when Ramírez approached him, offering a bunch of rolled-up paintings. The doctor was so impressed with Ramírez's work that he made sure the artist had plenty of drawing materials to use. Soon Pasto began collecting Ramírez's work and showed it to a num-ber of artists, including Jim Nutt, who arranged an exhibit of Ramírez's paint-ings with an art dealer in Sacramento. Other exhibits soon followed—in New York, Chicago, Sweden, Denmark, Houston, among other places—and

Ramírez, the perfect outsider, was a dazzling revelation at the exposition "Outsiders" in London's Hayward Gallery.

In a controversial text written in June 1986 to commemorate an exhibit, "Hispanic Art in the United States: Thirty Contemporary Painters and Sculptors," at the Corcoran Gallery in Washington, D.C., Octavio Paz, the 1990 winner of the Nobel Prize in literature, claimed that Ramírez's pencil-and-crayon drawings are evocations of what Ramírez lived and dreamed during and after the Mexican Revolution. Paz compared the artist to Richard Dadd, a nineteenth-century painter who lost his mind at the end of his life. As Carlos Fuentes, the Mexican novelist and diplomat, claimed in his book *The Buried Mirror,* the mute painter drew his muteness, making it graphic. And Roger Cardinal, the British author of *Figures of Reality,* argued that the artist's achievements should not be minimized as psychotic rambling and categorized him as "a *naïf* painter." To make sense of Ramírez's odyssey, Dr. Pasto concluded that Ramírez's psychological disturbances were the result of a difficult process of adaptation to a foreign culture. Ramírez had left Mexico at a turbulent, riotous time and arrived in a place where everything was unfamiliar and strange to him.

Ramírez's plight is representative of the entire Hispanic cultural experience in the United States. Neither a diluted Mexican lost in a no-man's-land nor a fully rounded citizen, Ramírez symbolizes the voyage of millions of silent itinerant *braceros* and legal middle-class immigrants bewildered by their sudden mobility, furiously trying to make sense of an altogether different environment. But Hispanics are now leaving his frustrated silence behind. Society is beginning to embrace Latinos, from rejects to fashion setters, from outcasts to insider traders. New generations of Spanish speakers are feeling at home in Gringolandia. (Etymologically, *gringo,* according to Webster's Dictionary, is derived from *griego,* stranger, but it may have been derived from the Spanish pronunciation of a slang word meaning fast-spender, *green-go*). Suddenly the crossroad where white and brown meet, where "yo soy" meets "I am," a life in the Spanglish hyphen, is being transformed. Many of us Latinos already have a Yankee look: We either make a conscious effort to look gringo, or we're simply absorbed by the culture's fashion and manners. And what is more exciting is that Anglos are beginning to look just like us— enamored as they are of our bright colors and tropical rhythms, our suffering Frida Kahlo, our legendary Ernesto "Che" Guevara. Martín Ramírez's silence is giving way to a revaluation of things Hispanic. No more silence, no more isolation. Spanish accents, our *manera peculiar de ser,* have emerged as exotic, fashionable, and even enviable and influential in mainstream American culture.

However, just as Ramírez's art took decades to be understood and appreciated, it will take years to understand the multifaceted and far-reaching implications of this cultural transformation, the move of Hispanics from periphery to center stage. I believe that we are currently witnessing a double-faceted phenomenon: Hispanization of the United States, and Anglocization of Hispanics. Adventurers in Hyphenland, explorers of El Dorado, we Hispanics have deliberately and cautiously infiltrated the enemy, and now go by the rubric of Latinos in the territories north of the Rio Grande. Delaying full adaptation, our objective is to assimilate Anglos slowly to ourselves.

Indeed, a refreshingly modern concept has emerged before American eyes—to live in the hyphen, to inhabit the borderland, to exist inside the Dominican-American expression *entre Lucas y Juan Mejía*—and nowhere is the debate surrounding it more candid, more historically enlightening, than among Hispanics. The American Dream has not yet fully opened its arms to us; the melting pot is still too cold, too uninviting, for a total meltdown. Although the collective character of those immigrating from the Caribbean archipelago and south of the border remains foreign to a large segment of the heterogeneous nation, as "native strangers" within the Anglo-Saxon soil, our impact will prevail sooner, rather than later. Although stereotypes remain commonplace and vices get easily confused with habits, a number of factors, from population growth to a retarded acquisition of a second language and a passionate retentiveness of our original culture, actually suggest that Hispanics in the United States shall not, will not, cannot, and ought not follow paths opened up by previous immigrants.

According to various Chicano legends recounted by the scholar Gutierre Tibón, Aztlan Aztlatlan, the archetypal region where Aztecs, speakers of Nahuatl, originated before their itinerant journey in the fourteenth century in search of a land to settle, was somewhere in the area of New Mexico, California, Nevada, Utah, Arizona, Colorado, Wyoming, Texas, and the Mexican states of Durango and Nayarit, quite far from Tenochtitlán, known today as Mexico City. Once a nomadic tribe, the Aztecs settled and became powerful, subjugating the Haustec to the north and the Mixtec and Zapotec to the south, achieving a composite civilization. Latinos with these mixed ancestries, at least six in every ten in the United States, believe they have an aboriginal claim to the land north of the border. As native Americans, we were in these areas before the Pilgrims of the *Mayflower* and understandably keep a telluric attachment to the land. Our return by sequential waves of immigration as wetbacks and middle-income entrepreneurs to the lost Canaan, the Promised Land of Milk and Honey, ought be seen as the closing of a historical cycle. Ironically, the revenge of Motecuhzoma II (in modern Spanish: Moctezuma; in its English misspelling: Montezuma) is understood differently in Spanish and English. For Anglos, it refers to the diarrhea a tourist gets after drinking unpurified water or eating chile and arroz con pollo in Latin America and the West Indies; for Hispanics, it describes the unhurried process of the penetration of and exertion of influence on the United States—*la reconquista,* the oppressor's final defeat. Yesterday's victim and tomorrow's conquistadors, we Hispanics, tired of a history full of traumas and undemocratic interruptions, have decided to regain what was taken away from us.

There is no doubt that the attempt to portray Latinos as a homogenous minority and/or ethnic group is rather recent. Within the various minorities, forces have always pulled unionists apart. As Bernardo Vega, a Puerto Rican social activist in New York City, wrote in his *Memoirs* in the 1940s:

When I came to [New York] in 1916 there was little interest in Hispanic culture. For the average citizen, Spain was a country of bullfighters and flamenco dancers. As for Latin America, no one could care less. And Cuba and Puerto Rico were just two islands inhabited by savages whom the Americans had beneficially saved from the clutches of the Iberian lion. Once in a while a Spanish theater company would make an appearance in New York. Their audiences never amounted to more than the small cluster of Spaniards and Latin Americans, along with some university professors who had been crazy enough to learn Spanish. That was it!

The constant growth of the Puerto Rican community gave rise to riots, controversy, hatred. But there is one fact that stands out: at a time when there were no more than half a million of us, our impact on cultural life in the United States was far stronger than that of the 4 million Mexican-Americans. And the reason is clear: though they shared with us the same cultural origins, people of Mexican extraction, involved as they were in agricultural labor, found themselves scattered throughout the American Southwest. The Puerto Ricans, on the other hand, settled in the large urban centers, especially New York, where in spite of everything the circumstances were more conducive to cultural interaction and enrichment, whether we wanted it that way or not.

Until the early eighties, Mexicans, Puerto Ricans, Cubans, Central and South Americans, and even Spaniards were considered independent units in the United States, never part of a unified whole. If culture is defined as the fabric of life of a community, the way its members react in a social context, then Hispanic culture in the United States is many cultures, as many as national groups from Latin America and the Caribbean, linguistically tied together—with Antonio de Nebrija, the first grammarian of the Spanish language, as a paternal figure. After the 1990 U.S. Census, which counted more than 22 million Hispanics—9 percent of the overall population (although at least 3 million wandering illegal immigrants should probably be added to that count)—we emerged as a solid political and social force. At that time the median income per Hispanic family was $23,446, whereas a white, non-Hispanic family earned an average of $35,975. The census also showed large concentrations of Hispanics in California and Texas, where 12 million or over half (53.8 percent) of all U.S. Hispanics live, followed by New York and Florida, where nearly 4 million, or about 17 percent, live. To put things into perspective, in 1980 Hispanics totaled 6.4 percent of the population, in 1990 9 percent of the population, and it is estimated that by the year 2000 Hispanics will exceed 31.2 million or 11.6 percent of the total U.S. population. Before the eighties our political struggles and social behavior were often associated, in the view of Congress and in governmental offices, with an image of some monstrous creature, inchoate, formless, inconstant, whose metabolism was difficult to define. Assimilation was analyzed according to our independent nationalities: For instance, many Cubans who came to the country after the 1959 Communist Revolution and before the Mariel boat lift in 1980 were educated upper- and middle-class people; consequently, their adaptation acquired a different rhythm from that of Puerto Ricans, who, mostly as *jíbaros* from rural areas near San Juan and elsewhere on their native West Indian island, arrived in the United States illiterate and without a penny. Although not all Cubans were well-off nor all Puerto Ricans miserable, many thought the two subgroups needed to be approached separately and as autonomous units. Things indeed have been reversed. Today the various parts making the Hispanic whole are approached by scholars more or less uniformly, as interdependent screws adding up to a sophisticated, self-contained machinery: Latinos are seen as an assembly of forces, in close contact with their Hispanic siblings under the border.

The discussion on how Hispanics have been assimilated has been greatly influenced by, among others, Juan Gómez-Quiñones, the dean of Chicano history; he wrote the groundbreaking 1977 essay on ethnicity and resistance entitled "On Culture," as well as studies of Chicano politics and the radical politics of the Mexican anarchist and anticlericalist Ricardo Flores Magón. This discussion has been centered for decades on what theoreticians called "negative assimilation." Immigrants from Spanish-speaking countries—anthropologists, sociologists, and historians believed—were ready to retain their ancestral heritage against all odds and costs; their daily existence in an alien, aggressive milieu provoked a painful chain of belligerent acts against Anglo-Saxon domination. According to this view, Mexicans in East Los Angeles, Puerto Ricans in Upper Manhattan's El Barrio, or Cubans in Key West and Miami's Little Havana silently yet forcefully engaged in a battle against the environment's imposing values. The Anglo, always the enemy, was seen as colonizing and enslaving, a view shared by many south of the Rio Grande since the time of the Spanish-American War. In a tantalizing poem, Lorna Dee Cervantes, a Chicana in California, author of *Emplumada,* wrote about the pilgrimage to a paradise without complete freedom: "I see in the mirror / my reflection: bronzed skin, black hair. / I feel I am a captive aboard the refugee ship. / The ship that will never dock."

At the end of the 1960s, a confrontational, bold, politically charged era emerged. The Chicano movement, led by César Chávez and the intellectually sophisticated Rodolfo "Corky" González,* which was intimately linked to the Vietnam War and the civil rights era, was, according to many, the apex of such social strife. The term *chicano* embodied the effort to overturn the dire conditions existing within the Chicano communities during the postwar period. And in their activism, Chicanos were joined by Puerto Rican revolutionary nationalists to form such organizations as the Young Lords, who fought for the independence and self-determination of Puerto Rico, equality for women, an end to racism, and better education in Afro-Indian and Spanish cultures. To oppose, to affirm one's own collective tradition, to remain loyal to the immigrant's culture, was considered essential and coherent with the Hispanic nature north of the Rio Grande. Such an attitude would often incorporate apocalyptic overtones. On the aesthetics of resistance, Gómez-Quiñones once wrote: "The forms and ethos of one art must be broken—the art of domination; another art must be rescued and fash-

---

*Unfortunately, when Anglicized, Spanish appellations and words often drop their accents. The explanation may be technological: Typewriters and word processors that are used in the United States either exclude them or have complex, laborious commands to bring them forth.

ioned—the art of resistance. . . . It is art that is not afraid to love or play due to its sense of history and future. It negates the exploitation of the many by the few, art as the expression of the degeneration of values for the few, the corruption of human life, the destruction of the world. At that point art is at the threshold of entering the dimension of politics."

Led by feminists such as Gloria Anzaldúa and Cherríe Moraga, whose work is devoted to analyzing "the mestizo world view" (the term *mestizo,* from the Latin *miscêre,* to mix, refers to people of combined European and American Indian ancestry), interpreters today are engaged in an altogether different frame of discussion. They suggest that Latinos, living in a universe of cultural contradictions and fragmentary realities, have ceased to be belligerent in the way they typically were during the antiestablishment decade. It is not that combat has disappeared or ceased to be compelling; it has simply acquired a different slant. The fight is no longer from the outside in, but from the inside out. We Latinos in the United States have decided to consciously embrace an ambiguous, labyrinthine identity as a cultural signature, and what is ironic is that, in the need to reinvent our self-image, we seem to be thoroughly enjoying our cultural transactions with the Anglo environment, ethnically heterogeneous as they are. Resistance to the English-speaking environment has been replaced by the notions of transcreation and transculturation, to exist in constant confusion, to be a hybrid, in constant change, eternally divided, much like Dr. Jekyll and Mr. Hyde: a bit like the Anglos and a bit not. Such a characterization, it is not surprising, fits the way in which Hispanics are portrayed by intellectuals in Latin America. Octavio Paz and Julio Cortázar once offered the *axolotl*—a type of Mexican salamander, a lizardlike amphibian with porous skin and four legs that are often weak or rudimentary—as the ad hoc symbol of the Hispanic psyche, always in profound mutation, not the mythical creature capable of withstanding fire, but an eternal mutant. And this metaphor, needless to say, fits perfectly what can be called "the New Latino": a collective image whose reflection is built as the sum of its parts in unrestrained and dynamic metamorphosis, a spirit of acculturation and perpetual translation, linguistic and spiritual, a dense popular identity shaped like one of those perfect spheres imagined by Blaise Pascal: with its diameter everywhere and its center nowhere. We are all to become Latinos *agringados* and/or *gringos hispanizados;* we will never be the owners of a pure, crystalline collective individuality because we are the product of a five-hundred-year-old fiesta of miscegenation that began with our first encounter with the gringo in 1492. What is applauded in today's multicultural age is a life happily lost and found in Spanglish, which the southern writer and scholar Rolando Hinojosa, the Chicano author of the Klail City saga, calls *el caló pachuco*: a round trip from one linguistic territory and cultural dimension to another, a perpetual bargaining. Bilingual education, which began in the 1960s in Florida in response to a request from Cubans who wished to allow their children to use Spanish in public schools, has reinforced the importance of our first language among Latinos. The tongue of Spain's Gold Age poets Luis de Góngora and Francisco de Quevedo, rather than fading away, is alive and changing, a crucial player in our bifocal identity. The hyphen as an acceptable in-between is now in fashion; monolingualism, people in the barrios of the Southwest enjoy saying, is curable. One of the best portrayals of Latino assimilation into the melting pot that I know of is found in Tom Shlamme's 1991 television film *Mambo Mouth,* in which the performance artist John Leguizamo (who wrote the original play as well) impersonates a Japanese executive trying to teach Latinos the art of "ethnic crossover." He claims that in corporate America there's no room for "Spiks," and thus elaborates a method by which Latinos can look and become Oriental. In the tradition of satirical comedy, Leguizamo ridicules Hispanic features: dietary and dressing manners, ways of speaking and walking, etc. As the monologue develops, we learn that the Japanese executive himself was once a Latino and that, occasionally, he longs for the *sabor hispano* of his past. Slowly, as in Chekhov's dramatic digressions—indeed, Leguizamo's piece is remarkably similar to Chekhov's tragicomic monologue "On Smoking and Its Dangers"— the character loses his integrity; while speaking, his feet suddenly run wild, dancing a fast-paced salsa rhythm. Obviously, the method for "ethnic crossover" has failed: Wherever we go, as Latinos we will always carry our idiosyncratic self with us.

Even before the publication of Oscar Hijuelos's dazzling novel *The Mambo Kings Plays Songs of Love* in 1989 and its subsequent receipt of the Pulitzer Prize, an explosion of Latino arts was overwhelming the country. Young and old, dead and alive—from William Carlos Williams to Joan Baez and Tito Rodríguez, from Gloria Estefan, Piri Thomas, Diego Rivera, Anthony Quinn, and Oscar Lewis to María Conchita Alonso, Celia Cruz, and Cortijo—novelists, poets, filmmakers, painters, and salsa, merengue, plena, rumba, mambo, and cumbia musicians are being reevaluated, and a different approach to the Latino metabolism has been happily promoted. The concept of negative assimilation has been replaced by the idea of a cultural war in which Latinos are soldiers in the battle to change America from within, to reinvent its inner core. Take the fever surrounding Latin America's magical realism, what the Cuban musicologist and novelist Alejo Carpentier first called *lo real maravilloso* after a trip to Haiti in 1943, and what has been used to describe, obtusely, Gabriel García Márquez's fictional coastal town Macondo, with its rain of butterflies and epidemic of insomnia. Incredibly marketable, magical realism exploited the tropics—largely forgotten in the international artistic scene, aside from the surrealist curiosity about primitivism, until after World War II— as an extrinsic geography, full of picturesque landscapes, a banana republic of magisterial proportions where treacherous army officials tortured heroic rebels. Foreigners' obsession with such images quickly transformed the region into a huge picture postcard, a kitsch stage where everybody was either a dreamer, a harlot, or a corrupt official. After intense abuse and massive commercialization, where Evita Perón was Patti LuPone singing an Andrew Lloyd Webber melody, the image has finally lost its magnetism, eclipsed by a focus on another scene: barrio nightclubs and alien urban turf. You don't need to travel to Buenos Aires or Bogotá anymore to feel the Latino beat. Miami, once a retreat for retirees, is now a laboratory where Latinization, as Joan Didion and David Rieff have both argued, is already a fact, and where, as the xenophobic media claims, "foreigners," especially Cubans and Brazilians, have taken over. It is *the* frontier city par excellence: It has incorporated 300,000 refugees from Latin America who seem to have come with a vengeance; bilingualism is the rule; there's little pressure to become a citizen of the United States; tourists are besieged and threatened and unhappy Anglos have fled; and huge investments pour in from wealthy entrepreneurs in Venezuela and Argentina, among other places.

Although some stubbornly persist in thinking that the so-called Third World begins and ends in Ciudad Juárez and Matamoros, the neighboring cities south of the Rio Grande, the fact is that Los Angeles, first visited by Spaniards in 1769 and founded as a town a few years later, is Mexico's second capital, a city with more Mexicans than Guadalajara and Monterrey combined. And New York City, originally a Dutch settlement called New Amsterdam, has turned into a huge frying pan, where, since the 1970s, the Puerto Rican identity has been actively revamped into Nuyoricanness, a unique blend of Puerto Ricanness and New Yorkese, and where numerous other Latino groups have proliferated since the 1980s. Welcome home, gringo! Claude Lévi-Strauss's *tristes tropiques* have just been relocated: Hispanics are now in the background, while Latinos, with their Jerome Robbins–choreographed, Stephen Sondheim–lyricized West Side stories, have come forth as protagonists in vogue.

> Tonight, tonight,
> The world is full of light,
> With suns and moons all over the place.
> Tonight, tonight,
> The world is wild and bright,
> Going mad, shooting sparks into space.
> Today the world was just an address,
> A place for me to live in,
> No better than all right,
> But here you are,
> And what was just a world is a star
> Tonight!

In quality and quantity, a different collective spirit is emerging, seasoned with south-of-the border flavors. The new Latino's ideological agenda is personified in the breathtaking prose of Sandra Cisneros and made commercial in the Madonna-like mercantile curiosity, in the Anglo arena, toward veteran musicians Tito Puente and Dámaso Pérez Prado. Again, the objective is to use the mass media, the enemy's tools, to infiltrate the system and to promote a revaluation of things Hispanic. For Hispanics Anglo-Saxon culture is, no doubt, still very much the villain, but the attitude is more condescending, even apologetic. As the poet Tato Laviera wrote in *AmeRícan*, a poem from which I quote two segments:

> We gave birth to a new generation,
> AmeRícan, broader than lost gold
> never touched, hidden inside the
> puerto rican mountains.

> we gave birth to a new generation,
> AmeRícan, it includes everything
> imaginable you-name-it-we-got-it
> society.

> we gave birth to a new generation,
> AmeRícan salutes all folklores,

european, indian, black, spanish,
and anything else compatible:

AmeRícan, defining the new America, humane
    america, admired america, loved
    america, harmonious america, the
    world in peace, our energies
    collectively invested to find other
    civilizations, to touch God, further
    and further, to dwell in the spirit of
    divinity!

AmeRícan, yes, for now, for i love this, my
    second land, and i dream to take
    the accent from the altercation, and
    be proud to call myself american,
    in the u.s. sense of the word,
    AmeRícan, America!

Our understanding of the evasive concept of borderland—a never-never land near the rim and ragged edge we call frontier, an uncertain, indeterminate, adjacent area that everybody can recognize and that, more than ever before, many call our home—has been adapted, reformulated, and reconsidered. Hyphenated identities become natural in a multiethnic society. After all, democracy, what Felipe Alfau called the tyranny of the many, asks for a constant revaluation of the nation's history and conviviality. And yet, a border is no longer only a globally accepted, internationally defined edge, the legal boundary dividing two or more nations; it is first and foremost a mental state, an abyss, a cultural hallucination, a fabrication. Latinos, as frontier dwellers, immersed in the multicultural banquet, can no longer afford to live quietly on the margins, parasites of a bygone past. For today's newly arrived immigrant, *la patria,* one's home nation, what Yiddish-speaking immigrants once called *der alter heim,* is, as Tato Laviera claimed, whatever one makes of today's United States. Animosity and resentment are put on hold, the semiburied past is left behind while the present is seized. Our generation is triumphantly ready to reflect on its immediate and far-reaching assimilation process, and this inevitably leads to a path of divided loyalty. Indeed, divided we stand, without a sense of guilt. Gringolandia, after all, is our ambivalent, schizophrenic *hogar*. We are reconsidering the journey, looking back while wondering: Who are we? Where did we come from? What have we achieved? Overall, the resulting hybrid, a mix of English and Spanish, of the land of leisure and futuristic technology and the Third World, has ceased to be an elusive utopia. Latin America has invaded the United States and reversed the process of colonization highlighted by the Treaty of Guadalupe Hidalgo and the Spanish-American War. Suddenly, and without much fanfare, the First World has became a conglomeration of tourists, refugees, and émigrés from what Waldo Frank once called *la America hispana, a sopa de razas e identidades,* where those who are fully adapted and happily functional are looked down on.

This metamorphosis includes many losses, of course, for all of us, from alien citizens to full-status citizens: the loss of language; the loss of identity; the loss of self-esteem; and, more important, the loss of tradition. Some are left behind en route, whereas others forget the flavor of home. But less is more, and confusion is being turned into enlightenment. In this nation of imagination and plenty, where newcomers are welcome to reinvent their past, loss quickly becomes an asset. The vanishing of a collective identity—Hispanics as eternally oppressed—necessarily implies the creation of a refreshingly different self. Confusion, once recycled, becomes effusion and revision. Among many, Guillermo Gómez-Peña has verbalized this type of cultural hodgepodge, this convoluted sum of parts making up today's Hispanic condition. "I am a child of crisis and cultural syncretism," he argued, "half hippie and half punk."

My generation grew up watching movies about cowboys and science fiction, listening to *cumbias* and tunes from the Moody Blues, constructing altars and filming in Super-8, reading the *Corno Emplumado* and *Artforum,* traveling to Tepoztlán and San Francisco, creating and de-creating myths. We went to Cuba in search of political illumination, to Spain to visit the crazy grandmother and to the U.S. in search of the instantaneous musico-sexual Paradise. We found nothing. Our dreams wound up getting caught in the webs of the border.

Our generation belongs to the world's biggest floating population: the weary travelers, the dislocated, those of us who left because we didn't fit anymore, those of us who still haven't arrived because we don't know where to arrive at, or because we can't go back anymore.

Our deepest generational emotion is that of loss, which comes from our having left. Our loss is total and occurs at multiple levels.

Loss of land and self. By accommodating ourselves to the American Dream, by forcing the United States to acknowledge us as part of its uterus, we are transforming ourselves inside El Dorado and, simultaneously, reevaluating the culture and environment we left behind. Not since the abolition of slavery and the waves of Jewish immigration from Eastern Europe has a group been so capable of turning everybody upside down. If, as W. E. B. Du Bois once claimed, the problem of the twentieth century was meant to be the problem of the color line, the next hundred years will have acculturation and miscegenation as their leitmotif and strife. Multiculturalism will sooner or later fade away and will take with it the need for Latinos to inhabit the hyphen and exist in constant contradiction as eternal *axólotls*. By then the United States will be a radically different country. Meanwhile, we are experiencing a rebirth and are having a festive time deciding to be undecided.

How can one understand the hyphen, the encounter between Anglos and Hispanics, the mix between George Washington and Simón Bolívar? Has the cultural impact of south-of-the-border immigrants in a country that prides itself on its Eurocentric lineage and constantly tries to minimize, even hide, its Spanish and Portuguese backgrounds, been properly analyzed? Where can one begin exploring the Latino hybrid and its multiple links to Hispanic America? To what extent is the battle inside Latinos between two conflicting worldviews, one obsessed with immediate satisfaction and success, the other traumatized by a painful, unresolved past, evident in our art and letters? Should the opposition to the English Only movement, Chicano activism, Cuban exile politics, and the Nuyorican existential dilemma be approached as manifestations of a collective, more-or-less homogeneous psyche? Are Brazilians, Jamaicans, and Haitians—all non-Spanish speakers—our siblings? Is Oscar Hijuelos possible without José Lezama Lima and Guillermo Cabrera Infante? Or is he only a child of Donald Barthelme and Susan Sontag? What does he as a Cuban-American share with Chicana Sandra Cisneros and Dominican-American novelist Julia Alvarez, author of *How the García Girls Lost Their Accents,* other than an amorphous and evasive ethnic background? Are César Chávez and twentieth-century Mexican anarchist Ricardo Flores Magón ideological cousins? Is Edward Rivera, author of the memoir *Family Installments* and an English writer and professor at City College of New York, in any way related to Eugenio María de Hostos, René Marqués, and José Luis González, Puerto Rico's literary cornerstones in the twentieth century? Is the Mexican-American writer Rudolfo A. Anaya, responsible for *Bless Me, Ultima,* a successor of Juan Rulfo *and* William Faulkner? Ought Richard Rodríguez be seen as a result of a mixed marriage between Alfonso Reyes and John Stuart Mill? Is Arthur Alfonso Schomburg—the so-called Sherlock Holmes of Negro History, whose collection of books on African-American heritage forms the core of the New York Public Library's present-day Schomburg Center for Research on Black Culture—our ancestor, in spite of his disenchantment with his Puerto Ricanness? How do Latinos perceive the odd link between the clock and the crucifix? Is there such a thing as Latin time? Is there a branch of Salvadoran literature in English? What makes gay Latinos unique? What is the role played by Spanish-language television and printed media in the shaping of a new Latino identity?

These are urgent questions in need of comprehensive answers and deserving many independent volumes. My objective in the following pages is to set what I judge to be an appropriate intellectual framework to begin discussing them. I shall therefore address the tensions within the minority group, our differences and our similarities, as well as the role played by popular and high-brow culture in and beyond the community. My approach, I should warn, isn't chronological. This, after all, is not a history of Hispanics in the United States but a set of reflections on our plural culture. (A chronology at the end of the volume offers a sequence of historical and cultural highlights.) Juxtaposing, when pertinent, some biographical information to enlighten the unaware, I shall comment on politics, race, sex, and the spiritual realm; discuss stereotypes; and consider the effects of a handful of writers, pictorial artists, folk musicians, and media luminaries on culture in the United States. I titled the book *The Hispanic Condition* because I am eager to show the multiple links between Latinos and their siblings south of the Rio Grande, a journey from Spanish into English, the northward odyssey of the omnipresent bracero worker, jíbaro immigrant, and Cuban refugee. In the fashion of the lifelong attempts by Zora Neale Hurston, Arthur Alfonso Schomburg, and the black artists and scholars during the Harlem Renaissance of the 1930s, who fought to disprove once and for all the common misconception that "Negros have no history," my overall hope is to demonstrate that we Latinos have an abundance of histories, linked to a common root but with decisively different traditions. At each and every moment, these ancestral histories determine who we are and what we think. As I am sure it can already be perceived, my personal interest is not in the purely political, demographic, and sociological dimensions, but, rather, in the Hispanic American and Latino intellectual and artistic legacies. What attracts me more than actual events are works of fiction and visual art, historiography as a cradle where cultural artifacts are nurtured. Idiosyncratic differences puzzle me: What distinguishes us from Anglo-Saxons and other European immigrants as well as from other minorities (such as blacks and Asians) in the United States? Is there such a thing as a Latino identity? Ought José Martí and Eugenio María de Hostos be considered the forefathers of Latino politics and culture? Need one return to the Alamo to come to terms with the clash between two essentially different psyches, Anglo-Saxon Protestant and Hispanic Catholic? The voyage to what William H. Gass called "the heart of the heart of the country" needs to begin by addressing a crucial issue: the diversity factor. Latinos, no question, are a most difficult community to describe: Is the Cuban from Holguín similar in attitude and culture to someone from Managua, San Salvador, or Santo Domingo? Is the Spanish we all speak, our *lingua franca,* the only unifying factor? How do the various Hispanic subgroups understand the complexities of what it means to be part of the same minority group? Or do we perceive ourselves as a unified whole?

Culture and identity are a parade of anachronistic symbols, larger-than-life abstractions, less a shared set of beliefs and values than the collective strategies by which we organize and make sense of our experience, a complex yet tightly integrated construction in a state of perpetual flux. To begin, it is utterly impossible to examine Latinos without regard to the geography we come from. We are, we recognize ourselves to be, an extremity of Latin America, a diaspora alive and well north of the Rio Grande. For the Yiddish writer Sholem Aleichem's Tevye the milkman, for instance, America was a synonym of redemption, the end of *pogroms,* the solution to earthly matters. Russia, Poland, and the rest of Eastern Europe were lands of suffering. Immigrating to America, where gold grew on trees and could easily be found on sidewalks, was synonymous with entering Paradise. To leave, never to look back and return, was an imperative. Many miles, almost impossible to breach again, divided the old land from the new. We, on the other hand, are just around the corner: Oaxaca, Mexico; Varadero, Cuba; and Santurce, Puerto Rico, are literally next door. We can spend every other month, even every other week, either north or south. Indeed, some among us swear to return home when military dictatorships are finally deposed and more benign regimes come to life, or simply when enough money is saved in a bank account. Meanwhile, we inhabit a home divided, multiplied, neither in the barrio or the besieged ghetto nor across the river or the Gulf of Mexico, a home either here or within hours' distance. José Antonio Villarreal's 1959 novel *Pocho,* for example, called by some critics "a foundational text" and believed to be the first English-written novel by a Chicano, is precisely about the eternal need to return among Chicanos: a return to source, a return to the self. And Pablo Medina's meticulous Cuban-American autobiography *Exiled Memories,* along the same lines, is about the impossibility of returning to childhood, to the mother's soil, to happiness. But return is indeed possible in most cases. Cheap labor comes and goes back and forth to Puebla and San Juan.

One ought never to forget that Hispanics and their siblings north of the border have an intimate, long-standing, love-hate relationship. Latinos are a major source of income for the families they left behind. In Mexico, for instance, money wired by relatives working as pizza delivery boys, domestic servants, and construction workers amounts to a third of the nation's overall revenues. Is this nothing new, when one ponders previous waves of immigration? Perhaps. Others have dreamed of America as paradise on earth, but our arrival in the Promised Land with strings attached underscores troublesome patterns of assimilation. Whereas Germans, Irish, Chinese, and others may have evidenced a certain ambiguity and lack of commitment during their first stage of assimilation in the United States, the proximity of our original soil, both in the geographic and metaphorical sense, is tempting. This thought brings to mind a claim by the Iberian philosopher José Ortega y Gasset, author of *Rebellion of the Masses,* among many other titles, in a 1939 lecture delivered in Buenos Aires. Ortega y Gasset stated that Spaniards assumed the role of the New Man the moment they settled in the New World. Their attitude was the result not of a centuries-long process, but of an immediate and sudden transformation. To this idea the Colombian writer Antonio Sanín Cano once mistakenly added that Hispanics, vis-à-vis other settlers, have a brilliant capacity to assimilate; unlike the British, for instance, who can live for years in a foreign land and never become part of it, we do. What he forgot to add is that we achieve total adaptation at a huge cost to ourselves and others. We become the New Man and Woman carrying along our former environment. Add the fact that we are often approached as traitors in the place once called home: We left, we betrayed our patriotism, we rejected and were rejected by the milieu, we aborted ourselves and spat on the uterus. Cubans in exile are known as *gusanos,* worms in Havana's eyes. Mainland Puerto Ricans often complain of the lack of support from their original families in the Caribbean and find their cultural ties tenuous and thin. Mexicans have mixed feelings toward *Pachucos, Pochos,* and other types of Chicanos; when possible, Mexico ignores our politics and cultural manifestations, only taking them into account when diplomatic relations with the White House are at stake.

Once in the United States, we are seen in unequal terms. Although England, France, and Spain were the chief nations to establish colonies this side of the Atlantic, the legacy of Iberian conquerors and explorers remains unattended, quasi-forgotten, almost deleted from the nation's memory. The first permanent European settlement in the New World was St. Augustine, Florida, founded by the Spanish in 1565, over forty years before the British established Jamestown in Virginia. Or simply consider things from an onomastic point of view: Los Angeles, Sausalito, San Luis Obispo, and San Diego are all Hispanic names. People know that during the U.S. Civil War, blacks, freed in 1863 from slavery as part of the Emancipation Proclamation (which covered only states in the Confederacy), fought on both sides; what is unknown or prehaps even silenced, what is left unrecognized, is that Hispanics were also active soldiers on the battlefield. When the war began in 1861, more than 10,000 Mexican-Americans served in both the Union and the Confederate armed forces. Indeed, when it comes to Latino history, the official chronology of the United States, from its birth until after World War II, is a sequence of omissions. Between 1910 and 1912, for instance, U.S. railroad companies recruited thousands of Hispanic workers, and nearly 2,000 braceros crossed the border every month to work for the railways. Also, Hispanic workers' unions are not a recent invention, and César Chávez was no sudden hero. Many Puerto Rican and Chicano rebellions occurred in the early stages of World War I, and organizers like Bernardo Vega and Jesús Colón were instrumental in shaping a new consciousness before the mythic La Causa movement took shape. For instance, after miners went on strike in Ludlow, Colorado, around the time that the Archduke Francis Ferdinand, heir apparent to the Austro-Hungarian throne, was assassinated in Sarajevo, more than fifty people, many who were Mexican-Americans, were killed by the National Guard. Puerto Rican and Chicano soldiers fought in World War II, and many more participated in the Korean War. Furthermore, Martí, Dr. Ramón Emetrio Betances, Hostos, and other revolutionaries were active in New York and elsewhere in the United States in the late nineteenth century, especially in the wake of the Spanish-American War. But very few are acquainted with these facts.

Flowing some 1,880 miles from southwestern Colorado to the Gulf of Mexico, the Rio Grande, the Río Turbio, is the dividing line, the end and the beginning, of the United States and Latin America. The river not only separates the twin cities of El Paso and Ciudad Juárez and of Brownsville and Matamores, but also, and more essentially, is an abyss, a wound, a borderline, a symbolic dividing line between what Alan Riding once forcefully described as "distant neighbors." The flow of water has had different names during several periods and along several different reaches of its course. An incomplete list, offered by Paul Horgan in his monumental Pulitzer Prize–winning book, *Great River: The Rio Grande in North American History,* follows: Gran River, P'osoge, Río Bravo, Río Bravo del Norte, Río Caudaloso, Río de la Concepción, Río de las Palmas, Río de Nuestra Señora, Río de Buenaventura del Norte, Río del Norte, Río del Norte y de Nuevo México, Río Grande, Río Grande del Norte, Río Guadalquivir, River of May, Tiguex River, and (by extension) the Tortilla Curtain. What's in a name? South facing north thinks of it as a stream carrying poisonous water; north facing south prefers to see it as an obstacle to illegal *espaldas mojadas,* a service door to one's backyard. The name game pertains to our deceitful, equivocal, and evasive collective appellation: What are we: Hispanics, *hispanos,* Latinos (and Latinas), Latins, *iberoamericanos,* Spanish, Spanish-speaking people, Hispanic Americans (vis-à-vis the Latin Americans from across the Rio Grande), mestizos (and *mestizas*); or simply, Mexican-Americans, Cuban-Americans, Dominican-Americans, Puerto Ricans on the Mainland, and so forth? And should I add *Spiks* to the list? (Pedro Juan Soto, who taught at the Universidad de Puerto Rico, once tried to trace the word's origins and mutant spelling to *Spigs,* used until 1915 to describe Italians, lovers of *spiggoty,* not *spaghetti,* and from *I no spik inglis*; the term then evolved to *Spics, Spicks,* and currently *Spiks*). Encyclopedias, at least until recently, described us as *Hispanic Americans* vis-à-vis the *Latin Americans* from south of the border. The confusion evidently recalls the fashion in which Black, Nigger, Negro, Afro-American, and African-American have been used from before Abraham Lincoln's abolition of slavery to the present. Nowadays the general feeling is that one unifying term addressing everybody is better and less confusing; but would anybody refer to Italian, German, French, and Spanish writers as a single category of European writers? The United States, a mosaic of races and cultures, always needs to speak of its social quilt in generally stereotypical ways. Aren't Asians, blacks, and Jews also seen as homogeneous groups, regardless of the origin of their various members? Nevertheless, in the printed media, on television, out in the streets, and in the privacy of their homes, people hesitate between a couple of favorites: *Hispanic* and *Latino.*

Although these terms may seem interchangeable, an attentive ear senses a difference. Preferred by conservatives, the former is used when the talk is demographics, education, urban development, drugs, and health; the latter, on the other hand, is the choice of liberals and is frequently used to refer to artists, musicians, and movie stars. Ana Castillo is Latina and José Feliciano is Latino, as is Andres Serrano, the controversial photographer, author of *Piss Christ*, who, alongside Robert Mapplethorpe, prompted conservative Senator Jesse Helms and others, in the late 1980s, to consolidate the so-called culture war against obscenity in modern art. Former New York City Schools Chancellor Joseph Fernandez is Hispanic, as are Congressman José Serrano and Bronx Borough President Fernando Ferrer. A sharper difference: Hispanic is used by the federal government to describe the heterogeneous ethnic minority with ancestors across the Rio Grande and in the Caribbean archipelago, but since these citizens are *latinoamericanos,* Latino is acknowledged by liberals in the community as correct. The issue, less transitory than it seems, invites us to travel far and away to wonder what's behind the name Latin America, where the misunderstanding apparently began. During the 1940s and even earlier, *Spanish* was a favorite term used by English speakers to name those from the Iberian peninsula and across the border: Ricardo Montalban was Spanish, as were Pedro Flores, Pedro Carrasquillo, and Poncho Sanchez, although one was Mexican and the others were Cuban and Puerto Rican. In Anglo-Saxon eyes, all were Latin lovers, mambo kings, and spitfires homogenized by a mother tongue. It goes without saying that from the sixteenth to the early nineteenth century, the part of the New World (a term coined by Peter Martyr, an early biographer of Columbus)* known today as Latin America was called Spanish America (and, to some, Iberian America); linguistically, the geography excluded Brazil and the three Guyanas. The term *Hispanic American* (*Hispanic* meaning "citizen of Hispania," the way Romans addressed Spaniards) captured the spotlight in the 1960s, when waves of legal and undocumented immigrants began pouring in from Mexico, Central America, Puerto Rico, and other Third World countries. (The term *Third World* is the abominable creation of Frantz Fanon and was largely promoted by Luis Echeverría Alvarez, a simpleminded Mexican president. Carlos Fuentes, in his volume on Spain and the Americas, *The Buried Mirror,* prefers the term *developing,* rather than *Third World* or *underdeveloped.*) When nationalism emerged as a cohesive force in Latin America, *Spanish-*

---

* See my book *Imagining Columbus: The Literary Voyage* (New York: Twayne-Macmillan, 1993), where I discuss the birth of the Americas in Europe's collective imagination.

American lost its value because of its reference to Spain, now considered a foreign, imperialist invader. The Spanish conquistadors were loudly denounced as criminals, a trend inaugurated by Fray Bartolomé de Las Casas centuries before, but until then not legitimized by the powers that be.

As Spanish speakers became a political and economic force, the term Hispanic was appropriated by the government and the media. It describes people on the basis of their cultural and verbal heritage. Placed alongside categories like Caucasian, Asian, and black, it proves inaccurate simply because a person (me, for instance) is Hispanic *and* Caucasian, Hispanic *and* black; it ignores a reference to race. After years in circulation, it has already become a weapon, a stereotyping machine. Its synonyms are drug addict, criminal, prison inmate, and out-of-wedlock family. Latino has then become the option, a sign of rebellion, the choice of intellectuals and artists, because it emerges from within this ethnic group and because its etymology simultaneously denounces Anglo and Iberian oppression. But what is truly Latin (Roman, Hellenistic) in it? Nothing, or very little. Columbus and his crew called Cuba, Juana and Puerto Rico, Hispaniola (the latter's capital was San Juan Bautista de Puerto Rico). One of the first West Indies islands they encountered, now divided into the Dominican Republic and Haiti, was known as Española (later, Saint Domingue and Hispaniola). During colonial times, the region was called Spanish America because of its linguistic preponderance, and then, by the mid-nineteenth century—with Paris the world's cultural center and romanticism at its height—a group of educated Chileans suggested the name *l'Amérique latine,* which, sadly to say, was favored over Spanish America. The sense of homogeneity that came from a global embrace of Roman constitutional law and the identity shared through the Romance languages (mainly Spanish, but also Portuguese and French) were crucial to the decision. Simón Bolívar, the region's ultimate hero, who was born in Venezuela and fought an ambitious revolution for independence from Iberian dominion in Boyacá in 1819, saw the term as contributing to the unification of the entire southern hemisphere. Much later, in the late 1930s and early 1940s, Franklin Delano Roosevelt's Good Neighbor Policy also embraced and promoted it. Yet historians and esthetes like Pedro Henríquez Ureña and Luis Alberto Sánchez railed against the designation: perhaps Hispanic America *and* Portuguese America, but please, never Latin America. Much like the name America is a historical misconception that is used to describe the entire continent—one that originated from the explorer Amerigo Vespucci (after all, Erik the Red, a Viking voyager who set foot on this side of the

Atlantic around the year 1000, and even poor, disoriented Cristóbal Colón, arrived first)—Latino makes little sense even if Romance languages in Latin America are true equalizers that resulted from the so-called 1492 discovery. This idea brings to mind a statement made by Aaron Copland after a 1941 tour of nine South American countries, "Latin America as a whole does not exist," he said. "It is a collection of separate countries, each with different traditions. Only as I traveled from country to country did I realize that you must be willing to split the continent up in your mind."

In mammoth urban centers (Los Angeles, Miami, New York), the Spanish-language media—newspapers and television stations—address their constituency as *los hispanos,* but hardly ever as *los latinos.* The deformed adjective *hispano* is used instead of *hispánico,* which is the correct Spanish word; the reason: *hispánico* is too pedantic, too academic, too Iberian. When salsa, meringue, and other rhythms are referred to, *latino* is used. Again, the distinction, artificial and difficult to sustain, is unclear; the Manhattan daily *El Diario,* for example, calls itself the champion of Hispanics, whereas *Impacto,* a national publication that is proud of its sensationalism, has as its subtitle "The Latin News" (notice: *Latin,* not *Latino*). Inevitably, the whole discussion reminds me of the Gershwin song performed on roller skates by Fred Astaire and Ginger Rogers in *Shall We Dance:* I say to-may-to and you say to-mah-to.

From Labrador to the Pampas, from Cape Horn to the Iberian peninsula, from Garcilaso de la Vega and Count Lucanor to Sor Juana Inés de la Cruz and Andrés Bello, the scope of Hispanic civilization—which began in the caves of Altamira, Buxo, and Tito Bustillo some 25,000 or 30,000 years ago ("the ribs of Spain," as Miguel de Unamuno would call them)—is indeed outstanding. Although I honestly prefer Hispanic as a composite term and would rather not use Latino, is there value in opposing a consensus? Or, as Franz Kafka would ask, Is there any hope in a kingdom where cats chase after a mouse? I herewith suggest using *Latinos* to refer to those citizens from the Spanish-speaking world living *in* the United States and *Hispanics* to refer to those living elsewhere. Which means that, by any account, a Latino is also an Hispanic, but not necessarily vice versa.

As for the pertinent art of Martín Ramírez, the mute Chicano artist whose drawings were shown at the Corcoran Gallery in the late 1980s, an Oliver Sacks–like "disoriented mariner" in an ever-changing galaxy, his quiet vicissitude in Gringolandia's labyrinthine mirrors will become my leitmotif. I am attracted to the striking coherence and color of his 300-

some paintings. Although produced by a schizophrenic, these images man-age to construct a well-rounded, fantastic universe, with figures like trains, beasts, automobiles, women, leopards, deer, *bandidos,* and the Vírgen de Guadalupe; they are characterized by heroism and a mystical approach to life. He is a true original, a visionary we cannot afford to ignore. Indeed, in terms of authenticity, Ramírez, it seems to me, reverses the syndrome of so-called unreal realism, of which the best, most enlightening examples are Chester Seltzer, who took the Hispanic name Amado Muro and pretended to write realist accounts of growing up Latino, and the now infamous Danny Santiago.

When Santiago's admirable first novel, *Famous All Over Town* (prophetically called, while in manuscript form and until its uncorrected galley-proof stage, *My Name Will Follow You Home*) appeared in 1983, reviews praised it as wonderful and hilarious. Chato Medina, its courageous hero, was a denizen of an unlivable barrio in East Los Angeles, the product of a disintegrating family who had a bunch of disoriented friends. The novel received the Richard and Hilda Rosenthal Award of the American Academy and Institute of Arts and Letters and was described as a stunning debut about adolescent initiation among Latinos. The author's biography on the back cover, which appeared without a photograph, stated that he had been raised in California and that many of his stories had appeared in national magazines. The arrival of a talented writer was universally acclaimed. Nevertheless, success soon turned sour. A journalist and ex-friend of Santiago, motivated by personal revenge, announced Santiago's true identity in a piece published in August 1984 in the *New York Review of Books*.

It turned out that Daniel Lewis James, the author's real name, was not a young Chicano, but a septuagenarian Anglo, who was born in 1911 into a well-to-do family in Kansas City, Missouri. A friend of John Steinbeck, James was educated at Andover and graduated from Yale in 1933. He moved to Hollywood and joined the Communist party, together with his wife Lilith, a ballerina. He worked with Charlie Chaplin, collaborating on *The Great Dictator,* and wrote, together with Sid Herzig and Fred Saridy, a Broadway musical, *Bloomer Girl,* which opened in 1944. During the 1950s, he devoted himself to writing horror movies. He was blacklisted during the McCarthy era, when the House Committee on Un-American Activities was investigating left-wing infiltration of the movie industry. The Lewises began a solid friend-ship with the East Los Angeles Chicano community, attending fiestas and inviting scores of Chicanos to their Carmel Highlands cliffside mansion. As a result of that relationship, James began to feel close to the Latino psyche, digesting its linguistic and idiosyncratic ways.

Subsequently, Father Alberto Huerta, a scholar who teaches at the University of San Francisco and has devoted a large part of his intellectual endeavors to analyzing the life and times of the outlaw Joaquín Murrieta, defended the beleaguered writer in the journal *The Californians,* accusing trendy Latino writers and New York intellectuals of "brown-listing" a genius. Father Huerta had kept a four-year-long correspondence with Santiago. It originated after the future author of *Famous All Over Town* reacted to one of Huerta's essays on Murrieta. They met at Santiago's Carmel Highlands home in 1984, and became friends. Father Huerta remains Santiago's most ardent defender. He is adamant about the unfair treatment the writer has been subjected to, and when I wrote critically of the controversial novel in 1993, he sent me a cordial but strong letter inviting me to change my opinions.

After the scandal erupted, an open symposium, sponsored by the Berkeley-based Before Columbus Foundation, entitled "Danny Santiago: Art or Fraud," took place in Modern Times Bookstore in San Francisco. The participants were Gary Soto, Rudolfo A. Anaya, and Ishmael Reed. James, of course, is a paradigm. Like the scandalous identity of Forest Carter, the white supremacist responsible for the best-seller *The Education of Little Tree,* and like other authors of buried background, it was an interesting career move to go from being a writer of low-budget movies to the darling of Latino letters. In spite of the aesthetic power of *Famous All Over Town,* Lewis personifies the feverish need in a nation consumed by the wars for identities to transgress. Authenticity and histrionics: in essence, Ramírez's silence and Danny Santiago's theatrical voice are opposites. They are the bookends of Latino culture.

Which brings me back to the culture itself. In a symbolic poem by Judith Ortíz Cofer titled "The Latin Deli" and published in book form in 1993, Hispanics north of the border are seen as an amorphous hybrid. Sharing heterogeneous backgrounds, they are summed up by an archetypal mature lady. The poet reduces the universe to a kind of curative store, a *bodega* in which customers look for a medicine to their disheartened spirit. This Patroness of Exiles, "a woman of no-age who was never pretty, who spends her days selling canned memories," listens to Puerto Ricans complain about airfares to San Juan, to Cubans "perfecting their speech of a 'glorious return' to Havana— where no one has been allowed to die and nothing to change until then," and to Mexicans "who pass through, talking lyrically of *dólares* to be made in El Norte—all waiting the comfort of spoken Spanish." Ortíz Cofer's image, incredibly inviting, is perfect to conclude this chapter. Latinos, while racially diverse and historically heterogeneous, an *ajiaco* (Cuban stew) made of diverse ingredients, by chance or destiny have all been summed up in the same grocery store called America. America, where exile becomes home, where memory is reshaped, reinvented. In the eyes of strangers, our hopes and nightmares, our energy and desperation, our libido, add up to a magnified whole. But who are we really? What do we want? Why are we here? And for how long will the *bodega* be owned by somebody else?

2

◆ ◆ ◆

Blood and Exile

In *The Repeating Island,* Antonio Benítez-Rojo, the exiled Cuban-American novelist and critic, claimed that the Caribbean, a basin pretty much unified by sugar and cacao plantations, is an archipelago made up of one single archetypal island, an island-of-islands, whose virtue is not lessened by its heterogeneity, a reality incorporating everyone in the region while allowing for individualities to persist. Something along the same lines ought to be said about Hispanic America: Syncretistic, essentially Indian, African, and European, and with *el sabor mestizo y mulato,* it is a result of the original miscegenation, the slave trade—what is known as the plantation economy in the Caribbean and *cacique* feudal systems elsewhere—as Simón Bolívar dreamed it, a nation of nations.

A handful of scholars and aficionados, the majority of them non-Hispanic, have tried with various degrees of success to tackle the collective Latino historical, political, and social minutiae. Most authors compare us to previous minorities to estimate our degree of adaptability and assimilation to the mainstream, from Joan W. Moore and Harry Pachon's 1985 sociological volume, *Hispanics in the United States*, as well as L. H. Gann and Peter J. Duigan's history of Hispanics north of the border, which appeared a year after, to Thomas Weyr's sociological study on breaking the melting pot, Linda Chavez's conservative treaty *Out of the Barrio: The Politics of Hispanic Assimilation*, and Earl Shorris's excessive, grandiloquent, overwritten, and unfriendly collective biography *Latinos*. What these authors frequently lack, first and foremost, is an insightful view of our cultural manifestations, so they at times confuse anthropology and folklore with art; second, they lack a regard for the Latin American link; that is, they stubbornly approach Hispanic issues from an American Studies perspective, with nearsighted results. What about the other way around? What happens when Latinos are seen as a Hispanic American branch reaching beyond the spiritual and geographic limits of a "U.S. minority"? After all, while we change, our siblings in the Caribbean and south of the border also transform themselves. As emissaries, attachés, and ambassadors, we, far and away, keep in close touch: We write, send monthly checks, telephone, send faxes and telecommunication signals, and, therefore, their daily language, their collective identity, their *weltanshauung* also change. Although it would be ridiculous to blame the 1992 riots in Los Angeles on poverty in Baja California and Sonora, and we Latinos ought not to be directly linked to the failures of any democratic regime in Argentina, Chile, or elsewhere, whatever we do or don't do in these latitude of opportunity, our brothers and sisters south of the border watch and listen to us closely—mainly through cable television, radio, books, correspondence, popular music, and the press—and imitate.

Imitation is dialogue. We imitate Anglo-Saxons; our brothers and sisters south of the border imitate us *and* Anglos: the way we speak, dress, think, and dream. And they jealously spy on us. An umbilical cord keeps us eternally tied together. If the world, as Marshall McLuhan claimed, is a small village, the Hispanic galaxy is just a neighborhood. To assume we have nothing to do with Latin America's intricate maze is to ignore a fundamental component of our daily existence. The three largest subgroups—Cubans, Puerto Ricans, and Chicanos—make up around 80 percent of the Latino population; Spaniards and Central and South Americans, such as Dominicans, Colombians, and Argentines, and especially Nicaraguans and Salvadorans, constitute a fourth major subgroup of our heterogeneous constituency. By paying careful attention to our origins, one gets a fresco of interconnected loyalties and long-standing racial and national rivalries. In one way or another, we are all children of lascivious Iberians and raped Indian and African maidens, and yet, diversity is our flag: We are blacks, Spaniards, Indians, mulattos, and mestizos. My goal in this chapter is to comment on our similarities and our heterogeneity, as well as to focus on politics and exile as motives for entering the melting pot.

Unlike the African and Asian minorities in the United States, we share one language (Brazilians, French Caribbeans, and Guayanans excepted); one cultural background; and a single religion, Catholicism (although other faiths coexist in the Hispanic world and lately a large number of believers have switched to Protestantism). Those who are aware of the tensions within the Latino community know, for example, that Cubans tend to look down on Dominicans, Dominicans minimize and ridicule Puerto Ricans, and so on: The Caribbean is a never-ending warfare of identities. And yet, as citizens of Chicago, San Antonio, Los Angeles, and Manhattan well know, miscegenation and interethnic marriages are common.

The collision of selves and idiosyncrasies acquires unique shades, depending on where one stands geographically. I still recall the scandal in the Latino community that came to be known as the Montaner affair. In 1989, Carlos Montaner, a Cuban novelist, newspaper columnist, and television commentator who lives in Spain and was on the staff of the evening program "Portada," the Spanish equivalent of "20/20," stated in a brief commentary that Puerto Rican women ought to be blamed for out-of-wedlock births and the desertion of their husbands. As expected, his words ignited a huge controversy, one that reached the headquarters of Hallmark Cards, at the time the owner of the program's television network in the United States, Univisión. Hispanic coalitions, as well as feminist groups, portrayed Montaner as racist, anti–Puerto Rican, and antiwomen. Agencies and companies with commercials made their positions clear by refusing to advertise on Univisión. They all demanded that Montaner be fired. While New York City's *El Diario*, a stronghold of Puerto Rican politics on the East Coast, dropped his weekly column, the network, on the grounds of First Amendment rights and freedom of speech, refused to let him go. The controversy subsided a couple of months later, and the incident is now only a footnote in the history of Latino relations.

Another cultural example of Caribbean rivalry in the United States can be found in *El Super*, a low-budget 1979 film by the exiled Cuban filmmakers León Ichazo and Orlando Jiménez Leal. In a scene toward the middle of the narrative, the protagonist, a melancholic Cuban superintendent in a New York City building, bitter about his exile in a cold, uninviting environment, plays dominoes in a dark, sordid cellar with a couple of old friends: One, also Cuban and a macho, lives eulogizing his past as a courageous army man during the Castro Revolution; the other is a Puerto Rican who came to the Big Apple looking for better economic opportunities and thus has trouble understanding why so much energy is wasted in discussing Caribbean political affairs. The conversation, to my mind, epitomizes the adversarial worldviews clashing in the segment of the U.S. Latino community that traces its background to Cuba and Puerto Rico. While the two Cubans support the idea that their island in the Caribbean is and will always be paradise on earth, no matter how disastrous Fidel Castro's regime ends up being, the Puerto Rican is more or less happy in his present condition—or at least considerably more so than his counterparts. Nothing stops him from traveling back to his native home, but he would not relocate because on the Mainland he nurtures the hope that his life might have a fruitful future. What he sees as the American Dream, his Cuban friends appreciate as the American Nightmare. As a result, they vehemently accuse him of complacency and, yes, mediocrity; he is not a Cuban like they are, which means his sense of heroism, as well as his political opinions, are not to be taken seriously. In the end, the discussion, having reached heated, quite offensive heights, concludes happily: The three men return to their original friendship, a fact signaling the unresolved status of their rivalry but, also, their desire not to take their animosity to an extreme.

In concrete terms, the Caribbean is as much a battleground as, say, the Middle East. (Although violence among us is mostly reduced to isolated acts of macho vengeance, it can acquire Israeli-Palestinian proportions, as when soldiers from the Dominican Republic massacred hundreds of Haitians during the bloody and corrupt dictatorship of Rafael Trujillo Molina.) Such tension does not debunk the nation-of-nations theory, but it makes me think that the Hispanic world is far less harmonious than it is often portrayed. A comment like Montaner's, to be honest, could come only from a Cuban because only the Cuban sense of superiority makes such a statement possible. Similarly, a metaliterary, Emersonian approach to literature, such as Jorge Luis Borges's, apparent in, say, his volume *Other Inquisitions*, could come only from Argentina, among the most cosmopolitan countries in Latin America; it could not come from a Costa Rican, a Peruvian, or a Guatemalan thinker, unless the person was an exception to the rule. The Montaner affair illustrates the way in which Latinos—Caribbeans in particular—respond to different stimuli. Unified perhaps by the sense that life is an eternal carnival, an ongoing performance—apparent in the way people speak, think, eat, dance, move, and sleep—the archipelago isn't a harmonious civilization, and it would be a mistake to think otherwise. Similarities and differences make factions, find allies and enemies, create alliances, and look for favors. Once Caribbeans emigrate to the United States, they adopt a new set of values. In the United States, Puerto Ricans, Cubans, Jamaicans, Haitians, and Dominicans retain distinct perceptions of themselves and their fellow West Indians.

The Caribbean's poignant history is a display of colonialism and resistance. The Commonwealth of Puerto Rico (originally Porto Rico, also known as Boriquén or Borinquén), since 1952 a self-governing entity associated with Washington, is, as José Luis González has suggested, a four-layered country. The first layer is made up of the Arawak Indians—the original inhabitants of the island, "discovered" by Columbus in 1493 and conquered by Juan Ponce de León, the Spanish explorer who also found La Florida, in 1508—as well as the black and mestizo peasantry (the latter resulting from a mixture of Spanish and Indian blood) and the ethnic hybrid created by blacks mixing with mestizos. The second layer was formed during the colonial period when a new class of white immigrants was encouraged to settle in Puerto Rico. The purpose of this immigration, now known as the Real Cédula de Gracias of 1815, was to whiten the population: After a series of recent black uprisings in Haiti, citizens of European ancestry feared they would eventually lose power to the Arawak Indians or even to African slaves who had been brought in to work the island's sugarcane plantations. The third and fourth layers— an urban professional class and a managerial class—were formed, according to Gonzalez, as a result of Governor Luis Muñoz Marín's expansive economic policies of the 1940s.

Cuba, called the Pearl of the Antilles, only ninety miles from Key West, was colonized in 1511 by Spain. The island, the largest in the West Indies, was used by Europeans as a transit port: Merchandise and exploration vessels would stop to recover from their journeys and to negotiate for supplies with their newly acquired cargo. Cuba's population was made up of European immigrants (mainly Spaniards) and African slave laborers. While other republics in South America became autonomous in the early nineteenth century, Cuba remained a colony, as a result of the inconclusive Ten-Year War. Compared to other West Indian countries, the island had a unique slave system, which allowed blacks to wander around and to influence the collective culture. Slavery was not abolished until 1886.

So is there one Caribbean or many? An example of an early harmonious link between these two nationalities, Borinquén and Cuban, is Eugenio María de Hostos and José Martí. Both were intellectual freedom fighters who were instrumental in the struggle that culminated in the Spanish-American War. Martí was a poet, essayist, children's book writer, and revolutionary who advocated Cuba's autonomy (he was called *el apóstol de la independencia*); and, together with Nicaraguan man of letters Rubén Darío, he was a supreme leader of the aesthetic *modernista* movement (a type of late-Romanticism that swept Hispanic America from about 1885 to 1915). He lived for a brief period in the United States, mainly in Florida and New York, where he founded the Partido Revolucionario Cubano in 1892 and edited *Patria,* a newspaper distributed among exiled conationals. (The suave actor Cesar Romero, the epitome of the Latin Lover who died in 1994, was Martí's grandson.) Martí idolized Walt Whitman, was highly influenced by Ralph Waldo Emerson ("we only speak through metaphors," he once said, "because nature as a whole is a metaphor of the human spirit"), and thought people who supported injustice and repression were animals, while those who fought for freedom honored their civilized spirit.

Martí's Puerto Rican comrade Hostos, *el ciudadano de América,* an educator who introduced modern pedagogical ideals into the region through works like *Social Morality* and *Scientific Education for Women,* was convinced of the superiority of ethics over art and dismissed writers who believed in art for art's sake. He thought that literature is the sister of politics and, like Martí, was politically and culturally active in New York City. A man whose pessimism and existential anxiety led to frequent depressions, he wrote "I need my days to be full of action, and they all pass by without my giving to the world any sign of myself. Each night, on retiring, fearful thoughts accost me, because I ask myself in vain what have I done, what I want to do. Dead, dead, dead. Life without will is not life: to live is to want and to do." He fought for an Antillian Federation, a conglomeration of republics united in a peaceful economic and cultural pact. Hostos was born in 1839 in Mayagüez and died at age sixty-four in Santo Domingo of "moral asphyxia," according to Pedro Henríquez Ureña. Hostos, author of *La peregrinación de Bayoán,* whose tormented, romantic hero struggles to establish the principles of independence for Latin America, was among the first novelists in Spanish this side of the Atlantic. While in Spain and as a follower of the neo-Kantian philosophy of German thinker Karl Friedrich Krause, he tried to influence liberals to support, under the First Republic, the cause of Hispanics in the Caribbean, which most Europeans considered a colony of colonies. Disappointed by the weak support he received, Hostos moved to New York, where he continued his political struggle, at one point meeting with President William McKinley to request Puerto Rico's freedom.

In their exile in the United States, Martí, who later became Fidel Castro's idol, and Hostos personified the joint effort to liberate the Caribbean from foreign intervention. They mobilized intellectuals, artists, and workers; delivered speeches; and signed petitions. In spite of their persistent pressure, at the end of the Spanish-American War, Puerto Rico was ceded to the United

States, and an administration with an American governor was set up in 1900. Cuba did not have a happier future: It finally became a republic, only to suffer recurrent periods of dictatorship (Gerardo Machado, Fulgencio Batista y Zaldívar, and Castro).

Martí was killed in 1895, at the beginning of the insurrection against Spanish domination. In 1901, in return for the withdrawal of foreign forces, Cuba accepted the Pratt Amendment, which, appended to a new constitution, granted Washington the right of intervention. (The amendment remained in effect until 1934). Freedom was scarce. In 1903, for example, the Havana government, under continuing pressure, agreed to lease to the United States in perpetuity 117 square miles, known today as the Guantánamo Naval Base.

Resistance and dependence, economic potential and political disgrace: Other West Indian countries, Spanish-speaking and otherwise, followed a similar pattern and, as I've stated, are frequently left out when defining Latin America. Jamaica, for example, has a history of repression and bloodshed. "Discovered" in 1494, it was settled by Spaniards, and captured by England in 1655. With a huge population of African slaves, who were brought to work on the sugar plantations, Jamaica was among the biggest sugar producers. After slavery was abolished, economic hardship, civil unrest, and British suppression of local authority followed, with violent consequences. It did not become an independent nation until the early 1960s, and since then has oscillated between right- and left-wing regimes and, as exemplified by the severe crisis brought on by Prime Minister Michael Manley's move toward socialism, has always struggled to define itself in economic terms.

Haiti, mountainous and densely populated, a third of the island of Hispaniola, still has Latin America's lowest per capita income and one of the highest rates of emigration. Sugar and coffee were always Haiti's main exports. Black slaves were brought from Africa with a sole objective in mind: to solidify the plantation economy, which would eventually bring the country to economic expansion. But social upheaval has been a constant in Haiti's history: Under French rule from 1679 on, the island was one of the leading producers of sugar and coffee in the region until tyrannical leaders who ruled mercilessly finally brought the Caribbean nation to political anarchy and financial bankruptcy. In 1844 Haiti had been divided and lost control of eastern Hispaniola, what is now known as the Dominican Republic. (Relations between the two have had numerous ups and downs, at times approaching war and at others establishing mutual cooperation.) Among the latest brutal dictators in Haiti is François "Papa Doc" Duvalier, who tortured many with his police force and was succeeded by his son, no less ruthless and undemocratic. Although slavery was abolished in 1801—under Toussaint-Louverture—chaos and violence have been the law of the land. This continues to the present, when the deposed president, Rev. Jean-Bertrand Aristide, with the economy in shambles, is reinstated from his exile in the United States.

Haiti's complement, the Dominican Republic, part of the Spanish colony of Santo Domingo during the sixteenth and seventeenth centuries, and at one point under Haitian rule, has also had a turbulent history. Bankrupted by civil strife after the murder of Ulysse Heureaux in 1899, just a year after the Spanish-American War, the young nation came under U.S. domination: the U.S. marines occupied it, and Washington exacted fiscal control until 1941. Trujillo's thirty-year dictatorship, which ended with his assassination, was followed by democratic elections and an enlightened reform president, Juan Bosch, but democracy, as usual, did not last long: Right-wing opposition caused a civil war between pro- and anti-Bosch factions. Washington once again intervened to pacify the prevailing animosity, and a 1966 election, supervised by the Organization of American States, restored the always fragile democracy.

A fragile political equilibrium. To be sure, the crossroads where blood and exile meet are not the exclusive property of the Caribbean. As children of the Iberian Counter-Reformation, the Hispanic world seems to be allergic to democracy. Waves of exiles have escaped in search of utopia, and millions are constantly relocated. For example, after Salvador Allende Gossens's downfall in the coup d'état orchestrated by U.S.-supported General Augusto Pinochet (as depicted in Constantin Costa-Gavras's political thriller, *Missing,* in the novels of Ariel Dorfman, and in Isabel Allende's powerful generational saga about Chile, *The House of the Spirits*), thousands of Chileans fled their homeland, a considerable number settling north of the Rio Grande.

Similarly, and to serve as counterpoint, Argentina, during the so-called dirty war, also forced many to remain abroad. This included the gay novelist Manuel Puig, author of *Kiss of the Spider Woman,* who, after a stay in Rome, worked in Air France's New York office. Nicaragua suffered civil strife during the first thirty years of this century, and again after tyrant Anastasio Somoza was overthrown in 1979 by the Sandinista National Liberation Front (named after an early guerrilla hero, Augusto César Sandino). Torture and civil unrest ultimately forced many to a better life in Miami and the Southwest, where they intermingled with Cubans, Chicanos, and other Hispanics. El Salvador, declared independent in 1821, after belonging to Agustín de Iturbide's

Mexican empire and the Central American Federation, has also failed to establish a peaceful democratic atmosphere and has been marked by guerrilla warfare. Countless refugees who came to the United States now have high per capita incomes, in spite of high unemployment rates.

Gregory Nava's melodramatic film about Guatemalan peasant immigrants north of the border, *El Norte*, illustrates their collective plight. The protagonists undergo drastic transformation from the moment they leave their home in rural Central America. Their first encounter with American culture is through the advertisements in women's magazines, where they are exposed to cosmetics, new technology, a pleasurable way of life—but only in these slick pictures. They also experience the military presence of the United States, against which they are ready to fight. They travel north in search of a better life, and are mistreated by Mexicans who they need to help them cross the border. Once in English-speaking America, the shock is tremendous. As lower-class immigrants they are forced to perform menial jobs to survive, and their lack of communication skills serves to oppress them further. Sentimental and manipulative, the film is nevertheless useful as a testimony of the plight of Guatemalans and other Central Americans north of the Rio Grande, a population that remains largely unknown and unrecognized.

Rubén Martínez's late-1980s reports about Central Americans' adaptation to East Los Angeles are an equally valuable testimony of blood and exile, as is Graciela Limón's 1993 novel *In Search of Bernabé*, the first work of fiction by a Salvadoran to be written in English. Dealing with her country's bloody civil war, Limón's narrative follows the life of a suffering mother, Luz Delcano, and her sons, two men who are moral opposites—one a revolutionary, and the other an army officer commanding a notorious death squad. Delcano is an enchanting large-eyed mestiza who was sexually abused by her grandfather when she was thirteen years old and gave birth to a bastard son, Lucio. Since she also descends from an illegitimate union—her grandmother had been an Indian servant to her aristocratic grandfather—she is forced to surrender her child to the prominent family who has rejected her. After taking a job as a servant in an upper-middle-class household, she has a liaison with her employer and bears another son, her beloved Bernabé, who appears destined for the priesthood. The 1980 assassination of Archbishop Oscar Arnulfo Romero appears in the first chapter: Bernabé, marching in the procession with his fellow seminarians, loses sight of his mother in the surging crowd and is separated from her; in the violent aftermath, she fears that he has been killed. The rest of the plot is concerned with her other son, Lucio, as he discovers the truth about his parentage and then resolves to destroy his half-brother. It also follows Luz Delcano's travels from El Salvador to Mexico City to southern California and back to her homeland. Among other things, Limón's novel offers a compelling account of the violent emotional ties that link the United States and Central America.

Incapable of escaping our treacherous, perfidious history, we Hispanics north of the Rio Grande are looking for space where freedom of speech and happiness are not forbidden. Remorse, introspection, disorientation, homesickness, nostalgia, and melancholia are our immediate symptoms. Martín Ramírez, the schizophrenic artist who was forced to leave Jalisco early on, always returned in his paintings to the memory of lived experiences; memory was a strategy for returning to a lost home. Muteness as a metaphor. While his hometown changed, he imagined its transformation from the seclusion of his psychiatric cell. Time stopped when he became mute, as it did when Adam and Eve were expelled from Paradise. When an émigré like Ramírez is suddenly forced to make a new beginning, losing his past means losing his self. The following corrido about the Juárez–El Paso border-crossing area, *Paso del Norte,* maps the loneliness felt by wetbacks who leave their homes and sweethearts behind:

Qué triste se encuentra el hombre	How sad man becomes
cuando anda ausente	When he is far away
cuando anda ausente	When he is far away
allá lejos de su patria	From his own country
Piormente si se acuerda	It is worse when he remembers
de sus padres y su chata	his parents and his girl
¡Ay que destino!	What a cruel destiny!
Para sentarme a llorar.	One could sit down and cry.
Paso del Norte	Oh, Paso del Norte,
que lejos te vas quedando,	How far I am leaving you,
sus divisiones	Your boundary lines
de mí se están alejando.	are getting farther and farther away.
Los pobres de mis hermanos	My poor brothers
de mí se están acordando.	are all thinking about me.
¡Ay que destino!	What a cruel destiny!
Para sentarme a llorar.	One could sit down and cry!

Paso del Norte	Oh, Paso del Norte,
que lejos te vas quedando.	How far I am leaving you.
Tus divisiones	Your boundary lines
de mí se están alejando.	are getting farther and farther away.
Los pobres de mis hermanos	My poor brothers
de mí se están acordando.	are all thinking about me.
¡Ay que destino!	What a cruel destiny!
Para sentarme a llorar.	One could sit down and cry.

The diverse flux of Caribbean immigrants to the U.S. mainland, including many with deep African roots, retains in number and strident power, in a unique fashion, Martí's and Hostos's painful ideological experience. Politics and literature always intertwine. Borinquén newcomers who came after 1945, unlike other Latinos, were granted citizenship following the Jones Act of 1917. They came from rural areas, looking for better opportunities. As American holdings in Puerto Rico's sugar economy increased, large corporations encroached on land used to grow subsistence food, and the resulting economic distress was not relieved until World War II. Encouraging industrial investment with tax incentives, Operation Bootstrap reinvigorated the economy, but changes were small and scattered. Racially, as well as culturally, the jíbaros share more with the blacks than with the Chicanos and Cubans. The Puerto Ricans—bringing bombas, plenas, and other peasant music and improvisational forms of discourse like the *décima* and *controversia* which encourage communal participation—once urbanized and entering a system already shaped by immigrant ancestors, soon acquired a distinct savoir faire. They retain a love-hate relationship with their native island. (Writers Pedro Juan Soto and Jaime Carrero exposed in their work the Nuyoricans' return home.)

According to the 1990 census, the 2.2 million Borinquéns, as they are known among Hispanics, rank the lowest of all Latinos on the economic scale, with 30.4 percent of their families living below the poverty line. Social and economic adaptation has proved elusive. Almost everybody in East Harlem and El Barrio is bilingual, with second-language skills acquired through formal education. While not a socially recognized asset, bilingualism and continued access to Spanish always end up reinforcing Puerto Ricans' cultural identity. As Juan Flores claimed in *Divided Borders*:

There seems to be a life cycle of language used in the community. The younger children learn Spanish and English simultaneously, hearing both languages from those who use them separately and from those who combine them in various ways. The older children and adolescents speak and are spoken to increasingly in English, which accords with their experience as students and as members of peer groups that include non-Hispanics. In young adulthood, as the school experience ends and employment opportunities begin, the use of Spanish increases, both in mixed usage and in monolingual speech with older persons. At this age, then, the Spanish skills acquired in childhood but largely unused in adolescence become reactivated. Mature adults speak both languages. Older persons are, for the present at least, Spanish monolingual or nearly so.

Entitled to unemployment and social security benefits, Puerto Ricans are ensnared in a web of governmental systems. Identified with blacks rather than with Cuban-Americans and Chicanos in their hardships and troublesome assimilation, the mass media perpetuate a stereotype of Puerto Ricans (about whom Karl Wagenheim and Olga Jiménez wrote insightfully in 1973), as criminals, drug dealers, irresponsible drinkers, incapable of articulating a self-redeeming identity—people, as John Sayles once wrote, you might cross the street to avoid meeting. When confronted by pushy journalists, Borinquéns will argue that their Puerto Ricanness is an injury. As Francisco Alarcón wrote in a bilingual poem:

I carry	*mis raíces*
my roots	*las cargo*
with me	*siempre*
all the time	*conmigo*
rolled up	*enrolladas*
I use them	*me sirven*
as my pillow	*de almohada*

Nuyorican (aka Neo-Rican) aesthetics, a rich product of their experience, developed solidly among migrants and U.S. natives like Carrero, Miguel Algarín, Miguel Piñero, Tato Laviera, José-Angel Figueroa, and Pedro Pietri (self-described as "a native New Yorker born in Ponce"), who were attempting to express in music and literature the bicultural experience of many Puerto Ricans. The spontaneous mandate was to verbalize and to translate into art the dehumanization and destruction of the Puerto Rican family, the island's political status, dilemmas of linguistic expression, and the labyrinthine assimilation process. Indeed, no adjective other than "spontaneous" describes such cultural development. As Faythe Turner has pointed out, while government-sponsored centers tried to attend to the community's cultural needs, in the late 1970s intellectuals and artists found their own center in the Nuyorican Poets Café. Created by Algarín, an outgrowth of informal meetings held in his Lower East Side apartment where poets and prose writers read their work, the Nuyorican Poets Café set up in an empty storefront across the street. Audiences from middle- and working-class backgrounds showed up, turning the place into a hangout for blacks, Germans, Japanese, and Irish, as well as Puerto Ricans. They eventually branched out to include a radio station.

Proto-Nuyorican figures, like newspaper columnist Jesús Colón, who was born in Cayey and died in 1974, count among the most illustrious Puerto Rican militants, linking words and action, advocating the improvement of life in the Puerto Rican community and an end to exile. Colón, a Bolshevik sympathizer already identified with left-wing causes in his hometown, at the age of seventeen stowed away on the SS *Carolina* bound for New York City, where he lived for five decades, continuing his socialist struggle and writing a regular column for the *Daily Worker,* the Communist party newspaper. After holding menial jobs like dishwasher, dock worker, and postal clerk, he presided over Hispanic Publishers, an imprint dedicated to Puerto Rican history, political, and literary books, which published collections of stories in Spanish by José Luis González, like *Five Tales of Blood.* Subpoenaed by the House Committee on Un-American Activities, he ran for the U.S. Senate on the American Labor Party ticket, and in 1969, the same year Norman Mailer ran for mayor, was defeated in a campaign for controller of the city of New York. Colón is the author of *The Way It Was and Other Writings,* a testimonial account of major Puerto Rican figures and organizations in New York. But he is better known for his landmark work of essays and reminiscences, *A Puerto Rican in New York and Other Sketches,* which consists of articles published in periodicals about Borinquén on the mainland, the working class in general, the link between Cuban and Puerto Rican roots, and the role that Latinos played in the early formation and activities of the U.S. Communist party.

Bernardo Vega, a lifelong *tabaquero,* born in 1885, was a friend of Colón, also had left-wing views, and was another crucial Puerto Rican activist. He participated in the early years of the Federación Libre de Trabajadores, a working-class organization on the island, and later became a charter member of the Partido Socialista, founded in 1915. Like his comrade, he carried his revolutionary goals with him when he moved to New York. Also under surveillance and a target of the House Committee on Un-American Activities during the McCarthy period, Vega quickly sympathized with the ideology of the Cuban Revolution of 1958 and pushed to consolidate Puerto Rico's Movimiento pro Independencia, a major political force on the island after World War II. His decades in the United States were full of activism and self-education, and, although he returned to Puerto Rico at the end of his life (he died in 1965), Vega was a fixture in the mainland community. His *Memoirs,* written in Spanish in the 1940s, remained unpublished until 1977. Vega's original goal, as his friend and editor César Andreu Iglesias claimed, was to narrate his life in the third person, creating a character called Bernardo Farallón, the surname referring to a rural area where he was born. But half-way through the narrative, he forgets to pursue the fictional aspect and continues in a strictly autobiographical tone. Unlike *A Puerto Rican in New York,* what makes the volume extraordinary is the historical data it provides on the creation of New York's Puerto Rican community and its discussion of the odyssey of exiles Ramón Emetrio Betances, Hostos, Martí, and other nineteenth-century ideological forefathers. Vega also referred extensively to Arthur Alfonso Schomburg, the Puerto Rico–born scholar and bibliophile attached to the Harlem Renaissance, whom I will discuss in the next chapter, and presented an account of the Partido Nacionalista under the leadership of Pedro Albizu Campos, who, considered a dangerous force as an early *independentista,* stood on trial in 1936 in San Juan's Federal Court and was sentenced to prison, an event that caused an uproar in New York's Hispanic community.

Have the Puerto Ricans at home and in the United States been too docile, too submissive? To this day, in spite of the furious fight by Colón, Vega, and others, stereotypes are the Borinquéns' worst enemy. As Linda Chavez shows in *Out of the Barrio: Toward a New Politics of Hispanic Assimilation*, since the 1960s governmental officials have often talked about "the Puerto Rican problem": criminality, the preponderance of drugs, the lack of education, poverty, and other forms of cyclical misery in El Barrio. Having exchanged their mountain homes for city buildings, their collective ties to the Caribbean island are diffuse, at least superficially. Puerto Ricans are represented as lacking character and self-esteem, domesticated, harmless, submissive, gentle to the point of naïveté, out of touch with themselves—"human trash" as far as the rest of the United States is concerned. This negative collective identity, their ghost life in U.S. cities, is thoroughly discussed, not only by American researchers and social analysts, but by Borinquéns in the island and abroad. Among the most famous discussants was René Marqués, who was a force in the renewal of Puerto Rican theater and culture. Born in 1914, a published poet at age twenty-five and an admirer of Miguel de Unamuno and Jean-Paul Sartre, he spent his artistic life exploring the concept of docility in plays about the social and historical patterns of his people at home and in New York City. Nationalism, for example, is the major theme of *Palm Sunday*, about a massacre in Ponce; in *The Oxcart*, a highly regarded play displaying a verbal style that projects explosive degradation and corruption, he deals with the pilgrimage of a jíbaro family from the Puerto Rican countryside to New York City's slums; and in *Mutilated Suns*, a play about progress, modernization, and the entrance of the American style of life on the island, he studies the inner life of three aristocratic sisters, hidden in their run-down mansion on Calle de Cristo in San Juan. In his essay "Docile Puerto Ricans," which was included in a volume that was translated into English in 1976, Marqués responded to Alfred Kazin's opinions about the island that were published in *Commentary*. "Docile," he writes, "from the Latin *docilis*, means 'obedient' or 'fulfilling the wishes of the one who commands.' Sainz de Robles cites, among other synonyms of the word, 'meek' and 'submissive,' which seems to be characteristic of the generally held meaning. For *docility* (the quality of being docile), the same scholar gives us 'subordination,' 'meekness,' 'submission.'" To tolerate the humiliations from abroad, Borinquéns, Marqués thought, see themselves as inferior, an admission that evidently injures their innermost self-esteem and takes the form of extreme reactions like antagonism and surrender. Thus, Marqués studied Puerto Ricans' resignation to their dependent condition (as a nation and as individuals) and the collective inferiority complex vis-à-vis Anglo-Saxons. Yet, his conclusion, it is sad to say, reinforced the acceptance of conditions: Since docility is historical, it is somehow acceptable. His complacent attitude reminds me of the remarks of José de Diego, a Puerto Rican statesman, poet, and political leader, who died in 1918 a fervent defender of the island's political independence. In an essay entitled "No," he claimed:

We do not know how to say "no," and we are attracted, unconscious, like a hypnotic suggestion, by the predominant *sí* of the world of thought, of the form of essence—artists and weak and kindly, as we have been by the generosity of our land. Never, in general terms, does a Puerto Rican say, nor does he know how to say, "no"; "We'll see," "I'll study the matter," "I'll decide later"; when a Puerto Rican uses these expressions, it must be understood that he doesn't want to; at most, he joins the *sí* with the *no* and with the affirmative and negative adverbs makes a conditional conjunction, ambiguous, nebulous, in which the will fluctuates in the air, like a little bird aimless and shelterless on the flatness of a desert. . . .

A landmark 1957 Broadway play at the Winter Garden Theater and an acclaimed film, *West Side Story* is an endearing retelling of Shakespeare's tragedy *Romeo and Juliet* reconciled as a social document. Although it tried to portray the explosive reality of Puerto Rican life in the slums of New York, it remains the venue for Anglos to approach mainstream Puerto Ricanness. Filmed in 1961 by Robert Wise, with music by Leonard Bernstein, *West Side Story* is set in a poor, racially diverse West Side neighborhood where Puerto Ricans are the minority. The feuding houses of Montague and Capulet have their counterparts in the rival gangs, the Sharks and the Jets, suspicious and alienated from each other and society. María is young, innocent, and virginal. Chino is her macho brother, intransigent, tyrannical, undaunted. Although the police are after both gangs in the neighborhood, the play certainly doesn't treat the opposing factions in similar terms; from the beginning, Puerto Ricans are harassed, offended by authority, and attacked verbally. Doom, disaster, death—in the end, the pessimistic message of *West Side Story* is that miscegenation and interracial encounters cannot come without suffering and loss. María, the only true survivor, is left alone without a courtier and a brother. If, as W. H. Auden once argued, *Romeo and Juliet* "is not simply a tragedy of two individuals but the tragedy of a city. Everybody in the city is in one way or another involved in and responsible for what happens," its musical adaptation is about the tragedy of urban racial stereotypes in a turbulent metropolis. Who are María, Bernardo, Anita, Pepe, and Consuelo? The male characters of Puerto Rican descent are machos longing for a less risky life in the tropics, whereas their women uniformly appreciate the challenge of the American Dream. Otherness is represented by brown-colored skin. (In the film, Italians have white skin and no accent). The hostility between Italians and Puerto Ricans, and the gang wars they undergo, only continues to perpetuate stereotypes about the size of Hispanic families, as well as the lust and violence inhabiting the Hispanic psyche. And yet, as with Dandy Santiago's *Famous All Over Town*, the film, which for quite some long time monopolized the fashion in which the United States approached Puerto

Ricans on the Mainland, is immensely enjoyable. At the time it was made it courageously dramatized segregation, ethnic strife, and miscegenation in an urban environment. A new generation might find it outdated and naive, but there was considerable talent in the production.

The Borinquén literature, written in English, full of first-person accounts, journalistic pieces, and autobiographical narratives about immigrant life in the slums, must always be considered in light of its counterpart in Spanish from the island. Such a cultural abyss separates them, such a profound sense of misunderstanding and betrayal, that I am tempted to portray them as twins that were separated at birth, each reacting to different aesthetic, political, and sociological stimuli, united only by their shared love-hate relationship with New York and a strange need to remember each other in bizarre, nostalgic terms. Linguistically, writers who reside on the Mainland can be divided into three groups: those who, involuntarily or by choice, embraced English as their creative language; those who didn't; and those, a solid number, who oscillate between English and Spanish. Although some critics would hesitate to include him, William Carlos Williams, the child of a Puerto Rican mother and an English father raised in the Caribbean, exemplifies the first group, alongside Nicholasa Mohr, Judith Ortíz Cofer, and New York Criminal Court Justice Edwin Torres. Luis Rafael Sánchez, the author of the outstanding novel *Macho Camacho's Beat,* who teaches at City College (an academic institution omnipresent in mainland Puerto Rican letters), belongs to the second group, together with Rosario Ferré and Julia de Burgos. Burgos, Puerto Rico's greatest female poet, lived both in Washington, D.C., and New York, a city she saw as cold and inhospitable and where she repeatedly suffered from alcoholism and was hospitalized (during one of these hospital stays, she wrote "Farewell in Welfare Island"). In 1953, on an indifferent street, she was found dead without any identification. Ed Vega, who has written novels in English and Spanish (or Spanglish), leads the third group, along with Miguel Algarín, who, together with the playwright Miguel Piñero, was the first to identify the group of writers known today as Nuyoricans.

As critic Eugene Mohr states in his study of Puerto Rican literature in the United States, *The Nuyorican Experience,* the tongue these authors use to write in does not preclude a concrete ideological position. Although it is generally unknown, the forefather of the entire mainland Borinquén movement was Francisco Gonzalo "Pichín" Marín, a typesetter who died fighting in Cuba and whose romantic poetry, in Spanish, like the prose of his successors Manuel Zeno Gandía and José de Diego Padró, offers a view of hopeless

Puerto Rican immigrant life in New York. Then came Jesús Colón, whose contemporaries who were active in Spanish included Marqués, Bernardo Vega, Pedro Juan Soto, and José Luis González. What makes Colón, the author of *A Puerto Rican in New York*, remarkable is that he switched to English to reach a wider audience, a decision that earned him the reputation of a sell-out among some peers and which I will discuss, in detail, in Chapter 7.

Actually, before Colón was William Carlos Williams, whose novel *A Voyage to Pagany* was published in 1928. Born in 1883, Williams had a life-long medical practice in Rutherford, New Jersey, the Paterson of his poems.* One of his most original semifictional works was *In the American Grain,* a collection of vignettes about Columbus, Hernán Cortés, Daniel Boone, Sir Walter Raleigh, and other crucial figures in the shaping of the Americas. This was a groundbreaking book in the Latino cultural progression. After a long silence came Piri Thomas, who wrote *Down These Mean Streets,* to be discussed in Chapter 6, followed by Pedro Juan Soto, born in Cataño in 1928, who may well be the most idiosyncratic Puerto Rican writer. Soto was a professor at the Universidad de Puerto Rico for many years, and his collection of stories, *Spiks,* is a remarkable piece of writing, considered by William Kennedy to be "pure gold as subject matter." Equally important are Nicholasa Mohr's *El Bronx Remembered,* a finalist for the National Book Award, and *Rituals of Survival: A Woman's Portfolio*; Ed Vega's *Mendoza's Dreams*; Judith Ortíz Cofer's *Silent Dancing*; and Martín Espada's socially conscious poetry in *Rebellion is the Circle of a Lover's Hands,* among other volumes. Espada's experience as a lawyer representing low-income residents, mostly Latinos, in Boston, through Su Clínica Legal, sharply marked his poetic voice. As he put it, his verses are "testimony, taken from my own life, and poems of advocacy, based on the lives of those customarily consigned to silence, who would make their own best advocates given the chance."

Miguel Piñero, who died prematurely in 1988 and whose prison drama *Short Eyes,* about power and prison violence, was awarded an Obie and the New York Drama Critics Circle Award for the best play of the 1973–74 season, is another outstanding member of the Borinquén literary progression. Piñero was born in Gurabo, Puerto Rico in 1946 and raised on the Lower East Side; as an adolescent he was often arrested for shoplifting and other crimes and was repeatedly sentenced to jail. Piñero began writing as a Sing Sing prison inmate for Clay Stevenson's theater workshop. "I write to sur-

---

*See Julio Marzán's interesting discussion in *The Hispanic American Influence in William Carlos Williams* (Austin: University of Texas Press, 1994).

vive," he once told an interviewer. Aside from other plays and poems, he wrote several screenplays and had cameo acting roles in *The Godfather* and *Fort Apache, the Bronx*. His themes are child molestation, racism, and an attack on middle-class aesthetics.

Among my favorite Puerto Rican writers in English is Edward Rivera, born in Orocovis, Puerto Rico, in 1944, and on the faculty of City College, New York, who is a most peculiar author in this tradition. Under the editorial guidance of Ted Solotaroff, he published segments of a memoir in prominent magazines and, with governmental funding, finished *Family Installments* in 1982, an enchanting account of growing up Latino in the United States. Another addition to the list is Abraham Rodríguez, Jr., whose collection of stories, *The Boy Without a Flag,* opens with a revealing epigraph from John Dos Passos's *The Big Money* (the third installment to his trilogy *U.S.A.*), "The language of the beaten nation is not forgotten in our ears tonight." The book includes seven narratives, about teenage mothers who leave their newborn babies alone as a sign of rebellion against the babies' irresponsible fathers, and about children of frustrated *independentistas* in New York who refuse to salute the American flag in school. Although the quality of the writing is uneven, the subject matter is gut-wrenching: the plight of dispossessed Puerto Ricans in the United States, forgotten by society. The harsh street jargon that Rodríguez uses, his themes, and his somber cast of characters—junkies and drug dealers, pregnant girls, and prison inmates—have been criticized by his fellow English-writing Puerto Rican literati, either in open attacks or in uncompromising silences. Thus, while Mohr and others have endorsed other less-exciting new voices, they have refused to acknowledge Rodríguez, and Ed Vega, once a friend and supporter, has accused him of benefiting from a Manichaean portrait of stereotypes. Rodríguez's *Spidertown* is written in broken English ("I don spee Englitch lie ju. *Soy hispano, puñeta*," a character claims) to re-create the violent reality of crack addicts and arsonists and other criminals. The novel follows the life of Miguel, a runner who works for the crack kingpin Spider, as he tries to distance himself from the milieu that made him rich and to remain loyal to his love Cristalena, a female protagonist with Victorian attributes, while Firebug, Miguel's roommate, accompanies him through an erotic, high-time fiesta. Dialogue is the author's unbeatable strength, and most chapters have numerous tête-à-têtes, a device that makes the plot move slowly but allows for an extraordinary study of the linguistic cadence of English-speaking Puerto Ricans.

Whereas most Puerto Rican immigrants were uneducated jíbaros, an intellectual elite made up of scientists, professors, and artists were attracted by appointments at prestigious academic institutions and better jobs and left the island during Muñoz Marín's modernization regime, in what Hispanic Americans call *fuga de cerebros*: an endless brain drain. A similar phenomenon took place in the Dominican Republic. In general, Dominicans, who have made New York City their capital in exile, lack a Nuyorican culture simply because fewer have left the Dominican Republic and their emigration is more recent. After the repressive Trujillo regime fell in 1961, social chaos and economic uncertainty prevailed, and waves of people moved to the United States, many prospering quickly and with little, if any, governmental support. The career and work of Julia Alvarez, an upper middle-class Dominican writer teaching at Middlebury College in Vermont, illustrates the division between educated immigrants and grass-roots workers. Much in the tradition of nineteenth-century Russian realism, and along the lines of the genuine porcelain narrative creations of Nina Berberova, Alvarez's first novel, *How the García Girls Lost Their Accents,* has as its protagonist the energetic, curious, and bellicose Garcías de la Torres, a rich family in Santo Domingo and its surroundings whose genealogical tree reaches back to the Spanish conquistadors. Through the García family's sorrow and happiness and the spiritual and quotidian search that leads to their exile in the United States, the dramatic changes of an entire era are recorded. The family's collective plight is a struggle to keep up with the times and to adjust to a foreign, often alienating culture. The plot focuses on Carla, Sandra (aka Sandi, following the Hispanic tradition of multiple individual appellations), Yolanda (Yo, Yoyo, or Joe), and Sofía (Fifi), their sisterhood and their aristocratic upbringing as SAPs (Spanish-American Princesses), from their "savage Caribbean island" to prestigious schools in New England and to middle-class life in the Bronx. The sisters' experiences with discrimination, linguistic misunderstandings, and difficult marriages illustrate the customary rite of passage of Latino immigrants into the melting pot. They discover, in Julia Alvarez's own words (written in a personal essay), that the in-between place in which they live "is not just one of friction and tension but one that offers unique perspectives, visions, energy, choices."

One of the factors that unifies the various Caribbean groups is the economy they were all part of. The Antilles, as I have stated, flourished thanks to its sugar and cacao plantations, a system that saw itself as an independent unit—a country within a country. So one is pushed to find a common denominator: Is there really such thing as the Caribbean people? Yes and no.

Puerto Ricans, Dominicans, Jamaicans, Haitians, and Cubans can be distinguished in numerous ways—by the language they speak, the history that shaped them, their worldview, their self-esteem, etc. Back at home, their patriotism is nurtured by ancestral differences that often amount to rivalries. Each nation has followed a considerably different pattern of development. But once the various citizens of the Caribbean become partners in the search for the American Dream, they create strange, unlikely alliances they would never agree to on their native soil. Tensions permeate inter-Caribbean relations; but when facing Anglos or even other Hispanics, the sense of unity becomes curiously inviting.

I shall now devote myself to the other important Caribbean subgroup. Among the most educated, well-off Latinos, Cuban-Americans, most of whom blame their migration on Fidel Castro's revolution, were members of educated upper- and middle-income families in Cuba who were reluctant to lose their class privileges when they came to the United States. Thus, their ascendance in the social hierarchy in this country was comparatively faster, easier, and more impressive than those of other Latino groups. According to the 1990 census, Cuban-Americans have the lowest unemployment rate (5.8 percent) and the highest per capita income ($33,500) of any Latino group. New Jersey and Florida (Miami, Hialeah, and Key West were already populated by Cubans in the late nineteenth and early twentieth centuries) have become urban centers for them. They have learned English faster than Chicanos and Puerto Ricans, and they are known for openly airing their ideological viewpoints. First-, second-, and third-generation Cuban exiles in Florida are torn between an imagined Eden left behind and their present status as secure American citizens. As a group, they are extremely influential in Washington affairs. Yet, they have not become totally assimilated (and are not likely to do so), simply because their attitude is colored by a melancholic rhythm, a vague commitment. While claiming to be ready to return to their native land when Castro's dictatorship falls, they contribute to producing and enjoying the irresistible fruits of the American Dream without fully embracing it. Indeed, Miami is known as a bastion of anti-Castro, often right-wing resistance, and *El Nuevo Herald,* a Spanish-language newspaper, has tremendous local and national political power. A handful of reporters and essayists have discussed the dilemma of Cuban exiles, most notably David Rieff, whose *The Exile: Cuba in the Heart of Miami,* published in 1993, is a thorough study of its beginning and foreseeable consequences. What these writers do best is explain the meaning of *el exilio,* a bizarre, phantasmagorical state of mind, what Czeslaw

Milosz called "the memory of wounds" and Julio Cortázar called "the feeling of being not all there." José Martí's immortal poem, "Dos patrias," known in English as "Motherlands," conveys the spiritual impact of exile. A segment:

Dos patrias tengo yo: Cuba y la noche.
¿O son una las dos? No bien retira
Su majestad el sol, con largos velos
Y un clavel en la mano, silenciosa
Cuba cual viuda triste me aparece.
¡Yo sé cuál es ese clavel sangriento
Que en la mano le tiembla! Está vacío
Mi pecho, destrozado está y vacío
En donde estaba el corazón.

I have two motherlands: Cuba and the night.
Or are they one and the same?
As soon as the sun withdraws
Its majesty, with long veils
And a carnation in her hand, silently
Cuba appears to me like a sad widow.
I know what that bloody carnation is
that trembles in her hand! Empty
my breast, destroyed and empty
Where once was my heart.

Such a nostalgic portrayal of exile reaches deeply into the Cuban-American community. *Cuba libre,* the dream, takes innumerable forms, including a mixed alcoholic drink, made of rum and Coke, which was devised after Castro's revolution and has become a Hispanic symbol. According to Joan Didion, the three most detested personalities in little Havana, are first and foremost, Fidel Castro, then Ted Koppel, anchor of ABC's evening program "Night-line"—because Cubans fail to appreciate the importance of open debate between opposing parties; they would rather liquidate—and last but not least John F. Kennedy, who ordered the ill-fated Bay of Pigs invasion and then forgot the support he had received from Miami's right-wing Cubans. When Kennedy was assassinated in Dallas in 1963, Cuban exiles were immediately targeted as members of the conspiracy. Oliver Stone's prize-winning, paranoid film, *JFK,* deals with the Cuban link to the assassination. In the film Cubans are portrayed as treacherous, obsessed with Castro's downfall; they often have strange physical mannerisms and an outrageous look. Among other things, Stone, it seems, wants to investigate the fashion in which the American imagination has used otherness to explain Kennedy's tragic end; but he becomes entangled in his own labyrinth: Cubans end up stereotyped, and the suggestion is made that unlike any other Latino community in the United States, they have access to power and have been involved in crucial events in U.S. history. (The only similar incident I can think of involving other Latinos dates back to November 1, 1950, when Oscar Collazo and Griserio Torresola, Puerto Rican nationalists, tried to kill President Harry S Truman, who at the time was temporarily living in Blair House while the White House was being renovated.) Memory and identity, memory and modernity. For us, exile is among our most painful, degradative, self-consuming, and tragic expressions of the labyrinth we inhabit.

Few question the importance of the Communist revolution as a coming-of-age event in the continent's modern history. Mexico, some fifty years earlier, had the continent's first pro-reform revolution in the twentieth century. But its dreams were betrayed and buried by subsequent corrupt regimes, the courage of its freedom fighters overcome by bureaucratic mediocrity. Fidel Castro's struggle, on the other hand, had an immediate echo in the Latin American intelligentsia. Many celebrated its triumph and naively embraced its left-wing ideology. In 1956, Fidel, his brother Raúl Castro, "Che" Guevara, and seventy-nine others set out from the Pacific coast of Mexico, in the yacht *Gramma,* to overthrow the Batista regime. The arrangements were botched, and only twelve survived the landing—an aborted uprising, a laughable incident had posterity not rewritten its lines. The Rebel Army—with the glorious name *Ejército Rebelde*—and Radio Rebelde, inaugurated by Che, took to the Sierra Maestra to launch the guerrilla campaign against the government.

Fulgencio Batista, a corrupt army sergeant, embraced a tyranny with close links to the United States. Cuba, during his tenure, was known as America's whorehouse, a tropical island where gambling and prositution reigned. The scorned Batista regime was divided in two parts. The first part lasted a decade, 1934–44. After Gerardo Machado was overthrown by Batista in 1933, Dr. Ramón Grau San Martín, president for less than a year, was forced out of office by the military. Then, in 1952, after a coup d'état, Batista overthrew the government of Carlos Prío Socarrás. (Sydney Pollack's embarrassing 1990 film, *Havana,* with Robert Redford and Lena Olin, is set in the final hours of Batista's second regime.) The Rebel Army's July 1953 attack on the Moncada Barracks marked the beginning of the insurrection against Batista, but the actual revolution did not take place until 1959. On New Year's Eve 1958, Batista fled the country, and on January 1, 1959, the Rebel Army under Che Guevara triumphantly entered Havana. The political impact was tremendous: In October 1960 the United States imposed an economic embargo with far-reaching consequences; this action was vilified by many Latin Americans as aggression, a reversal of Roosevelt's Good Neighbor Policy. In early 1961 Washington permanently broke diplomatic relations with Cuba, and the pressure by Cuban-Americans in Florida for Washington to remain steadfast suddenly increased and would grow stronger in the following decades. When a literacy campaign was launched in Cuba (illiteracy abruptly dropped from 24 percent to 4 percent in one year), Castro declared the socialist nature of the revolution. In 1965, the Communist party of Cuba was formed, two years before Che was killed in Bolivia and three years before the last private businesses in Cuba were nationalized. Considering sugarcane as Cuba's principal source of production and income in the international market, Castro orchestrated an ill-fated campaign for a ten-million-ton harvest, which prompted his regime, albeit reluctantly, to revaluate its economic and political goals and potential.

Tensions between Miami and Havana have escalated since Castro has been in power and as a result of the embargo. In 1975 Cuban troops were sent to Angola, and two years later, President Jimmy Carter signed an agreement to exchange diplomats and regulate offshore fishing. But Ronald Reagan and George Bush increased the hostilities toward Fidel Castro's government, and it was not until the Clinton administration that U.S. citizens, invited by Castro, traveled to Cuba. This newly extended invitation had a clear strategy behind it: to bring hard currency into a suffocated system. While Miami and Havana live back to back, since Castro has been in office, communication between them comes in the form of shrieks. They constantly accuse each other of betrayal and lack of patriotism. They spit on each other's faces, and each other's names.

A crucial chapter in United States–Cuban relations is known as *el diálogo*. In 1978 a group of Cuban-Americans founded the Committee of Seventy-five, whose aim was to establish a dialogue between the exile community and the island authorities. An explosion in diplomatic relations occurred in April 1980, when twelve Cubans who were seeking asylum crashed a minibus through the gates of the Peruvian Embassy in Havana. Cuba's government announced that anyone who wished to leave Cuba could be picked up at the port of Mariel. Some 125,000 people left the country, a number of whom were criminals and other prisoners held in Cuban jails, including Reinaldo Arenas, whose autobiographical work is discussed in Chapter 4. (Nestor Almendros's and Jorge Ulla's film *Nobody Listened* deals, in part, with echoes of this incident.) The Mariel incident caused much debate in both countries. Finally, in December 1984 Cuba and the United States signed an Immigration Accord whereby Cuba agreed to take back 2,746 Mariel "excludables" and the United States accepted an annual quota of 20,000 Cubans. Once again exile and memory were wedded. The Mariel boat lift retains a special place in the Cuban-American imagination. The novelist Reinaldo Arenas was one of the many that came to the United States at the time, and his writing is full of disappointment and fury. His anger against the tyrannical Castro regime, rather than disappearing, was reshaped once he got to Florida. He was ridiculed and stigmatized among Cuban-Americans because of his gay identity. (Almendros courageously addressed the issue of homosexuality in Cuba under communism in his 1983 documentary *Improper Conduct*.)

As a rule, the U.S. media portrays Cubans and Cuban-Americans in stereotypes, as power-driven or as individuals obsessed with memory and exile. In the movie *El Super* the protagonist is consumed by a desire to return to the tropical paradise of his youth. In Oliver Stone's *JFK*, Cuban-Americans appear to have played a detonating role in Kennedy's assassination. What is perhaps the most atrocious portrait of a Latino in a Hollywood movie is Brian De Palma's *Scarface* (the screenplay adaptation is by Oliver Stone himself), a three-hour-long carnival of blood and bullets. Al Pacino, incapable of carrying his Hispanic accent all the way through, plays Tony Montana, a Mariel refugee who refuses to perform menial jobs—the movie begins with real television footage of the 1980 incident—and, instead, becomes a paranoid drug lord. Montana turns memory and exile into macho strength. He loves his family but is unable to understand their needs. Rather than assimilating to the American Dream, he adapts the dream to his own needs. (Ironically, Montana has become a mythical figure among rap musicians who glorify his meanness and individualism.)

Memory and its pervasive echoes tend to be the key elements in literary re-creations of Cuban-Americans and this is also the tune of Oscar Hijuelos's oeuvre: the art of yearning as a spiritual sport. Hijuelos's first novel, *Our House in the Last World*, published when the author was thirty-two, was, in Nicolás Kanellos's words, "a typical ethnic autobiography, capable of attracting Hispanic writers to the trade market." Then came the extraordinary success of *The Mambo Kings Play Songs of Love,* a moving account of brotherly love in the New York of the 1950s, which traced the impact and influence of Latin rhythms north of the border. Hijuelos followed up his novel of urban ambitions with something as far from a sequel as one could imagine: *The Fourteen Sisters of Emilio Montez O'Brien,* a pastoral narrative of a Cuban-Irish family living in a bucolic small town in Pennsylvania, written with a genuine feminine sensibility. Influenced by an intriguing mix of writers, from William Butler Yeats to Flann O'Brien, Hijuelos signals a trend by the new generation of Cuban-Americans and shies away from politics, as does Julia Alvarez in her fictional study of well-off Dominican girls in the United States.

Cristina Garcia's first novel, *Dreaming in Cuban,* is about the search for identity and self-esteem of the del Pino family, especially of its four women, the matriarch Celia del Pino, her two daughters, Lourdes Puente and Felicia Villaverde, and her granddaughter, Pilar. A Cuban-American journalist born in Havana in 1958 and raised in New York City, where she attended Barnard College, Garcia has firsthand knowledge of her subject. Her novel seems to be an autobiographical portrait, an attempt by a second-generation immigrant to narrate the ever-changing adventures of her relatives in Cuba and in el exilio. But it is also something more: In lyrical, enchanting prose, the book is a fascinating dissertation on the culture of exile and how different people survive its miseries or perish from nostalgia. Indeed, Garcia's last name has suffered from the acculturation she talks about—the Spanish accent now absent in the English spelling. Precisely that type of transformation, linguistic and spiritual, affects every one of her characters. The plot travels back and forth from the Cuban village of Santa Teresa del Mar to Havana, to Brooklyn and Czechoslovakia, as if the Latino identity is incarnated in an eternally divided diaspora, a bridge broken to pieces. Survival strategies vary: Each protagonist has to adapt to the milieu while history seems to undergo drastic changes that are difficult to grasp. The process of adaptation does not occur without suffering. Unhappy as a painter and student in New York City, Pilar dreams in English but hopes to return to the island, to her grandmother's side, to regain control of herself, to dream in Cuban. The fact that she tries to end her exile is a statement on her status as a citizen in the United States; she uses this culture, but is still a member of the other. Yet, in 1980, when she finally makes it back to a surreal Havana packed with revolutionary billboards and streets full of old Oldsmobiles, just as the Mariel boat lift is about to begin, she understands the maxim immortalized by Thomas Wolfe: You can't go home again! Home is a hallucination.

Cuban nostalgia has also become an engine for success. Take the case of Ricky Ricardo, the orchestra leader portrayed by Desi Arnaz, who thinks his wife should stay home; who, in spite of the dissenting voice of cubanistas, remains the ultimate Cuban-American success story and a rebuttal of melancholia as a way of life. From October 1951 to May 1957, America's favorite pastime was viewing the 179 half-hour episodes of "I Love Lucy" on CBS television. As Bart Andrews argues in his book-long account of the television show, *Lucy & Ricky & Fred & Ethel: The Story of "I Love Lucy,"* the Ricardos and the Mertzes were so popular that more people watched the 1953 episode depicting the birth of little Ricky than the inauguration of President Dwight D. Eisenhower the next day or even the coronation of Queen Elizabeth six months later.

The only child of a Cuban senator and mayor of Santiago, Desi Arnaz was born Desiderio Alberto Arnas y de Acha III in 1917. The family owned 100,000 acres, an enormous house in the city, a private island in Santiago Bay, and numerous speedboats, automobiles, and racehorses. The father wanted Desi, as he was called, to study law at the University of Notre Dame in Indiana and then return home to practice. But the first Batista coup d'état in 1933 created considerable problems. As he described it in his 1976 memoir, *A Book*, Desi's father was jailed, and his property was confiscated. Desi and his mother sailed to Miami. He attended St. Patrick's High School, where one of his classmates was Al Capone's son. He worked at numerous jobs to pay the rent, while fighting to liberate his father: cleaning out canary cages, truck driving, train-yard checking, bookkeeping. His English was poor. According to Andrews, once when Desi ordered a meal at a restaurant, he mistakenly was served five bowls of soup. He began playing music in nightclubs and soon made it to New York, where he landed a leading role as a Latin football player in a musical. He met Lucille Ball in 1940 at a Hollywood studio where he had been summoned to reprise his Broadway role in a film adaptation. The director introduced them.

About a decade later, Ball became disenchanted with her film career. Arnaz was still playing with his band in nightclubs, along with occasional roles in films and plays. Ball had a radio show, "My Favorite Husband," which CBS wanted to transfer to television. At first, the executives refused to have Arnaz as her costar, but Ball would not accept any alternative. What resulted was a sitcom in which Latin music and a Spanish accent were essential ingredients. Arnaz was not only a force behind the enormous success of his wife, but was the brains behind many prime-time series, including "The Untouchables."

Why was the Cuban so popular? As Andrews claimed, a foreign-born relative with an embarrassing accent is somewhere in the background of every American. Ricky Ricardo, a Latin with a thick Cuban accent, is loved by every-body. (Arnaz would sometimes make mistakes translating Lucy's English into Spanish.*) By sharing their respect for him, does the audience appease its conscience? Strictly speaking, in spite of its hilarious nature, "I Love Lucy," just like West Side Story, perpetuated a set of stereotypes about Latinos and women in general: Ricky Ricardo would sing a chorus of "Guadalajara," "Babalú," and "Cuban Pete"; the Mertzes would celebrate a wedding anniversary at the Copacabana; and Lucy would decorate her apartment "like Cuba," with palm trees, sombreros, a flock of chickens, and even a mule; but no pro-found understanding, no honest regard for human differences, was displayed. Granted, the television show was billed as pure entertainment. Yet, its laughter ultimately managed to pervert reality, rather than unravel its complexities. In the eyes of the TV audience, Arnaz emerged as the ultimate Latin lover and spitfire. In one episode, an item in a morning gossip column prompts Lucy to assume that Ricky is seeing another woman. To apologize for what she believes is a lack of wifely faith, she quickly prepares his favorite dinner. Lucy is constantly aware of language reveries and addresses the whole country's linguistic discomfort with foreign accents. In another episode, ashamed of the effects his sloppy English may have on her soon-to-be-born baby, she hires a tutor after asking Ricky: "Please promise me you won't speak to our child until he's nineteen or twenty." Arnaz's ordeal, as Hijuelos knows (the now-famous beginning of his second novel circles around a rerun of a half-hour episode of "I Love Lucy"), is every Latino's dream of making it big in America. And among Latinos, Cuban-Americans symbolize success and progress, assimilation but also self-awareness.

Miami, as David Rieff showed, has become a Cuban-American political stronghold. In 1985 Radio Martí, an anti-Castro station that broadcasts to Cuba, was launched in Miami, and Cuba suspended the Immigration Accord. And half a decade later, after Mikhail Gorbachev of the former Soviet Union visited Cuba, and senior army and state security officers in Cuba including a hero of the republic, General Arnaldo Ochoa Sánchez, were tried and executed on drug-trafficking charges, TV Martí broadcast the trial via a balloon anchored off the Florida Keys. There is no doubt that the ambivalence of Cuban émigrés

*Gustavo Pérez-Firmat discusses Arnaz's linguistic intricasies in Life on the Hyphen (Austin: University of Texas Press, 1994).

has created a number of far-reaching side effects, including the volatile atmosphere of Cuban radical politics in Miami, with Jorge Mas Canosa, founder and head of the dogmatic, right-wing Cuban-American National Foundation, as its most virile exponent. Canosa's dictatorial style—he is yet another installment in the almost infinite list of tyrants from the Caribbean and elsewhere in Latin America, where the collective psyche generates such extreme power egomaniacs—is apparent in his "antidefamation" campaign of vilification against the Spanish daily *El Nuevo Herald*, which his supporters have compared to the organ of the Communist party in Havana. One more consequence of the Cuban-American's ambivalence is the wholehearted commitment by Cubans in the United States to bilingual education, a movement that actually started in Dade County in the early 1960s as a result of the refusal of wealthy and ideologically active émigrés to allow their children to live and be educated solely in English. Cuban émigrés have a self-conscious and precise perception of themselves and their people. "Cuba was, is, and will again become the Eden" is the collective approach to a lost reality. The Cuban obsession to celebrate themselves and to glorify their nation's past is often taken to absurd limits. (Once again, the film *El Super* offers an enlightening example.) The difference in perspective is frequently evident across generations: While direct victims of Castro's nationalization and persecutions tend to be more involved, and thus need to view the future in drastic terms, the new generation of Cuban-Americans, who are less politically involved and more inclined to accept the American Dream, prefers to take a noncommittal attitude. What is unquestionable is that many in Miami eagerly await the crucial redemptive date, and their patience is running short. There is already a government in exile, with its necessary president and cabinet, and investigations into the legal reappropriation of lost real estate in Cuba are under way, with observers closely watching the procedures unraveling in Russia and Eastern Europe.

Whatever the attitude of Cuban-American exiles to their native island's future, as a struggle, as a way of life, as a condition, displacement is, and will remain, a Latino signature. Political upheaval is everywhere, in all things. South of the Rio Grande, our historical contradictions are immense, which means that there will never be a final revolution, no end to the sequence of ideological transformations that sweep people up. To be expelled from home, to wander through geographic and linguistic diasporas, is essential to our nature. Once in the United States, things become harder. In exile in the belly of the beast, the Anglo's friendly hand, both detestable and lovable, simultaneously opens a cozy shelter and subjugates as a victimizer.

Many histories, one archipelago. Let me now return to the initial theme of this chapter: the fragmentation of the Caribbean basin. When talking about Hispanics in the United States, one needs to remember that two of the three major groups trace their ancestry to the Antilles. Strictly speaking, the basin, in its idiosyncrasy and history, is strikingly different from Latin America. To begin with, the region is populated by multiple languages and resulted from a process of syncretism quite different from that of, say, Mexico, where the African slave was practically nonexistent. Then there is the issue of pan-nationalism. Cuba, Puerto Rico, the Dominican Republic, Haiti, Jamaica, and other smaller islands: Each has its distinctive past and lives in its own isolation. Overall, Caribbeans perceive the universe as a never-ending performance. Their religious and spiritual motifs could not be further from those found in Central America, for instance. Should we then continue addressing these people as Latin Americans, in spite of their own discomfort with the term? Should we persist in reducing into one single category cultures that have trouble understanding themselves as siblings?

From time immemorial, the Caribbean has been known as a transit point, a stage of departure and encounter, the harbor in which ships from and to Europe and the Americas would arrive. This transitory port of ports had a profound effect on the various cultures. When talking about Cuba, the scholar Gustavo Pérez-Firmat uses the concept of "translating culture": the original that comes from abroad is adapted, reimagined, reinvented to suit a need at home. The psychology behind this device is unlike that in Argentina or Uruguay or Mexico, countries known not as transient stops but as ends in themselves. All this suggests that it is a mistake to throw all Caribbeans into one sack, and that sack into another with all Hispanics. *Primero muerto que cubano*, a Puerto Rican would say. And vice versa. As Judith Ortíz Cofer writes in her poem "The Latin Deli," while Cubans prepare their speech for a glorious return to Havana, Puerto Ricans complain that it would be cheaper to fly to San Juan than to buy a pound of Bustelo coffee. Ironically, Antonio Benítez-Rojo believes that the crucial unifier of the Caribbean experience isn't language, history, or geography, but the sugar and cacao plantation. I talked earlier in this chapter of the presence in the collective mind of a continuity in the region's literature, music, and art. In other words, what makes the Caribbean basin more or less a unified whole is an economic system and not, as others would want to believe, a shared codex of information. The plantation is a unique Caribbean experience rarely shared in the other Americas.

3

❖ ❖ ❖

At War with Anglos

Viva la revolución! Our home is in the diaspora!

On August 29, 1970—months after civil rights demonstrations in Denver and elsewhere led by César Chávez and other leaders—Rubén Salazar, activist, radio producer, and *Los Angeles Times* reporter, was killed by the Los Angeles police. The Chicano movement, also known as La Causa and El Movimiento, was at its apex. Shortly before, as can be seen in Jesús Treviño's documentary *Requiem 29,* over 30,000 people attended the National Chicano Moratorium Committee's march against the Vietnam War in East Los Angeles.

Salazar, together with two friends, had been covering a protest that turned into a riot and had stopped momentarily at the Silver Dollar Bar on Whittier Boulevard in the Laguna Park section of L.A. Thinking an armed Chicano activist was inside, a few sheriff's deputies, after sealing the entrance door and shouting for the man to come out, used tear gas and fired a shell that struck Salazar in the head and killed him. The gunman, a deputy, was later identified but never arrested. Salazar's death was epoch-making and is ubiquitous in the Chicano collective consciousness. Monuments to the journalist abound: From California to Texas, parks, libraries, and housing projects are named in his memory. His life and funeral, his thought and image, have inspired murals and other forms of graphic art, and as symbols of resistance they appear, for example, in Lucha Corpi's 1992 thriller *Eulogy for a Brown Angel* and in *The Revolt of the Cockroach People* by Oscar "Zeta" Acosta, the militant Chicano lawyer who is the inspiration for the three-hundred-pound Samoan in Hunter S. Thompson's *Fear and Loathing in Las Vegas.* Earl Shorris dedicated his book *Latinos* to Salazar because he understood the intricate marriage of sword and pen. Probably killed because his newspaper essays and reports embarrassed governmental agencies and denounced injustices committed against Chicanos, Salazar used his forums, the newspaper and radio shows, to verbalize the internal and external plight that Chicanos were undergoing. Thus, he personifies the fashion in which art and politics are intimately intertwined among us Chicanos.

This chapter is devoted to the clash between Latinos and Anglos, as expressed, primarily although not uniquely, in Chicano art and history. Whereas mainland Borinquéns, as stated in the previous chapter, are probably closer to U.S. blacks than to any Latino subgroup, Mexican-Americans, *mexicanos,* Pochos, La Raza, or simply Chicanos (from Me*chicanos*), have experienced a different type of exile than have other Hispanics and easily identify with native Americans. Although most Mexican Americans today either crossed the border as seasonal agricultural laborers during or after World War II or are descendants of *braceros,* we Mexican Americans proudly trace our status as the oldest inhabitants of the continental United States to the Treaty of Guadalupe Hidalgo, which ended the Mexican-American War in 1848 and resulted in the sale by Mexico to the United States of territories in what is now California, New Mexico, Arizona, and Texas for $15 million. From early on, the Chicano psyche has been belligerent. Silent resistance, a refusal to accept their new status, always colored the lives of Mexicans north of the Rio Grande.

I should add that not all Mexican-Americans are in the Southwest. New York in the eighties, for example, could have been renamed New Mex City: In 1992, there were an estimated 200,000 Mexicans in the metropolitan area, mostly under the age of thirty, mostly from Puebla, Oaxaca, and other southern Mexico states. Chicago's South Lawndale neighborhood has been renamed La Villita because Mexican culture is ubiquitous. And that doesn't begin to cover the rest of the Midwest at all.

We, the Chicano intelligentsia, portray ourselves as fighters for equality and justice in a long-standing resistance to external dominating forces, often personified by Anglos. Only through organized efforts have things actually changed. The Orden Hijos de América, for example, formed in 1921 in San Antonio to promote voter registration and political action by Mexican-Americans, helped create a climate of understanding. And cultural organizations were formed in the Southwest to celebrate Mexican and U.S. patriotic holidays on an equal basis, even if one of the assurances that resulted from the Guadalupe Hidalgo Treaty was that Spanish, and Hispanic, fiestas would be respected. But aside from scattered cases (the most important one is that of Miguel Antonio Otero, who in 1897 became the first Chicano to be elected governor of the territory of New Mexico), Latino politicians, as a group, did not hold public office until recently. As William Carlos Williams, a Puerto Rican sympathizer, stated: "History, history! We fools, what do we know or care? History begins for us with murder and enslavement, not with discovery. No, we are not Indians but we are men of their world. The blood means nothing; the spirit, the ghost of the land moves in the blood, moves the blood. It is we who ran to the shore naked, we who cried, 'Heavenly Man!'" To fight, to persevere against oppressive, larger-than-life external forces, is at the core of our being. Struggle, contention, fight, endeavor. Opposition, of course, is the immigrant's energetic statement against life as an underdog.

Most Chicanos came north and entered, illegally or otherwise, as guests. Immigration laws monitor their entrance, although not their assimilation as Latinos; they also label newcomers, establishing the way in which society will perceive them afterward. In 1917, for instance, the United States passed the Immigration Act, which required all immigrants except Mexicans to pay a head tax and to fulfill a literacy requirement. Seven years later, the Johnson-Reed Act refined the immigration quotas first instituted in 1921: The government strictly limited all immigration except from the nations of northern and western Europe, which officially meant that Hispanics—underdogs, *escoria social*—were treated as second-rate after Europeans like Jews and Italians and accused of taking jobs away from other people. A segment of Jimmy Santiago Baca's poem "So Mexicans Are Taking Jobs from Americans" reads:

O Yes? Do they come on horses
with rifles, and say,

     Ese gringo, gimme your job?

And do you, gringo, take off your ring,
drop your wallet into a blanket
spread over the ground, and walk away?

I hear Mexicans are taking your jobs away.
Do they sneak into town at night,
as you're walking home with a whore,
do they mug you, a knife at your throat,
saying, I want your job?

Our history, as that of Caribbeans, is a painful chain of traumatic relationships with societies more powerful than us, from the Portuguese-Iberians to the French, British, and Americans. The Plan de San Diego, written in 1915 in San Diego, Texas, called for Mexican-American opposition in the South. In 1932–33, the Cannery and Agricultural Workers Industrial Union organized and led the San Joaquín Valley Cotton Strike, opposing substandard minimum wages and miserable working conditions. Can a suffering culture become a culture of success? We first worshipped *bandidos* like Juan Cortina—who led a revolt in 1859 to protest Anglo-American mistreatment of Mexican Americans in Texas—Gregorio Cortez, Juan Flores, Jacinto Treviño, Tiburcio Vásquez (the subject of a play by Luis Valdez), and, perhaps better known, Joaquín Murrieta (whose name is sometimes spelled with only one *r*). Throughout this century, we have perfected the arts of activism, and the link between the two, agony and triumph, is obvious: Outlaws moved from the periphery of the culture to center stage.

Father Alberto Huerta, from San Francisco, California, has devoted a huge amount of energy to deciphering the historical and metaphorical implications of the plight of the legendary nineteenth-century Mexican *canaille* Murrieta in Fresno County. Murrieta was a kind of Robin Hood, who fought the Anglo establishment out of grief and outrage, giving money and happiness to the poor and dispossessed. His death, like that of Pancho Villa, has been turned into a myth.* During the Gold Rush, Murrieta traveled from Sonora, Mexico, to California with his brother, wife, and probably other relatives and friends. His fate remains obscure. Apparently, a bunch of drunken Anglos raped his wife, tortured him, and hanged his brother. During the next few years, disguised as an old man, an Indian, or what have you, he searched for every one of his torturers and killed them. The U.S. authorities placed a bounty on his head after he turned into a vengeful criminal, a symbol of the Chicano animosity toward the English-speaking establishment. The time was the 1880s, when Tiburcio Vásquez and others were branded as *bandidos* by the mainstream press for resisting the seizure of Chicano lands by Anglos in California. Here is one of the several corridos about Murrieta:

Yo no soy americano	I am not an American
pero comprendo el inglés.	but I understand English
Yo lo aprendí con mi hermano	I learned it with my brother,

*See my essay "¿Dónde está la cabeza de Pancho Villa?" *La pluma y la máscara* (Mexico City: Fondo de Cultura Económica, 1993).

al derecho y al revés.
A cualquier americano lo hago
temblar a mis pies.

Cuando apenas era un niño
huérfano a mí me dejaron.
Nadie me hizo cariño,
a mi hermano lo mataron.
Y a mi esposa Carmelita,
cobardes la asesinaron.

Y me vine de Hermosillo
en busca de oro y riqueza.
Al indio pobre y sencillo
lo defendí con firmeza.
Y a buen precio los sherifes
pagaban por mi cabeza.

A los ricos avarientos,
yo les quité su dinero.
Con los humildes y pobres
yo me quité mi sombrero.
Ay, que leyes tan injustas
fue llamarme bandolero.

A Murrieta no le gusta
lo que hace no es desmentir.
Vengo a vengar a mi esposa,
y lo vuelvo a repetir,
Carmelita tan hermosa,
cómo la hicieron sufrir.

Por cantinas me metí,
castigando americanos.
"Tú serás el capitán
que mataste a mi hermano.
Lo agarraste indefenso,
orgulloso americano."

Mi carrera comenzó
por una escena terrible.

from beginning to end.
I make any American
shake his feet before me.

When I was still a child
I was left an orphan.
Nobody gave me affection,
and my brother was killed.
And my wife Carmelita,
was assassinated by some cowards.

I came from Hermosillo
in search of gold and fortune.
I defended with courage
the poor and simple Indian.
And the sheriffs would pay
a good price for my head.

I took away the money
from the stingy rich.
Next to the humble and poor
I respectfully took my hat off.
Ah, it was unfair by the law
to call me an outlaw.

What Murrieta does not like
he would never hide.
I came to avenge my wife,
and I repeat:
Carmelita the beautiful,
they made her suffer.

I entered cantinas
to punish Americans.
"You must be the leader
of the squad that killed my brother.
You killed him unarmed,
proud American!"

My career began
with a terrible scene.

Cuando llegué a setecientos	After I traveled seven hundred miles,
ya mi nombre era temible.	my name was already feared.
Cuando llegué a mil doscientos	When I reached twelve hundred,
ya mi nombre era terrible.	already my name was terrifying.
Yo soy aquel que domina	I am the one that dominates
hasta leones africanos.	even African lions.
Por eso salgo al camino	That's why I wander around
a matar americanos.	to kill Americans.
Ya no es otro mi destino	Such is my fate:
¡por cuidado, parroquianos!	beware, countrymen!
Las pistolas y las dagas	Guns and knives
son juguetes para mí.	are toys for me.
Balazos y puñaladas	Gunshots and knife injuries,
carcajadas para mí.	laughing matter for me.
Ahora con medios cortados	Now with a little violence,
ya se asustran por aquí.	they get scared around here.
No soy chileno ni extraño	I am neither a Chilean nor a stranger
en este suelo que piso.	in this soil I stand on.
De México es California	From Mexico to California,
porque Dios así lo quiso.	because God so wanted
Y a mi sarape cosida	I have my honor
traigo mi fe de bautismo.	stamped in my serape.
Qué bonito es California	How beautiful is California
con sus calles alineadas	with its symmetrical streets.
donde paseaba Murrieta	Where Murrieta wandered around
con su tropa bien formada,	with his well-structured troops,
con su pistola repleta	his loaded gun,
y su montura plateada.	and his silver horse sit.
Me he paseado en California	I have wandered through California
por el año cincuenta.	around the year 1850.
Con mi montura plateada,	With my silver horse sit
y mi pistola repleta.	and my loaded gun.
Yo soy ese mexicano	I am the Mexican
de nombre Joaquín Murrieta.	people call Joaquín Murrieta.

Inured to violence, ready to kill as many enemies as possible, Murrieta inaugurated, or at least perpetuated, the image of the aggressive Hispanic: ready to avenge, to attack, to allow his barbaric spirit to emerge. It is not surprising that this character has metamorphosed into a hero among Chicanos. Many have written about him, often giving him different homelands and identities. In 1881, an anonymous short fictional text appeared under the title *Las aventuras de Joaquín Murrieta*. Both Irineo Paz, Octavio Paz's grandfather, and Yellow Bird (John Rollin Ridge) wrote about him, the latter in his 1925 *Life and Adventures of a Celebrated Bandit: Joaquín Murrieta*. Jill L. Cossley-Batt saw him as "the last of the California rangers" in 1928, and Walter Noble Burns saw him as "The Robin Hood of El Dorado" in 1932. Before them, Joaquin Miller published a poem in which he described the outlaw as follows:

No moral man his like has seen.
And yet, but for his long serape
All flowing loose, and black as crape,
And long silk locks of blackest hair
All streaming wildly in the breeze,
You might believe him in a chair,
Or chatting at some country fair
With friend or señorita rare,
He rides so grandly at his ease.

Pablo Neruda, the 1971 Noble Prize winner, portrayed him as a Chilean in a poetic dramatization, "Fulgor y muerte de Joaquín Murrieta." In 1967 Rodolfo "Corky" Gonzáles wrote his epic poem *I Am Joaquín/Yo Soy Joaquín,* about the identity and struggle of Chicanos. The poem is considered one of the most inspiring pieces of literature of the Chicano movement, and Luis Valdez turned it into a movie. At the center of the poem is the *vato* of El Barrio, a frustrated social type without much interest in education; he suffers from a mental block and cannot speak Spanish. He feels intimidated, forced to abandon his roots. Rodolfo "Corky" Gonzáles was born in Denver in 1928 into a family of sugar beet workers. Like Floyd Salas, the Chicano author of *Buffalo Nickel* and other novels, he was a boxer—a Golden Gloves champion who turned pro and was a featherweight contender from 1947 to 1955. In 1957 he became the first Chicano district captain for the Democratic party. He then entered the bail-bond business and opened an auto insurance agency. But he remained active in the community, and in 1963 he organized Los Voluntarios, a group against police brutality. After that he became director of the War on Poverty's youth program in Denver, but was fired for his involvement in a walkout. In Gonzáles's poem, Joaquín Murrieta becomes a metaphor for his entire people:

> I am the sword and flame of Cortez
>> the despot.
> And I am the Eagle and serpent of
>> the Aztec civilization.
> . . .
> I am
> the black shawled faithful woman
> who die with me
> or live
> depending on time and place.
> I am
>> faithful,
>> humble,
>>> Juan Diego
>>> the Virgin of Guadalupe
>>> Tonatzin, Aztec Goddess too.
> . . .
> I rode the mountains of San Joaquín
> I rode as far East and North as the Rocky Mountains
>> and
> all men feared the guns of
>> Joaquín Murrieta.
> I killed those men who dared
>> to steal my mine,
>> who raped and killed
>> my Love
>> my life. . .

Joaquín Murrieta continues to fascinate. Richard Rodríguez devoted an entire chapter to Murrieta in his 1992 book, *Days of Obligation*. In fact, in the book, Rodríguez is obsessed with finding Murrieta's bounty-branded head—according to some rumors it was returned by state troopers for reward money after he was killed in July 1853. But where is it? Who has it? Rodríguez comes across Father Alberto Huerta, the Chicano academic and friend of Danny Santiago, who is anxious to find it so he can bury it with dignity as a gesture of reconciliation. Huerta claims: "All of us need to face our guilt and fears, if we are to reconcile with one another." Turned into detectives, the writer and Huerta follow one clue after another until they eventually meet a curious antiquarian, who claims that the deformed and monstrous head he keeps hidden is that of Murrieta. In imaginatively exploring the life of such a myth, Rodríguez comes to see the Rio Grande as a psychic injury dividing the idiosyncrasies of Mexico and the United States. Murrieta is an emblem, a symbol of divergence, part American and part Mexican.

Always combative, Chicano letters have a couple of clear venues: an urban setting and the itinerant rural life of migrant workers. Until fairly recently, most Chicano writers came to the craft without much education, as "Corky" Gonzáles did. As Rudolfo A. Anaya once put it: "The Hispanic writer never quite learned his craft. He is self-taught and has been writing for ages. He just sits and writes, and writes until overtaken by exhaustion and hemorrhoids." In the next few paragraphs I shall list the most distinguished Mexican-American works of literature. They are all marked by a common leitmotif: a sense of affirmation and resistance, the struggle to continue "an internal revolution." These writers convey the need to recognize that one's own house is curiously located in the diaspora. Although Chicanos are at home in the United States, it isn't that they came north, as other Latinos, but that *el norte* came to them. Through narratives and poems, writers are submerged in a political journey of collective discovery.

Considered the first novel by a Mexican-American, *Pocho,* by José Antonio Villarreal, published in 1959, is a bildungsroman, in which Richard Rubio, a teenager in Santa Clara, California, struggles to decipher the enigmas of his Mexican-American identity. Born in Los Angeles in 1924, Villarreal was in the U.S. Navy from 1942 to 1946; received a bachelor's degree from the University of California, Berkeley, in 1950; and did graduate work at the university some eight years. He worked as a consultant, a supervisor of technical publications and public relations, an assistant professor of English at the University of Colorado, and as writer-in-residence at the University of Texas at El Paso. He then moved to Mexico in 1973, where he worked as a freelance writer, travel agent, translator, and newscaster, although he often returns to the United States to lecture.

Reading Villarreal is helpful in understanding the conflict between Anglo and Chicano cultures. His work highlights the clash Hispanics undergo as they enter the Anglo mainstream. In a review in *The Nation,* John Bright wrote: *Pocho* "is notable not only for its own intrinsic virtues, but as a first voice from a people new in our midst who up to now have been almost silent." Early critics praised the writer's style and structure, suggesting it was the very first fictional account of growing up Mexican-American in the Southwest, in which a desire to first fight the establishment and then become part of it is thoroughly discussed.

Richard Rubio faces a number of sexual, emotional, and intellectual challenges as he tries to discover his role as an American citizen of Mexican descent. Villarreal begins by offering an unrelated panoramic view of the Mexican Revolution, in which Richard's father fought and from which he is forced to escape to survive. A bookish adolescent, Richard struggles to understand his father's idiosyncratic behavior, which he compulsively idealizes, in a milieu in which women are increasingly asking to be respected as equals. Comparatively, Richard's mother, apparently better suited to life in a non-Hispanic environment, finally throws her womanizing and abusive husband out of the house, asking for Richard's support, which he reluctantly offers. As Charles M. Tatum and others have suggested, Richard is not an altogether convincing character, especially in his boyhood philosophical musings. He seems to have an intellectual maturity that is well beyond his years. The novel also feels unbalanced. The first segment on the Mexican Revolution has little bearing on the rest of the narrative, and the end, in which Richard must decide between an education and the army, is abrupt. Ultimately, the protagonist and the novel fail to awaken the reader's sympathy and ultimately become unmemorable creations.

Villarreal is the author of a couple of other novels, less important in nature, tone, and impact. *The Fifth Horseman,* which stands as the background for *Pocho* and seems predictable and disengaging, focuses on the Mexican Revolution, an armed struggle in which the writer's father was active before emigrating to the United States. The novel's protagonist is Heraclio Inés, an exploited *peón* who joins Pancho Villa's army and eventually grows disenchanted. In an introduction to the work, the critic Luis Leal talks about the novel's literary antecedents, relating it to works by Juan Rulfo (*Pedro Páramo*), Carlos Fuentes (*The Death of Artemio Cruz*), Martín Luis Guzmán (*The Eagle and the Serpent*), Mariano Azuela (*The Underdogs*), and Agustín Yáñez (*On the Water's Edge*), among many others. Notwithstanding, Villarreal's book stands on its own, in that it was published some seventy years after the peasant's struggle and, even more strikingly, unlike all precursors it was originally written in English. In that sense it's closer to John Dos Passos's *The 42nd Parallel*, which includes a chapter ("The Camera Eyes, Newsreel XVII") dedicated to revolutionary Mexico, as well as Stirling Dickinson's *Death Is Incidental* and titles by Malcolm Wheeler-Nicholson, Carleton Beals, and Richard Carroll. Villarreal's third novel, *Clemente Chacón,* stands as a possible sequel to *Pocho* and follows a young Mexican who becomes successful as a businessman in the United States. While it attracted little attention when published in 1984, critics like Tomás Vallejos claim it is Villarreal's most accomplished work of fiction, with a display of characters also not quite noteworthy but at least better-rounded.

Villarreal's importance as a Chicano and Latino writer is double-faceted. First, he was among the first to switch from Spanish to English to reach a wider audience, and is thus considered a sell-out among radical Chicanos. In an interview in *Contemporary Authors* he said, "As [a child] I knew only Spanish. It was not until my second year at school that I began to write and converse in English, and by the fifth grade, although I read and wrote in Spanish and spoke Spanish exclusively within our home, the idiom had become my second language. By then I knew that I wished to be a writer and attempted to write vignettes about my people. When I was perhaps thirteen years old, I realized that the non-Mexican population in my country did not know about us, did not know we existed, had no idea that we could be part of the mainstream of America and contribute to what I believe is . . . the melting pot. I resolved then that I would write about my people. I wished that the American public would know of us. I believed, and still do, that I could best accomplish this through fiction." Villarreal also opened up a new narrative field by introducing a distinctively Mexican-American perspective dealing with identity and cultural conflicts. Shortly after *Pocho* appeared, John Rechy's explosive *City of Night,* about gays, hustlers, and Mexican-Americans in the border region, appeared, followed by the works of Richard Vásquez and Tomás Rivera, all influenced by Villarreal. And yet, subsequent Latino, and particularly Chicano, authors in the United States have not looked to Villarreal for inspiration. Successors have found affinities in other minority figures, often depicting *Pocho* as a traditional work of fiction by a boring realist. Many haven't even read his work, and in Mexico, where Villarreal has lived since 1974, he is totally unknown as his work has never been translated into Spanish. His significance and literary standing remain the sole property of U.S. scholars and researchers. Villarreal's legacy can be found in the culture clash that keeps on occupying the attention of Chicano and Latino intellectuals and artists. He is a cornerstone, a compass, a map.

Although the Chicano novel as a literary genre did not appear full blown until the 1960s, many wrote epic dramas and poetry before then, from Cabeza de Vaca, discussed in Chapter 4, to Gaspar Pérez de Villagrá, responsible for the 1598 epic poem *History of New Mexico* and the pageant-drama *Moors and Christians*. A few literary works were published in Spanish before the Treaty of Guadalupe Hidalgo: *Los Comanches,* an 1822 allegorical drama which circulated anonymously; Fray Gerónimo Boscana's 1831 rhetorical, discursive, unremarkable diary, *Chinigchimich;* and María Amparo Ruíz de Burton's 1885 novel, *The Squatter and the Don.* As territories were acquired and ruled by the United States, legends, in the form of folk songs and corridos, began to circulate about treacherous bandidos like Gregorio Cortez and Juan Chacón, who were not ready to accept Anglo rule. (Robert M. Young's film about Cortez, *The Ballad of Gregorio Cortez,* is outstanding, as is Beverly Sánchez Padilla's experimental video, *The Corrida of Juan Chacón.*) One of the first Latino novels in Spanish, Eusebio Chacón's *El hijo de la tempestad,* appeared in 1892. Then came Benjamín Padilla's humorous vignettes, published in a series called Kaskabel in southwestern newspapers from 1910 to 1929.

After the Hispanic American *modernista* movement (framed between 1885 and 1915 and led by Rubén Darío, Delmira Agustini, Julián del Casal, Manuel Gutiérrez Nájera, and José Martí), a number of exiles who lived in New York, Washington, D.C., Miami, and Los Angeles, including José Juan Tablada, kept Spanish letters alive in the United States in the form of haiku and other vanguard poetic experiments. In 1935, Miguel Antonio Otero published his memoir *My Life on the Frontier 1865–1882,* and a couple of years later *Esquire* published some stories by Roberto Torres on the Mexican Revolution. As World War II began, Roberto Félix Salazar published his poem "The Other Pioneers." In 1945 Josephina Niggli published *Mexican Village,* portraying the alienation of being part Mexican, part Anglo; and Mario Suárez displayed his considerable narrative talents in short stories published in the *Arizona Quarterly* between 1947 and 1948 (he was one of the first writers to use the term *Chicano* in print). After Villarreal, the flourishing of the Chicano intelligentsia was patent. Richard Vásquez's epic novel, *Chicano,* appeared in 1970, followed by Rolando Hinojosa's *Sketches of the Valley and Other Works* in 1973, and Ron Arias's magic realist novel *The Road to Tamazunchale,* a tribute to Gabriel García Márquez's baroque style and Borges's metaphysical concerns, started its chain of numerous editions in 1975.

Chicano novelist Aristeo Brito's *El diablo en Texas,* a *Spoon River Anthology* of sorts, is a remarkable story about Presidio, a ghost border town frequently visited by the Devil, part Mexican, part Anglo, and whose history of desolation and poverty is told symphonically by lawyers, renegades, unborn children, and dead agricultural workers as perceived in three different moments (1883, 1942, 1970). In this novel and at the core of the Latino progression are two unifying motifs: memory and democracy. Along the same lines is Miguel Méndez's *Pilgrims in Aztlán,* first published in Spanish in 1974 and now available in English in David William Foster's wonderful translation. Victor Villaseñor's epic *Rain of Gold* is the Latino equivalent of Alex Haley's *Roots,* and Rudolfo A. Anaya's *Bless Me, Ultima,* is a classic tale of coming of age in the Southwest. Tomás Rivera, considered by many to be the grandfather of Chicano letters, wrote, originally in Spanish, . . . *And the Earth Did Not Part,* a collection of vignettes on itinerant rural life that is highly regarded by Latino critics. Rivera, who died in 1984, was born in Crystal City, Texas, in 1935 and received a doctorate in romance languages and literature from the University of Oklahoma. A true man of letters, he was a poet, novelist, short story writer, literary critic, college administrator, and educational specialist whose work deserves an English-speaking audience.

A handful of forceful Chicana writers who aggressively fought for a voice are finally sharing the stage. Latin American women novelists, one ought to remember, took some 450 years to find, paraphrasing Virginia Woolf, a room of their own in the library of regional literature. With the exception of Sor Juana Inés de La Cruz, a seventeenth-century nun who astonished the Spanish-speaking world with her conceptual sonnets and philosophical prose, it has not been until recently that the feminine intellect has been allowed to enlighten the eclipsed dimension of the Hispanic psyche. Rosario Castellanos, Isabel Allende, Elena Poniatowska, and Gabriela Mistral (the latter received the 1945 Nobel Prize), to name a few of the best, have explored and dissected a facet of reality left unapproached for far too long. A list of Latinas, equally combative, who write in English might begin with Sabine Ulibarrí, whose short stories *Tierra Amarilla: Stories of New Mexico* appeared in the early 1970s; others were included in the anthology of feminist writing, *This Bridge Called My Back,* edited by Cherríe Moraga and Gloria Anzaldúa, which was published in 1981, the same year as Lorna Dee Cervantes's *Emplumada.*

Sandra Cisneros, best-selling author of *The House on Mango Street,* has become the ultimate symbol, the Frida Kahlo of her generation. During an interview, she once said that she began to write when she couldn't see herself in the novels and stories she was reading. Born in 1954, her most famous work, *Woman Hollering Creek and Other Stories,* is a mosaic of voices of Latinos who joke, love, hate, and comment on fame and sexuality. To call them "stories" may not always be accurate. They are verbal photographs, memorabilia, reminiscences of growing up in a Mexican-American milieu, San Antonio in particular. Cisneros's intention isn't only to explain a trauma or to re-create a certain flavor of childhood or a long-lost feeling for a beloved or an acquaintance, but to offer a persuasive portrait of Chicanas as aggressive and independent. Candid, engaging, rich in linguistic tricks, her style, a bit slick to my taste, is always ideologically charged: She is a writer of opinions, an intellectual attacking society's weaknesses. In her text "Eyes of Zapata," for example, she reevaluates the 1910 Mexican Revolution from the female perspective. It is not that the *soldados* alone are fighting the war but their women also have a fundamental role: They function as a compass. Although intimate and domestic, their battle is equally important. And her piece "The Malboro Man," about a macho who is also a homosexual, reminds me of Nash Candelaria's brilliant tale "The Day the Cisco Kid Shot John Wayne," in which Wayne's anti-Mexican animosity in film is contradicted by the fact that in life he married a woman named Pilar or Chata—a Mexican. Cisneros's major contribution to Latino letters can be found in her strength of approaching the Hispanic experience north of Rio Grande in a non-apologetic, authentic fashion.

Alongside Cisneros, and also among the most representative of Chicana writers, is Ana Castillo, veteran novelist, poet, translator, and editor, whose books were published by small presses in Arizona, Texas, and New Mexico. She is among the most daring and experimental and, as Robert Coover and William Gaddis know, experimentation costs. Born in 1953 in Chicago, Castillo is the author of *Sapogonia. An Anti-Romance in 3/8 Meter,* published in 1989, and *The Mixquiahuala Letters,* an avant-garde epistolary novel that to me is her most memorable work. Built around the friendship of a couple of independent Latino women, Alicia and Teresa, whom we accompany through introspective letters from their youthful travels to Mexico to their middle years in the U.S., this unconventional narrative is an open tribute to Julio Cortázar's *Hopscotch,* a novel typical of the French *nouveau roman* and designed as a labyrinth in which the writer suggests at least a couple of possible sequences for reading. Castillo's book offers three sequences: one for conformists, one for cynics, and one for Quixotic readers. Her obsession is to turn popular and sophisticated genres upside down, to revisit their structure by decomposing them. Her third novel, *So Far from God,* parodies the Spanish-speaking *telenovela.* Framed within two decades of life in Tome, a small hamlet in central New Mexico, it tells the story of a Chicana mother, Sofia, and her daughters: La Loca, Fe, Esperanza, and Caridad—names recalling a famous south-of-the-border melodrama. We are in the terrain of overt sentimentality: Magic realism is combined with social satire as prostitutes, miracles, prophecies, resurrections, and a visit to the Chicano activism of the 1960s are intertwined.

As I have been arguing, readers need not go too far to hear the everlasting Chicano outcry. It's everywhere in literature, music, and art. The official account of the Mexican-American experience is Rodolfo Acuña's book, *Occupied America: A History of Chicanos.* As the author, who teaches at California State University at Northridge, once put it, the first edition was influenced by Third World writers like Frantz Fanon and was filled with moral courage. That tone indeed has only slightly subsided in the next two editions. Eight years after it first appeared, the second edition, a bit calmer, was much more documented. It offered enormous data to explain injustices suffered by Chicanos in New Mexico, Texas, and California. And the third standardized edition, published in 1988, the one best known to researchers and students, has slowly become the official history of the Chicano movement. Divided into eleven chapters, it details the conquest of Mexico's northwest, the colonization of New Mexico and Texas (his analysis of the Alamo incident, for instance, is full of fury), and the occupation of Arizona. From there, Acuña studies the building of the Southwest between 1900 and 1930, examines the Great Depression from the perspective of Mexican-Americans, and centers his attention in the upheaval of the 1960s, only to finish with two sections unified by the title "The Age of the Brokers," in which Ronald Reagan's administration is dissected. Acuña describes the ways in which racism and discrimination were common after the Treaty of Guadalupe Hidalgo was signed: Those who acquired the lands in New Mexico, California, Texas, and the other southern regions, while refraining from keeping slaves, treated Hispanics as dogs. In 1877, the El Paso Salt War was waged by Mexican-Americans when Anglo Texans denied them their salt rights. Among the first attempts to organize agricultural unions occurred in Texas in 1883; in 1888 Las Gorras Blancas, a precursor of civil rights organizations, defended the rights of Mexican-Americans against Anglo homesteaders and cattle and lumber companies in New Mexico; a year later the United People's party, organized by Las Gorras Blancas in New Mexico, ran Mexican American candidates for office in local elections for the first time. At the same time, a desire to see history from the victim's perspective arose among intellectuals. Novels, memoirs, plays, and accounts, such as Mariano Vallejo's 1875 history of California, circulated.

Meanwhile, on the other side of the border, Porfirio Díaz led a successful coup d'état in 1876 in Mexico, after which he exercised absolute power for thirty-three years. As often happens in Latin America, his tyrannical regime, which imposed new taxes on just about everything, offered an interregnum for the economy to develop. Since the War of Independence some six decades before, opposing political factions and foreign powers had struggled to retain control of the country. Díaz (whose image, after blunt attacks by successive south-of-the-border governments, was finally rehabilitated in textbooks in the 1980s under the administration of Carlos Salinas de Gortari) stabilized Mexico, brought in foreign investment, introduced technology, and built a useful rail system. But Chicanos did not participate in such a transformation: We were sold as merchandise and forgotten. The trauma would remain for many decades, and Chicanos still retain a sense of rivalry vis-à-vis their Mexican counterparts. Memory is incredibly painful and does not disappear. Tino Villanueva's poem "Scene from the Movie *Giant*," referring to the film version of Edna Ferber's novel, is about a Chicano finding his own cultural identity by transforming his experience with racism into literature:

What I have from 1956 is one instant at the Holiday
Theater, where a small dimension of a film, as in
A Dream, became the feature of the whole. It
Comes toward the end . . . the café scene, which
Reels off a slow spread of light, a stark desire

To see itself once again, though there is, at times,
No joy in old time movies. it begins with the
Jingling of bells and the plainer truth of it:
That the front door to a roadside café opens and
Shuts as the Benedicts (Rock Hudson and Elizabeth

Taylor), their daughter Luz, and daughter-in-law
Juana and grandson Jordy, pass through it not

Unobserved. Nothing sweeps up into an actual act
Of kindness into the eyes of Serge, who owns this
Joint and has it out for dark-eyed Juana, weary

Of too much longing that comes with rejection.
Juana, from barely inside the door, and Serge,
Stout and unpleased from behind his counter, clash
Eye-on-eye, as time stands like heat. Silence is
Everywhere, acquiring the name of hatred and Juana

Cannot bear the dread—the dark-jowl gaze of Serge
Against her skin. Suddenly: bells go off again.
By the quiet effort of walking, three Mexican-
Types step in, whom Serge refuses to serve . . .
Those gestures of his, those looks that could kill

A heart you carry in memory for years. A scene from
The past has caught me in the act of living: even
To myself I cannot say except with worried phrases
Upon a paper, how I withstood arrogance in a gruff
Voice coming with the deep-dyed colors of the screen;

How in the beginning I experienced almost nothing to
Say and now wonder if I can ever live enough to tell
The after-tale. I remember this and I remember myself
Locked into a back-row seat—I am a thin, flickering,
Helpless light, local-looking, unthought of at fourteen.

Our twentieth century began with workers' unions organizing to defend
their constituencies. The Clifton-Morenci Mine Strike in 1903, for example,
although unsuccessful, politicized Mexican-American workers in Arizona and
New Mexico. A fascinating chapter in Latino politics concerns the Flores
Magón brothers, Ricardo and Enrique. (Douglas Day, the biographer of
Malcolm Lowry, wrote a novel about the period.) Opposing the Díaz regime,
the Flores Magón brothers, anarchists, were exiled in Texas. In 1905, they
began publishing the influential magazine *Regeneración,* and a couple of years
later founded El Partido Liberal Mexicano (the infamous PLM), a syndicalist
anarchist political party, in the southern United States. The party had a gazette,
Aurora, in which Sara Estela Ramírez, poet, PLM organizer, and an early
activist for women's rights, edited columns. The Magóns' ideological voice

had far-reaching echoes, and the Mexican Revolution, led by Emiliano Zapata and Pancho Villa, which began in 1910, caused the first large-scale migration of poor *campesinos* northward. The Flores Magón brothers were found guilty of violating the U.S. Espionage Act and sentenced to prison in 1912. Nevertheless, their ideology lived on, and during the Chicano uprising in the 1960s, their anarchy acquired a new breadth. Regeneration became a ghost, the spirit behind the anarchism that prevailed.

Immigration and its discontents: Its ups and downs always depend on the need for cheap labor, and regulations are irremediably unfair. One of the crucial stages of the U.S. government's relationship with Latin America began in 1924 with the so-called Quota Law, which reduced the total number of immigrants and fixed the number from each nation of origin, favoring Europeans and effectively barring Asians and Hispanics. In 1933, the Good Neighbor Policy, implemented by President Roosevelt, declared the government's opposition to armed intervention in Latin America. About a decade later, Washington instituted the Emergency Labor Program, known as the Bracero Program, to import Mexican workers during World War II, because soldiers—blacks, whites, Asians, and others—were busy fighting the enemy. "You need the hands, we need the money," seemed to be the slogan. In 1965 an amendment of the 1952 exclusionary McCarran-Walter Immigration and Nationality Act replaced national quotas with hemispheric limitations, providing for acceptance of political refugees. Thus, the Tortilla Curtain, as the Rio Grande is called, could be considered simply a transit point: Until the 1994 North American Free Trade Agreement, the flux of cheap labor was overwhelming and the United States and the Mexican economy were dependent on the mobilization of such human energy.

By 1940 Chicano adolescents, mainly in California, already came to be known as *Pachucos*. As a Guggenheim fellow and still a young man, Octavio Paz spent time in Los Angeles in the late 1940s. World War II had just concluded, and California's Latino population was becoming notably visible. The result of Paz's tenure in the region was his groundbreaking volume *The Labyrinth of Solitude,* the first chapter of which is devoted to *Pachucos*, radical children of Mexican parents born north of the border. He writes: "[Mexican-Americans] have lived in the city [of Los Angeles] for many years, wearing the same clothes and speaking the same language as the other inhabitants, and they feel ashamed of their origins; yet no one would mistake them for authentic North Americans. I refuse to believe that physical features are as important as is commonly thought. What distinguishes them, I think, is their furtive, restless air: they act like persons who are wearing disguises, who are afraid of a stranger's look because it could strip them and leave them stark naked." He also argues that *Pachucos* react to the hostility around them by openly affirming their personality. He portrays them as lone Mexicans, orphans lacking positive values, lost souls without a whole inheritance: language, religion, customs, beliefs. It isn't difficult to understand why Paz has infuriated so many Chicano intellectuals: His views of Mexicans north of the Rio Grande are negative, reductive. Rather than feeling admiration for the hybrid that is being formed in front of his eyes, he rejects the Hispanic culture of the Southwest as illegitimate and inauthentic. Not surprisingly, since his 1950 classic was published, his remarks have been discussed time and again among Latinos—as if, in the act of antagonizing Paz, a new consciousness is being forged.

In 1968 Chicano high school students conducted a boycott in Los Angeles to protest educational deficiencies in the public schools. During the boycott, nearly 3,500 students did not attend classes for eight days. The stage was ready for César Chávez, née César Estrada Chávez, creator of La Causa, a nonviolent organization that fought to make Chicanos and, indirectly, Latinos realize the advantages of the American Dream. As a political entity, Chávez, five feet six inches, never an eloquent speaker or a *simpático*, father of *la huelga*, and an admirer of Mahatma Gandhi, advocated resistance to prejudice and discrimination and affirmed biculturalism. It was the 1960s, and Latino life would never be the same. Unlike his grass-roots predecessors, Chávez managed to organize farmworkers into a unified group. His National Farm Workers Association, later called the United Farm Workers, joined a grape pickers' strike in 1966, and together with leader Dolores Huerta, an important Chicana activist (others are Virginia Musquiz, Luna Mount, Linda Benítez, Francisca Flores, Vicky Castro, and María Hernández), led farmworkers on a three-hundred-mile march from Delano, California, to Sacramento. An unprecedented number of urban Chicanos and non-Chicanos supported the strike, thus accelerating the transition of a labor movement into what became the Chicano civil rights movement. Other figures joined Chavez in the struggle. In Denver, for instance, Rodolfo "Corky" Gonzáles led the Crusade for Justice; in New Mexico, Reies López Tijerina organized La Alianza Federal de Mercedes; and in Crystal City, Texas, José Angel Gutiérrez formed La Raza Unida party. Student support and activity were also important components of the Chicano movement and were represented, after 1969, by the Movimiento Estudiantil Chicano de Aztlán. Resistance continued. The grape boycott quickly spread to Canada and Europe, and Chávez acquired enormous political power and an aura of sainthood.

The grape boycott was followed by a period of upheaval in which, for example, political leaders stormed into courtrooms in Tierra Amarilla, New Mexico, to free colleagues held in custody, and student activists founded the Brown Berets in Los Angeles, a militant organization modeled on the Black Panthers. As a result, an awareness of things Latino in general became widespread, and, in the 1970s and later, Chicano studies programs were established at universities in Arizona, California, Colorado, New Mexico, Texas, the Midwest, and the Pacific Northwest.

New York and other major cities of the Northeast were not too far behind. Inspired by the Black Panthers and their Chicano counterparts, Puerto Rican activists organized in the early seventies and even before, forming groups like the Young Lords. Through riots in East Harlem, violent clashes with the police, and other forms of protest, they sympathized with their Mexican-American siblings on the other coast. Calling themselves "revolutionary nationalists," their demands included Puerto Rico's independence, the end of racism and discrimination, and economic and educational improvement for the Borinquén community. The Anglo establishment was perceived as evil. Animosity reigned among Latinos. It was an open war without compromises.

César Chávez, the force behind so much of this change, was born in 1927, near Yuma, Arizona, the second of five children of Juana and Librado Chávez. His father's parents had migrated from Mexico in 1880. César spent his childhood on the family's 160-acre farm. But during the Great Depression, the family lost its farm. Along with thousands of other families in the Southwest, the Chávezes sought a new life in California. They found it picking carrots, cotton, and other crops in arid valleys, following the sun in search of the next harvest and the next migrants' camp. César never graduated from high school. As his obituary in the New York Times claimed when he died in early 1993, Chávez once counted sixty-five elementary schools he had attended "for a day, a week or a few months." His parents settled in San Jose in 1939, where his father became active in an effort to organize workers at a dried-fruit packing plant. The experience was decisive and remained in his mind forever. Chávez served two years in the navy during World War II, then resumed his life as a migrant, married Helen Fabela in Delano, and had eight children. Deeply influenced by professional radicals, he helped Chicanos organize into a political bloc in the early 1950s. He joined organizations devoted to community service, helped register Pochos to vote, and later criticized the organizations for being dominated by non-Hispanic liberals. He quit these organizations and returned to Delano and formed the National Farm Workers Association.

The 1960 census claimed that Chicanos, 3,842,000 of them, were the second largest minority population in the United States. In 1965, the same year that President Johnson signed the Voting Rights Act eliminating all discriminatory qualifying tests for voter registration, Chávez's National Farm Workers Association joined the Filipino farmworkers in the Delano, California grape strike. By 1965, as the *New York Times* claimed, Chávez had organized 1,700 families and persuaded two growers to raise wages moderately. His fledgling union was too weak for a major strike. But 800 workers in the virtually moribund Agricultural Workers Organization Committee went on strike against grape growers in Delano, and some of the members of Chávez's group demanded that they join the strike.

That was the beginning of five years of *la huelga*, in which the frail labor leader became internationally famous as he battled the economic power of the farmers and corporations in the San Joaquin Valley. In 1966 Chávez and Reies López Tijerina led Alianza members in reclaiming part of the Kit Carson National Forest in New Mexico. And in an Albuquerque walkout, fifty Chicanos protested their lack of representation on the Equal Employment Opportunity Commission. It was also the year when the Black Panther party, the black revolutionary party, was founded in Oakland, California, by Huey Newton and Bobby Seale.

Like Gandhi, Chávez often went on hunger strikes to accentuate his pleas, and he became an international leader around 1968 when his most visible campaign took place: He urged Americans not to buy table grapes produced in the San Joaquin Valley until growers agreed to union contracts. The boycott proved to be a huge success; a public opinion poll quoted by the *New York Times* found that 17 million Americans had stopped buying grapes because of the boycott. In July 1970, after losing millions of dollars, the grape growers finally agreed to sign—it was the highest point in Chávez's career, in particular, and of any Latino leader's, for that matter. His angelic struggle also had a dark side. As a good Hispanic dictator, intolerant, undemocratic, authoritarian, he purged his union of non-Latino officials. He built a commune-style union headquarters called La Paz in a former sanatorium in

Keene, near Bakersfield, California. (Chávez's ordeal is portrayed in the 1972 film *Yo Soy Chicano*.)

Folklore, as Américo Paredes claims, is of particular importance to minority groups because their basic sense of identity is expressed in a language with an unofficial status, different from the one used by the official culture. Our folklore is multifarious, complex. We paint, we write, we scream, we dance: pictorial expression, literature, music, body movement. Graffiti and street art are our favorite forms of protest. Since, as John Berger states, paintings underscore an act of possession, we transgress, encroach, infringe, and disobey. By attacking the aesthetic of Western civilization, we create a chaotic alternative: murals on enormous walls and indecipherable signs on urban walls. As Tomás Ybarra-Frausto, the art critic, points out, a signature of Chicano street art, a form of protest, is the initials *c/s*, meaning *con safos*; this motto typically appears at the bottom of a piece of graffiti or a mural in barrio calligraphy and serves as a charm against defacement. It also warns that any insult happening there will also occur at the offending party's place. The sign is also used to link murals created by Chicanos to graffiti, a fundamental form of political activism, albeit anarchic, omnipresent in the 1960s and still a large part of the way urban youths manifest their discontent. Crucial to the understanding of graffiti is *rascuachismo,* a term suggesting a unique aesthetic embodied by these arts: the attempt to introduce low-brow culture into sophisticated art.

Muralism and graffiti, of course, are siblings. And urban muralism is perhaps the best exponent of *rascuache* art. Chicano art in the United States, public and private, has been deeply influenced by *los tres grandes,* the trio of Mexican muralists—José Clemente Orozco, Diego Rivera, and David Alfaro Siqueiros—who, during the 1930s, in what some critics called *la fiebre mexicana,* painted New Deal art projects north of the Rio Grande: glorious murals in California, Michigan, New Hampshire, and New York about the post-revolutionary reality at home and in the vast Hispanic orbit. From the mid-nineteenth century to the 1930s, Latino pictorial art remained a shadow in the Anglo-Saxon world. In the United States, around 1929, Antonio García, considered a precursor to Chicano artists today, began producing paintings, such as *Aztec Advance,* that were based on pre-Columbian themes and strengthened the value of Hispanic roots. His contribution and that of his Chicano contemporaries remained unknown until the left-wing Mexican muralists came on the scene and slowly began to be recognized. Although other artists, including lampooner José Guadalupe Posada—whose *calaveras* draw heavily on the socialist revolution and who will be discussed further in Chapter 4—also remain inspiring forces, the three muralists have received enormous popular acclaim. Orozco was hired to paint at Pomona and Dartmouth colleges, as well as at the New School for Social Research, and Rivera was hired to paint at the Detroit Institute of the Arts and at Rockefeller Center. Siqueiros, somewhat of an anomaly, came to the United States as a political exile and was the only orthodox Marxist of the group; he ended up deplored by friends and comrades who considered him to be dangerous and more of a radical than Rivera. Siqueiros painted murals in Los Angeles in 1932 that attacked imperialism, racism, and corruption; he participated in the Spanish Civil War, and was involved in the 1940 assassination of Leon Trotsky in Coyoacán, a suburb of Mexico City. Art historian Richard H. Pell has described how Mexican artists, in era in which Edmund Wilson persuaded artists to confront daily life—to act, to commit themselves—became an inspiration to many U.S. intellectuals, including Chicanos, as they embraced the "twin doctrines of community and collectivism."

As expected, the craze eclipsed after a decade. Orozco, Rivera, and Siqueiros returned to their native country, World War II broke out, and a change in political mood swept the United States. Admiration soon changed to disgust. Abstract expressionism took over the art world, and political matters, at least temporarily, were relegated to a second place. Even the political Left began to feel uncomfortable with the muralists' direct, impolite message. Anti-Stalinists and Trotskyites began attacking Siqueiros for his role in the 1930s. Some of Rivera's murals in the United States, including one at the California School of Fine Arts and another at Rockefeller Center in New York City, were destroyed or covered up in that decade or afterward, because they didn't fit with the spirit of the exhibits at that time; other paintings were stored in boxes and not viewed by the public for years. Sometime in 1934, after the destruction of the Rockefeller Center mural which generated controversy and countless opinion pieces, Rivera produced at the National Palace of Fine Arts in Mexico City a later version of his Rockefeller Center mural, as revenge.

Before the meltdown surrounding the Mexican muralists, artistic interest in things Hispanic reached a climax in 1940 with *Twenty Centuries of Mexican Art,* an exhibit sponsored by the Museum of Modern Art in Manhattan and the Mexican government. This was an ideological coup to sell Mexican art to the United States, which, half a century later, would again be repeated at the same institution. This first exhibit occurred after Lázaro Cárdenas's controversial nationalization of the oil industry and antigringo sentiment south of the border became widespread; an effort was made to promote an image of the Mexican psyche as ancient, balanced, and rich in tradition and religious symbolism and as having emerged from a country with an abundance of historical dramas and in constant search of its identity. The objectives of the second major exhibit of Mexican art at the Metropolitan Museum of Art in 1990 were similar: to show Mexico as a friend, a politically stable neighbor that was ready to orient its sights to the north and become part of the North American Free Trade Agreement with the United States and Canada.

Curiously, the first exhibit failed to attract any interest in Rivera's physically and psychologically troubled wife, the artist Frida Kahlo. The descendant of a Hungarian Jewish father and a Mexican mother, Kahlo had been crippled in a traffic accident in adolescence. As her biographer Hayden Herrera noted, she was raised as a conservative Catholic, but later in life became a vociferous political ideologue and a member of the Communist party, encouraging native painters to turn away from European easel art toward art inspired by Marxist literature and Mexican folklore. An admirer of Emiliano Zapata, she was a feminist and an indigenista who strongly supported the growth of Mexican nationalism. Paradoxically, she admired William Blake and Paul Klee, Paul Gauguin, and Henri Rousseau's primitivism, but, more than anything else, she was in touch with the female essence of the Hispanic spirit. Late in the 1980s, Kahlo acquired a second chance, thanks to her surrealistic interpretations. Kahlo's pictorial art, in a critic's words, sometimes seems like a complaint metamorphosed into images.

Although Kahlo's work had been ignored in the United States, politicians, artists, and rock superstars, Latino and otherwise, from Madonna to Luis Valdez and Gloria Estefan, would eventually embrace Kahlo as a true political martyr in the broadest sense: intimately, as an embattled woman betrayed time and again by her womanizer husband with whom she shared a tormented, if artistically stimulating relationship, and publicly, as a struggling militant ready to sacrifice to advance the cause of women in society. Soon her painting began to surpass Rivera's, in attention and in monetary value, and it is not surprising that, since the 1960s, numerous Chicana painters have found in Kahlo the perfect idol. For instance, Yrenia D. Cervantez's 1978 *Homaje a Frida Kahlo,* which toured the United States in the late 1980s as part of an extraordinary exhibit called "CARA. Chicano Art: Resistance and Affirmation," is full of Kahlo's favorite motifs—pregnancy, blood, flowers, and nudity—and is a sound tribute to a south-of-the-border influence.

Latino music, directly influenced by Violeta Parra, Victor Jara, Caetano Veloso, Silvio Rodríguez, the *Nueva trova cubano,* and typified by the songs of Rubén Blades and the lyrics of blind Puerto Rican songwriter José Feliciano, is less politically outspoken than other Latino arts. Performed in nightclubs to arenas, Latino music seems to prefer to oscillate between existential dilemmas and folklore. (Rubén Blades has a song about spitfire Pedro Navaja's accidental death at the hands of a prostitute.) Musicians such as Teresa Covarrubias, Suzanne Vega (stepdaughter of Puerto Rican novelist Ed Vega), Eddie Cano, Ritchie Valens, Los Caifanes, Los Illegals, and Los Lobos, all have sung about daily occurrences, possessive love, revenge, and obsessive encounters with the opposite sex. This personal, belligerent Latino identity has also been forged in film, even beyond national borders. An early movie about Chicanos, Alejandro Galindo's *Campeón sin corona,* is about Robert "Kid" Terranova, a boxer from the slums who lacks the self-confidence to become a star and who is psychologically cowed by Joe Ronda, a Mexican-American given to shouting in English during the matches. Using authentic Mexico City slang, the plot deals with the Latino inferiority complex, a topic discussed in Chapter 4, in the context of the Latino racial and sexual identity. Crucial historical incidents have also been explored in films about Chicanos. For instance, the controversial, independently made 1954 film, *Salt of the Earth,* about a strike involving Chicanos in Silver City, New Mexico, was produced by the International Union of Mine, Mill, and Smelter Workers and had a cast that included Mexican actress Rosaura Revueltas, who was deported from the United States for her association with the film.

To this day, Latino art retains a belligerent tone, not only because it introduces ideological messages, but, more important, because it promotes and uses indigenous folklore to solidify an evasive collective identity with an unofficial status. In the 1930s as los tres grandes were hailed by Anglos, Chicano artist Patrocinio Barela, a New Mexican carver, gained national recognition also for his santos, which reached deep into Mexican-American folklore for inspiration and continue to appeal to modern art collectors. At the end of the 1940s, another major breakthrough for Latino art came when Armando Baeza's sculpture of the Vírgen María won a prize in Los Angeles and was immediately recognized by *Newsweek* and other media channels. In retrospect, the sporadic recognition of these highlights signaled a time of creative insemination, in preparation for the overwhelming explosion of visual images.

Latino art, politically committed, profoundly rooted in the Hispanic tradition, acquired true relevance and significance in the 1960s, primarily among Chicanos, as an integral part of the upheaval of César Chávez's United Farm Workers Union, a movement made up of disenfranchised land-grant owners, urban working-class people, and students in California, Texas, and New Mexico, who were ready to stamp their signature in the nation's mind. Street art, the type immortalized by los tres grandes, became pertinent again in posters and murals expressing popular anger and anxiety that appeared, like a rainbow after a storm, throughout the Southwest and as far away as Chicago. A crucial ideological influence was the Cuban Revolution. Meanwhile the revolution also seemed to usher in a new age of printmaking, whose art was largely based on a dreamlike infatuation with a benign Hispanic utopia. (Since 1959, Fidel Castro and Che Guevara were, naturally, the postermakers' idols.) Exhibits of Cuban posters announcing campaigns against illiteracy and for vaccination, attacks against foreign imperialism, and the adulation of Soviet culture influenced artists in other countries. *The Art of Revolution: Castro's Cuba: 1959–1970,* a large, illustrated volume, reached workshops in California, New Mexico, and Texas, and exhibits of Cuban artists in Latino galleries north of the Rio Grande were received with great excitement. (Understandably, of the Latino groups who were active at the time, Cuban-Americans, most of whom had been in the United States only a few years, were the least enthusiastic and committed and the most ambiguous about the radical hopes expressed during the 1960s.)

El Grito de Aztlán, the first Chicano art gallery, opened in Denver in the late 1960s. Capturing the spirit of the times, Ester Hernández's poster *Sun Mad Raisins* was a valuable synthesis of the collective animosity: us against Anglos, an ancient liberation struggle, a need to repossess what was lost. The Farm Workers Movement also produced a forum through which Chicano artists could express themselves: *El Malcriado: The Voice of the Farm Worker.* This bilingual biweekly, which began publication in 1964, included cartoons by its staff cartoonist Andy Zermeño that were reminiscent in their ironical approach to historical events of Mexican lampooner José Guadalupe Posada's illustrations (whose engravings would appear on the cover). The cartoons recorded the activities of Richard Nixon and Chávez's grape boycott; Don Sotaco, one of Zermeño's characters, was a kind of underdog who was always abused by others, again signaling the era's dichotomy between oppression and liberation.

The goal of my overview of Latino art is to show how creativity has been a vehicle for conflict and resistance. The continual lack of access to mainstream institutions and the sense that life has to be lived in the periphery has forced artists to assume, to be committed to, a political voice. Such a voice has led to a sense of cultural nationalism. Through theater, through novels, poems, and stories, through pictorial art, the community has created a distinction between "us" and "you," between a dominant culture and an oppressed culture. Consequently, a lot of mythologizing, an incredible amount of propaganda, goes into the shaping of a work of art. Because a physical place to feel comfortable is nonexistent, the artist is called to create a new abstract space where Hispanics north of the Rio Grande can feel at home—an imaginary geography that often inverts social roles. "We, not you, are in power here!" the artist seems to imply. Ironically, the war fought through art ends up opening new doors to militancy, which means that Latino artists see creativity as sister to politics. To create is to transform, to accuse, to make suffering evident.

In the 1960s, the overly ideological facet of Latino art openly expressed anti–Vietnam War sentiment. Posters were created to promote antiwar rallies that were organized as early as 1967 by a number of Chicano leaders like "Corky" Gonzalez and López Tijerina, as well as to show support, mainly among Chicanos, for the American Indian Movement. At this time Native American groups were becoming more visible in their political activities; for example, the former prison on Alcatraz was occupied, and Navajos and Hopis occupied their former lands. These actions reminded Mexican-Americans of their own native roots before the arrival of the Spanish conquistadors and resulted in neoindigenism, an aesthetic concept, manifest in literature, music, and visual art, which suggested that the people of Aztlán were actually *más mexicanos que los meros mexicanos* (even more authentic Mexicans than their siblings south of the border), simply because the Aztecs, as a cohesive civilization, had originated in California and New Mexico. (The concrete original geography changed from one interpreter to another.) Aboriginal images, already present in the art of Posada, Siqueiros, Orozco, and Rivera, acquired a refreshing tone under Chicano muralists and oil painters, and the search for a collective identity through strong religious, mystical, and spiritual ingredients was intimately linked to accusations of racism and discrimination from Anglos and freedom from oppression in general.

Scholarly works on Latino art began to appear in the early 1970s, accompanied by a sense of collective accomplishment. Jacinto Quirarte's *Mexican-American Artists*, a historical survey of Chicano art and artists published in 1973, offered an encyclopedic view of the development of the pictorial tradition and legitimated the collective craft. At about the same time, the Los Angeles County Museum of Art held an exhibit of an artistic quartet, known as *Los Four*—Carlos Almaráz, Frank Romero, Beto de la Rocha, and Gilbert Luján—and many other exhibits of Chicano painters followed.

The Chicano movement and the growing importance of Mexican-Americans in the Southwest inspired a handful of cinematic explorations of uneven quality, from Pepito Romay's 1973 *De sangre chicana,* which was well received in Los Angeles, to low-quality movies such as *Soy chicano y mexicano* and *Chicano grueso calibre.* These latter were made for the growing number of uneducated, often illegal residents in East Los Angeles and environs who, amounting to several million, were a lucrative market for south-of-the-border producers. Alfonso Arau, an actor-director with residences in Mexico and Hollywood and the husband of novelist Laura Esquivel, made *The Promised Dream,* about Mexican illegal workers in the United States, and *Chicano Power,* a satire of the Chicano movement of the 1960s. Nevertheless, political activism soon faded away. One can say that, overall, Latinos achieved a sense of self-esteem and the certainty that the country would pay attention if the uproar was boisterous and tumultuous enough. Yet, I cannot fail to feel a sense of general defeat: None of the objectives expressed at that time—justice, freedom, upward mobility—changed the actual social conditions of Chicanos, Puerto Ricans, and Central and South Americans in the United States. Although extraordinary Latin American painters (Rufino Tamayo, Fernando Botero, Jacobo Borges, Alberto Gironella, Roberto Matta) have achieved international recognition hand in hand with world-class magic realist writers from such countries as Colombia, Peru, and Argentina, considerably smaller interest has been shown in most things Latino, pictorial or literary.

The generally accepted belligerence of Latinos has ostracized those representing compliance. Thus whereas Joan Baez, author of the memoirs *Daybreak* and *And a Voice to Sing With,* whose politically committed songs and convictions have probably been strengthened by her difficult personal life, is applauded, Anthony Quinn, actor and painter who wrote an autobiographical account, *The Original Sin: A Self-Portrait,* symbolizes the sellout: *el vendido.* Consumerism obviously ameliorates the ideological message. A didactic movie like Ramón Menéndez's *Stand and Deliver*—based on the life of Jaime Escalante, a Colombian-born mathematics teacher in a poor Los Angeles neighborhood who found a persuasive technique for helping his unprepared students pass a difficult algebra exam—stressed the intellectual potential of Latinos, leaving politics aside. Playwright and film and stage director Luis Valdez is an example of an artist who has consistently embraced an ideological message in his work. Born to migrant farmworkers in Delano in 1940, Valdez has seen his work produced from an early age (his first full-length play, *The Shrunken Head of Pancho Villa,* was staged at San José State College in 1964) and then matured into a dramatist with a resonant theatrical voice. *Zoot Suit,* his 1978 play, among the best performed by his troupe, Teatro Campesino, was the first Chicano play to open on Broadway; it was made into an astonishing experimental film directed by Valdez in 1981, with Edward James Olmos portraying a rioting zoot suiter. As critic Jorge Huerta argues, the play, dealing with the infamous Sleepy Lagoon murder trial of 1942, exposes social ills and is close in style to the docudrama, owing much to Bertolt Brecht: A didactic technique is used throughout the play; newspaper clips are used as set decorations, and the narrator, El Pachuco, representing the Aztec concept of *el nahual,* an other self, often stops the action to make a point. From *La carpa de los Rascuachis* to the staged re-creation of a television sitcom in *I Don't Have to Show You No Stinking Badges!* and the movie *La Bamba*—in which the Chicano musician Richard Valenzuela, after taking the name Ritchie Valens to write and record "Come On, Let's Go" and "Donna," dies in a 1959 plane crash alongside Buddy Holly—Valdez's plays and films retain a remarkable authenticity in their attempt to study Latino myths and stereotypes.

Art and politics—the crossroads where the two meet is a thermometer that charts the heat at the heart of the Latino community. The development of a collective identity among Hispanics north of the border can be divided into three clear-cut stages: (1) from 1848 to the mid-1940s, with the Sleepy Lagoon incident and the Zoot Suit Riots, in which artists began to understand their role as speakers for the silent masses; (2) from the end of World War II to the Chicano movement, in which art was injected with an explosive ideological message; and (3) from the mid-1970s to the present, an era in which Latinos have slowly traveled to center stage, using their art as a mirror to the soul, never substituting the political for the nonpolitical but, because of the multicultural craze, being accepted by society at large as a victimized minority that needs to be heard. From an art produced for communal consumption to one reaching a non-Latino audience, concrete stages can be traced. Through art a fierce war has been fought against the Anglo establishment, one in which the winner might have lost one or two battles but perseverance and commitment added up to a final victory. Again, one should remember that since Latin American societies are incredibly repressive the move to the United States, the search for freedom, is all the more passionate. And once the juices of freedom are tasted one is not likely to reject its delicious flavor. Since colonial times Hispanic art has been imbued with politics—as a new stage, the United States only accentuates certain tonalities. In short, to be a fashionable Latino today is a result of a long ideological struggle fought throughout the decades. Sandra Cisneros cannot be understood without precursors like Posada, Rivera, and Frida Kahlo, without César Chávez and "Corky" Gonzáles. Rubén Salazar, to return full circle, is an essential role model: a rebel, a revolutionary whose words were weapons. Discontent and rebellion are, par excellence, the artistic banner of Chicanos: to fight, to resist, to rebel. Our odyssey is targeted toward the *reconquista,* an attempt to regain full control over what was taken away from us. Will the struggle succeed? Italo Svevo's remarkable novel *The Confessions of Zeno,* about a man whose entire life is spent trying to quit smoking, comes to mind. When the protagonist finally overcomes his addiction, at the end of his life, he suddenly realizes that trying to stop smoking was an end in itself, a way of living, and neither smoking nor not smoking makes sense anymore. The end is swapped with the means, the goal replaced by the struggle's energy. Among Chicanos, whenever possible, the word *opposition* is highlighted: opposition and violence, opposition and rebellion, even when aggression is not a desired act but a simple reaction, as in the poem "Stupid America" by Abelardo Delgado.

Stupid america, see that chicano
with a big knife
in his steady hand
he doesn't want to knife you
he wants to sit on a bench
and carve christfigures
but you won't let him.
stupid america, hear that chicano
shouting curses on the street
he is a poet
without paper and pencil
and since he cannot write
he will explode.
stupid america, remember that chicanito
flunking math and english

he is the picasso
of your western states
but he will die
with one thousand masterpieces
hanging only from his hand.

4

◆ ◆ ◆

Ghosts

"Happy the nation, fortunate the age, whose history is not diverting," said Benjamin Franklin in *Poor Richard's Almanac*. To this I would add unhappy the nation whose ground was born out of greed. Whereas the Puritans in the Thirteen Colonies approached the New World as Paradise on Earth, a new home, a door closed to the Mother Country, the Spanish Crown sent explorers and conquistadors to appropriate the lands across the Atlantic: to dominate, possess, and subdue them. The conquistadors were not educators, persons of vision, technological innovators, or philosophical visionaries. Their tacit goal was to expand the domains of the Spanish empire, not to create a new homeland. The Iberians who came to conquer belonged to the worst segments of society: proud scoundrels, brutal criminals, greedy gold seekers, and ambitious military men whose awkward morality was still feudal at a time when more advanced Europeans were experimenting with free thinking and bourgeois capitalism.

We, the Latino people, are inhabited by a sense of outward pride. Indeed, to carry one's pride everywhere is a person's real commitment in life. Status is not achieved but inherited: A child of *extranjeros*, light-skinned, blond, and blue-eyed, is protected by a benign aura, regardless of his or her overall individual characteristics. A family with economic resources, unless given to frequent misconduct, is regarded as possessing outward pride. We are concerned with *lo que piensen los demás*, other people's views. Merit and achievement are ever-vanishing phantoms in our houses. We inhabit a palace of shifting mirrors, a labyrinth where fiction and reality intertwine, foreign, in the Anglo-Saxon world, where power swifts from liberals to conservatives and back again while the future is always open.

On December 10, 1830, less than a week before his death, Simón Bolívar is said to have pronounced, after a physician insisted that he confess and receive the sacraments: "What does this mean? . . . Can I be so ill that you talk to me of wills and confession? . . . How will I ever get out of this labyrinth?" Linear and circuitous, inextricable and impenetrable, the maze—complex, curved, distorted, wandering, winding, with constant double tracks—is a map of the Latino psyche. The apparent confusion it projects is only an illusion, a mask that is designed to entrap the mind, a concealment ready to catch you, to fool your senses in spite of your most purified awareness. A metaphor of metaphysical ambiguity, a figure that changes according to perspective, it confuses, infuriates, and disorganizes, but in its lack of organization, in its chaos, it is an example of perfected craftiness.

We are unstable. We simultaneously incorporate clarity and confusion, unity and multiplicity. It was not by accident that Gabriel García Márquez devoted an entire novel to unveiling what Bolívar truly meant by the labyrinth. And Márquez was not the only one: Jorge Luis Borges spent his life imagining perfect labyrinths: lineal, rectangular, and circular; spacial and temporal; material and spiritual. He envisioned a maze of mazes, one sinuous spreading labyrinth that would encompass the past and the future and in some way involve the stars. Octavio Paz, in *The Labyrinth of Solitude*, portrayed Hispanics as trapped in a maze of nostalgia and introspection. René Marqués's blunt attack on the Americanization of Puerto Rico and Miguel Piñero's strong realistic theater are about the labyrinths of violence and domination. Cristina Garcia's prose is about memory as a maze, and Oscar "Zeta" Acosta's *The Autobiography of a Brown Buffalo* is about politics and identity as a spider web.* Julio Cortázar's first published work under his own name, *The Kings,* is about the myth of the Minotaur. The Mexican comedian Cantinflas's verbal pyrotechnics were an entanglement. Graffiti is a visual paradox. Cuban-American painter Emilio Falero's art, including his oil painting *Findings,* explores a complex syncretism of styles. Diego Velásquez's *Las Meninas,* a 1656 painting about painting and the painter, is an exercise in self-reflection. Spanish painter Joan Miró was never a stranger to labyrinths, designed to puzzle and entertain, and neither was the Spanish filmmaker Luis Buñuel. In cultural terms, of course, the fountainhead, the source of sources, is the

*See my book *Bandido* (HarperCollins, 1995).

great Spanish writer Miguel de Cervantes, who was the perfect example of a man trapped in the labyrinthine corridors of reason and madness, enlightenment and obscurantism, Erasmus and Machiavelli. His alter ego, Alonso Quijano (aka Quejado or Quezada)—Don Quixote—may well be the ultimate Hispanic character, a knight incapable of distinguishing between reality and dreams, a topic essential to the Latino condition.

We are Quixotic, anarchic, and fatalistic at heart, imprisoned in our own individuality and sense of time, eternal inhabitants in a traumatic garden of history. La Mancha, where huge windmills are giant enemies and poor maidens are decorous ladies, is our eternal geography. Take cities, which, in the Jungian sense, express through architecture the collective mind of their inhabitants. Maps of Latin American cities are extremely baroque. We deliberately exhaust design possibilities with ornamentation and excess. Take any city, from Montevideo to Lima to Bogotá. Alejo Carpentier, in an insightful essay entitled "The City of Columns," argues that in Havana, a metropolis with innumerable columns, it is almost impossible to find two that are alike; each belongs to a different architectural style or, as Carpentier puts it, they are simply horrible creations, each different in its own way, a mixture of aesthetic views that never constitute a homogenized whole. From the simplicity of a convent to the baroque delirium of an aristocratic mansion, Carpentier saw only confusion and orderly disorder in our architecture: a lack of originality and, ironically, artificial authenticity. Our cities lack urban planning and suffer from poorly designed traffic routes, sewer systems, and electrical and telephone wiring. Like a pyramid, they are made of additions, levels or surfaces added to previous ones, but without the foundation to carry the weight and sophistication of the complete structure.

Hispanics, it goes without saying, are not the sole owners of a Platonic maze. What, if not the labyrinth, is Franz Kafka's kingdom? But the Czech's complex mental mapping is light years from that of Hispanics. Ours is neither a bureaucratic labyrinth nor a psychological one. We view the world as half lie, half truth. The Spanish conquistadors are symbols not of *laissez-faire,* but of the perverse accumulation of strength and authority. History is a labyrinth of forking ethical paths. Death brings birth brings death. Therefore, it is not surprising that the Spanish word for both history and story, past and fiction, is *historia.* Our past is a pantheon of mythical heroes, fabulous and often anachronistically artificial, fabricated to please the regime, stripped of their innermost rebellious spirit—men with courageous spirits who ended up as street names and in textbooks without any real value. Official history—

the established, government-controlled approach to the past—is always exclusive, never inclusive. Porfirio Díaz, who ruled Mexico from 1876 to 1910, was a villainous tyrant or the promoter of economic growth, depending on who is depicting him and when. He was the cause of the bloody Mexican Revolution, which killed millions and pushed the country into chaos, or the promoter of unequaled stability. José de San Martín, Esteban Montejo, Che Guevara, and Enriquillo, born Guayocuya, the colonial Dominican fugitive, are viewed as liberators or lunatics, saints or martyrs, visionaries or fools, and stimulators of progress or supporters of regression.

Our history is a mirage, an invention. Not without reason did Ch'n Shih Huang Ti, emperor of China at the time of Hannibal, order the construction of the Great Wall and, simultaneously, decree the burning of every book written before he came to power. To abolish the past and to reinvent the present: to shape the future. His goal was to build a self-protected, autonomous universe where things gone by can be reinvented, a reality where history is controllable and humans are not at its mercy. Umberto Eco, the author of *The Name of the Rose,* once talked about how spaghetti with meatballs is an American creation. In nineteenth-century Italy spaghetti was the solution to times when meat was scarce; thus, mixing pasta and meat is a typical American anachronism: to invent, to start from scratch, to reshape the past. The sweetness of future success is the only reward.

Hispanics, on the other hand, are stuck in our bastardized origin. Rather than having a sense of what's right and wrong, we value things for the benefits they offer. Friendship promotes contacts, enhances careers, and is a step in the ascending road to power. Afraid of the future, we hide in the past: a traumatic past in which we were forced to assume the colonizer's identity, a mask. Spanish missionaries, characterizing natives as idolatrous, decapitated the religions they found, replacing aboriginal gods with "civilized" European objects of worship. Quetzalcóatl and Coatlicue became Jesus Christ and the Virgin Mary. In this case, however, despite the decapitation, the body was left intact. Astonished by the traumatic reaction of the Indian population to losing their spiritual epicenters, the Spanish decided to replace them with Spanish ones. Thus, churches were built on pyramids and temples, which means that the substructure of Hispanic Catholicism is populated by syncretic theological images. On top of truncated idols the church founded a sanctuary.

As an architectural structure, the pyramid is built by adding new, smaller platforms to existing ones. Because pre-Columbian religions were already accustomed to additions, the imposition of the Spanish contribution was taken somewhat naturally, as illustrated by the legend of Quetzalcoatl's second coming as a bearded white man, a premonition that allowed Hernán Cortés free reign. This illustration also signals the density of our culture. When parishioners pray on their knees to Saint Lázaro in the Caribbean, they also pay tribute to Babalú, although their temples are separated. Catholicism and Yoruban spirituality, Catholicism and Aztec myths, cohabit. In a Cuban parable, a bum called Lázaro goes to the house of Bulón de Rich. He is thrown out, and Bulón's dogs go after him. When Lázaro goes to heaven, Bulón goes to hell, where he asks Lázaro for help. The parable resembles a *Pataquí*, a Yoruban legend, accepted and read in Cuba as a Catholic and as an African legend, in which a deity refuses to feed a Babalú condemned to hunger and sickness, and as the tale included in the New Testament.

Such a religious strategy, to decapitate, to acculturate, is radically different from that of the Pilgrim colonizers in what became the United States; this difference arises simply because native tribes north of the Rio Grande were too spread out to oppose effectively the English colonizers. Lacking a center, our mestizo and mulatto styles are ever changing, allowing a multicultural identity, one that negotiates in spiritual and linguistic translations. José María Arguedas, a professor of anthropology of Quechua descent at the University of San Marcos in Peru and the author of *Yawar Fiesta,* was incapable of finding a solid bridge between his Indian and European backgrounds. Forced from childhood through adulthood to live eternally divided, between Quechua and Spanish, instinct and intellect, he committed suicide. He was, however, an exception. No matter how fragile a compromise, the art of translating oneself, linguistically and otherwise, is at the very core of our popular consciousness, although some approach it as if it was a devil's kiss. The following stanza by Sor Juana Inés de La Cruz makes this point:

En confusión, mi alma	In confusion, my soul
se divide en dos:	is divided:
una es esclava de la pasión,	one is passion's slave,
la otra sirve a la razón.	the other, reason's to command.

Perhaps the perfect allegorical map of our collective psyche, a metaphysical expression of loss in the labyrinth, evidence of the perplexing encounter with chaos, is Cabeza de Vaca's life, starting with his journey through Florida, as part of a 1527 expedition to conquer the region north of the Gulf of Mexico. The author of *La Relación* (also known in its second edition as *Naufragios* and translated into English as *Adventures in the Unknown Interior of America*), Alvar Núñez Cabeza de Vaca was born about 1490; grew up in Jeréz, a small town in Andalucia known for its sherry; and began his military career in his teens. He fought in the battle of Ravenna and served as ensign at Gaeta outside Naples. He was part of the three-hundred-man expedition to the New World, headed by the one-eyed, red-bearded Pámfilo de Narváez. Having been shipwrecked by a hurricane on an island off the coast of Texas, the men made it to the mainland and set out on foot, traveling northward. For eight years they wandered across Texas, New Mexico, Arizona, and northern Mexico, and their numbers were reduced from 300 to four. Captured by Indians and then a fugitive, Cabeza de Vaca's account offered Europeans the first information on the Southwest: its climate, flora and fauna, and the customs of the natives. Cabeza de Vaca was the first to see an opossum and a buffalo, the Mississippi and the Pecos, pine-nut mash and mesquite-bean flour. His is also the first known literary description of a West Indies hurricane. Cabeza de Vaca returned to Spain in 1537 and offered his report to King Charles V.

When Hernando de Soto received the royal commission for Florida, the king made Cabeza de Vaca an *adelantado*, a governor, of the South American provinces of the Río de la Plata, to which he sailed in 1540. He tried to rescue the beleaguered and diseased colony of Assunción and made an expedition, 1,000 miles across the unknown and supposedly impenetrable jungles, mountains, and villages, barefooted, between 1542 and 1543. He then became obsessed with another goal: to penetrate Paraguay and find the lost golden city of Manoa, but a mutiny destroyed his dreams. He was the target of intrigue and jealousy and eventually was deposed and brought back to Spain in chains in 1543. He was tried and sentenced to banishment in Africa for eight years. However, the king annulled the sentence, awarded him a pension, and gave him a job. He died in 1557. His account of his South American journey, known as *Comentarios,* appeared two years before his death.

Cabeza de Vaca's journey became an odyssey through the labyrinth. Although he stood in the tradition of all the colonizers who were ready to discover a new reality in the king's name, his only achievement was the realization of his own limitations. In more than one way, Cabeza de Vaca's adventures bring to mind Joseph Conrad's *Heart of Darkness,* published in 1899, and now considered the door to a new consciousness about the European impact on Africa. Both works move psychologically toward climactic insight. They are full of unobtrusive symbolic imagery. They penetrate anthropological time and space, tracing the deceptively long path from the primitive to the civilized world and suggesting that the triumph of reason and order does not necessarily bring forth tranquillity and a higher form of society.

Cabeza de Vaca's and Conrad's accounts illustrate that colonialism is not a happy path—that it eventually causes violence and hate and a clash of different cultures. Both deal with the idea of man attempting to explore and understand the universe and state that truth is in the eye of the beholder. The preternatural stillness of the jungle and the voices of a fallen envoy and a missionary are symbols of power and its discontents and ineffectuality. Indeed, Kurtz's last words in *Heart of Darkness,* "The horror! The horror!" summarize Cabeza de Vaca's pilgrimage. On his arrival, he believes (as he has been taught) that he is superior. As the expedition's treasurer and provost marshal, he helps Governor Pámfilo de Narváez organize the men and is ready to seize the territories from the River of Palms to what he calls "the cape of Florida." But the fury of nature and the aborigines have been underestimated.

Cabeza de Vaca survives, but not without undergoing a profound transformation. He adapts to the customs of a tribe that has captured him and helps cure their sick. He pretends to have prophetic power by praying and using common sense as well as his precarious yet useful knowledge of medicine and first aid. Nevertheless, the Indians are brighter than he is. They undress him, they make him dance and sing, they reshape him. In short, Cabeza de Vaca is the first Spaniard to lose control of the historic situation in which he embarked and to be molded by the aborigines. His odyssey brings to mind a masterly contemporary short story by the Guatemalan fabulist Augusto Monterroso, "The Eclipse." A favorite of Irving Howe, it is about Brother Bartolome Arrazola, who is lost in a Central American jungle. The sun is strong, and he has almost given up hope. He falls asleep, and when he awakens, he is surrounded by a group of natives who are ready to sacrifice him on an altar. He is frightened and looks for ways to escape. Suddenly, he comes up with a solution, "an idea he considered worthy of his talent, universal culture and the deep knowledge of Aristotle." He remembers that a total eclipse is to take place that day. With his limited knowledge of aboriginal languages, he tells his victimizers that he can darken the sun at its height. The story ends a couple of hours later, with the priest's blood spilled on the sacrificial stone "while one of the natives recited without raising his voice, unhurriedly, one by one, the infinite dates in which there would be solar and lunar eclipses, that the astronomers of the Mayan community had foreseen and written on their codices without Aristotle's valuable help."

The ultimate expression of the Hispanic labyrinth is the carnival, an occasion to set spiritual and physical ghosts free, making in the fashion of Calderón de la Barca the entire world a stage, full of surprises and secrets—and that, precisely, is how we Latinos understand reality: as a larger-than-life theater, a space of leisure and never-ending performances. Progressively integrated into the modern-day parade (or, as Borinquéns call it, *la parada*), the carnival is a larger-than-life blender, where individual identity is simultaneously hidden behind masks and openly revealed, lost and reshaped, where people momentarily cease to be themselves. The dense Hispanic identity allows for sacrificial rituals, liberating repressed energy, and suspending the rules of morality. Men dress as women, and vice versa, which means that the transgressor is androgynous for a day. Our tropical life, as Guillermo Cabrera Infante claimed in *Three Trapped Tigers,* is like show time: *Señoras y señores.* Ladies and Gentlemen. Welcome to *el cabaret más famoso del mundo,* a landscape of supernatural beauty, *el mundo maravilloso y extraordinario!* Its exotic ways spread through the most varied systems of signs: music, song, dance, myth, language, food, dress, and physical expression.

Brazilian and Caribbean carnivals—in San Juan, Havana, Caracas, and Rio de Janeiro—are particularly famous. The event's metabolism is directly linked to the sociocultural density of the region. For example, during *Día de Reyes,* a carnival for slaves in preindependence Cuba, a day allowed by the regime as well as by religion, blacks danced near the ruler's palace. The governor or whoever was ruling, together with his ministers, would enjoy the dance and then throw money at the slaves, all of whom were free for that day. People continued dancing through the streets of Havana until late at night. In a sacrificial dance (see Nicholás Guillén's "Sensemayá"), blacks killed the serpent, an act that symbolized their hope for a slavery-free future. Governors, slave owners, plantation owners, and the rest of the people in power allowed such behavior so that the animosity against them would be channeled in a less threatening way than direct confrontation.

A number of critics, beginning with the Russian literary critic Mikhail Bakthin, author of an intriguing study on Dostoyevsky, have studied the carnival. Bakthin believes that the carnival is an opportunity to ridicule, to make fun of the authoritarian power controlling society. Umberto Eco, from a different standpoint, argues that the carnival, in essence unofficial, is official during

a precise period, which means that the regime incorporates its own rebelliousness, allowing the forces that oppose it to express their animosity without
punishment in a specific space and time. René Girard, a Frenchman, claims
that the carnival is the social representation of a sacrifice, and that every sacrifice implies the metaphorical need for the blood of those you hate, which
means that through the carnival people channel their rebelliousness against
the system. The best description I know of our carnivals, by Antonio Benítez-
Rojo, proves that there is something extraordinarily androgynous in this fiesta:

> Its flux, its diffuse sensuality, its generative force, its capacity to nourish
> and conserve (juices, spring, pollen, rain, seed, shoot, ritual sacrifice—
> these are words that come to stay). Think of the dancing flourishes, the
> rhythms of the conga, the samba, the masks, the hoods, the men dressed
> and painted as women, the bottles of rum, the sweets, the confetti and col-
> ored streamers, the hubbub, the carousel, the flutes, the drums, the cornet
> and the trombone, the teasing, the jealousy, the whistles and the faces, the
> razor that draws blood, death, life, reality in forward and reverse, torrents
> of people who flood the streets, the night lit up like an endless dream, the
> figure of a centipede that comes together and then breaks up, that winds
> and stretches beneath the ritual's rhythm, that flees the rhythm without
> escaping it, putting off its defeat, stealing off and hiding itself, imbedding
> itself finally in the rhythm, always in the rhythm, the beat of the chaos . . .
> [that is the universe].

Carnivals, parades, fiestas: color, masks, theatricality. We are queens and
kings of the fiesta. Néstor García Canclini, an anthropologist who studied in
Paris under Paul Ricoeur and teaches in Mexico, claims, in his volume
Transforming Modernity about popular culture south of the Rio Grande, that
the fiesta in the Hispanic world "can be regarded as a staging of fissures
between the country-side and the city, between Indian and Western elements, their interactions and conflicts. This is demonstrated by the coexistence of ancient dances and rock groups, by hundreds of Indian offerings to
the dead being photographed by hundreds of cameras, by the crossing of the
archaic and modern rituals in peasant villages, and by the hybrid fiestas with
which migrants in industrial cities invoke a symbolic universe centered
around corn, earth, and rain." What characterizes the Latino fiesta is the possibility of dissolving racial, cultural, and social boundaries. The fiesta opens
up the spirit and allows for alliances that otherwise could not take place; it is

a result of the ethnic and cultural density and lack of social mobility. In contrast to parties in the United States, which are simple and do not break rules of behavior, Latino fiestas are complicated, dense, and labyrinthine. Everyone participates in frantic movement, sound, and eroticism; we drink, dance, laugh, and love, losing ourselves in the crowd and ignoring our spiritual injuries. The fiesta ought not to be understood as a transcendental interruption of everyday life, but as a way of affirming what a hostile nature or an unjust society denies us. Through the fiesta, an entire town or neighborhood comes together, the sum of individual energies becoming an overwhelming explosion of energy. Rhythm is the heartbeat of the community, the union through movement and expression. We live to enjoy and enjoy to live.

Although the carnival's time is eternal, Latin time is slow, mythical, ahistorical. Disagreeing with Luther's belief that solid actions are statements, we procrastinate: *Hoy no, mañana*. We care less about the act of doing than about the act of being. As Carlos Fuentes once said at a Harvard commencement speech:

> Some time ago, I was traveling in the state of Morelos in central Mexico, looking for the birthplace of Emiliano Zapata, the village of Anenecuilco. I stopped and asked a *campesino*, a laborer of the fields, how far it was to the village. He answered: "If you had left at daybreak, you would be there now." This man had an internal clock which marked his own time and that of his culture. For the clocks of all men and women, of all civilizations, are not set at the same hour. One of the wonders of our menaced globe is the variety of its experiences, its memories, and its desires.

Each culture has its own clock. Fuentes's campesino measures time in a unique fashion, not by European standards, but in an internal, intuitive, unhurried manner. Anglos save time; we waste it. I once attended an international writers' meeting in which a guest from Argentina arrived late. His tardiness was deliberate. Since we shared a room in the hotel, I knew he would wake up before dawn, shower, and have breakfast, but when the time came for him to go somewhere, he would wait ten or fifteen minutes, just sit and wait. He was aware that people were waiting for him, which is why he would arrive late. It wasn't plain inconsiderateness, nor was it a power play. It also wasn't one more example of wasting time. It was my colleague's duty to arrive late—as if he lived a quarter of an hour behind the rest of the world. In Latin America, time wouldn't be lost if so many people wouldn't kill it. Our siesta often lasts two or three hours. Businesses close, and activity comes to a halt. García Márquez's "Tuesday's Siesta" is an illustration of this peculiar attitude: A poor woman arrives in a distant town with her daughter to trace the remains of her late son, Carlos Centeno, shot while trying to break into a house in the middle of the night. Making their way into the church at noon, they discover that the priest, the church keeper, and everyone else in the town pretend to be asleep—and refuse to cooperate. Nobody cares. Time stands still.

Religion and earthly life, eternity and circularity—these are our habitat. In *Hunger of Memory*, Richard Rodríquez juxtaposed the clock with the crucifix, connected artifacts in our hyphenated soul:

> I grew up a Catholic at home and in school, in private and in public. My mother and father were deeply pious *católicos*; all my relatives were Catholics. At home, there were holy pictures on a wall of nearly every room, and a crucifix hung over my bed. My first twelve years as a student were spent in Catholic schools where I could look up to the front of the room and see a crucifix hanging over a clock.

Metaphorically, the arrival of Iberians in *l'Amerique latine* during the sixteenth century marks the entrance of Hispanics to Western time schedules. Aztecs, Nahuas, and others inhabited a sequence of nonlineal, nonprogressive calendars. The conquistadors initiated the natives in the manners of the Old World, forcing their spiritual life on the "idolaters." The result was trauma and suffering. The attempt to narrate, to poetize our labyrinthine accumulation of external and internal forces, to verbalize the sound of our internal clock, gave birth to a baroque spirit and a rich cast of phantom types. *Indios* and *negros,* for example, each with their internal time, are ubiquitous, eternal ghosts, indelible "guests" in our art and letters. They may be seen in Gloria Anzaldúa's *Borderlands/La Frontera: The New Mestiza;* Alejo Carpentier's first novel, *Ecué-Yamba-O;* Lydia Cabrera's *Yemayá and Ochún;* Juan Rulfo's *Pedro Páramo;* the masterpiece *Men of Maize* by Guatemalan Miguel Angel Asturias, who won the 1967 Nobel Prize for Literature; and any of the numerous epic novels by Jorge Amado, a traditionalist whose multicast plots recall the art of Charles Dickens and who documents the hybrid identity of Brazilians and other South Americans, a mixture of Portuguese or Spanish, African, and native people. Transculturation in Latin America is a process where ethnic and cultural promiscuity result in a superimposition of different internal clocks. So when one looks for the clock of clocks, the unifying one, what one finds is a colossal fracture. The Hispanic world is so akin to a baroque style because the collective soul is a blender where different times collide—African, Indian, European, and the consequent mixture of these three basic racial components.

Time and race are thus directly related. One cannot be understood without the other. Amado's books—perfect examples of what in intellectual circles throughout the southern hemisphere are known as "total novels," ambitious, comprehensive literary projects in which every single aspect of society, every class, faith, and ideological concern, is represented—include archetypal scenarios full of *candomblé* cult leaders, virginal maidens, poor urban workers, ambitious university professors, corrupt politicians, and newspaper reporters. Amado's clear objective is to re-create the dynamics of race, power, and money in a milieu that is constantly dancing to the syncopated drumming of the samba. In one narrative, for instance, Saint Barbara of the Thunder, a Christian saint merged with the female spirit Oyá Yansan in syncretistic African-Christian religions, undergoes a miraculous physical mutation from motionless to living entity. She awakens to the smell of cinnamon and tobacco, ready to rescue a misbegotten believer. Her disappearance ignites a furor and opens up all sorts of subplots in which detectives and journalists try to make sense of the bizarre mystery. *Orixá* spirits, *ossé* offerings, saints, and ornamental artifacts abound. Soon the personality of Saint Barbara of the Thunder becomes a metaphor for Brazil's collective soul: Neither Christian nor African, she is a sum of parts, a religious entity in need of translating herself to parishioners who celebrate her double identity, European and native. Like Virgil showing Dante the way, Amado, who was born in 1912 on a cacao farm in southern Bahia, guides us through an underworld of superstition and idolatry without the obtuse and patronizing perspective of Western superiority. His stunning magical journey is a reminder that Hispanics are many things at once: multicolored, multiethnic, multicultural. The multiplicity of race is taboo among us, and is rarely openly discussed by Hispanics. Thus, Cuban critic Fernando Ortíz's famous statement, "Caribbean culture is *blanquinegra*—black-n'-white," is, in essence, profoundly ironic simply because, while as a people we are an ethnic composite, ethnic issues are not discussed. Amado's work is a mirror whose reflection never ignites continental debate. What, then, may be expected from Latinos, ancestral carriers of such a taboo, who are living in a reality where, from Crown Heights to Watts, many die in ethnic urban wars, where race is a hot topic of discussion? Perplexity. From bronze-skinned to mulatto, from snow white to *indio*, ours are wide-ranging colors—but a long-standing, rampant racism running through our blood remains unanalyzed. Yes, *racismo*. Society is silent when the word is uttered. Nobody takes responsibility. Nobody listens.

In the United States, a nation obsessed with racial and cultural wars, we Latinos are ambiguous, suspicious, and uncomfortable. *Gallo, caballo y mujer, por su raza has de escoger,* a Mexican-American saying goes: Should we reevaluate our ancestral approach to race? Piri Thomas spent most of his adolescence and early adulthood shifting between his Puerto Rican and black identities. Aztlan and mestizo roots are omnipresent in Miguel Méndez's and Alejandro Morales's fiction, in Lorna Dee Cervantes's poetry and Cherríe Moraga's narrative work. The latter writes in *The Last Generation*: "*Aztlan*. I don't remember when I first heard the word, but I remember it took my heart by surprise to learn of that place—that 'sacred landscape' wholly evident en las playas, los llanos, y en las montañas of the North American Southwest. A terrain that I did not completely comprehend at first, but that I continue to try, in my own small way, to fully inhabit and make habitable for its Chicano citizens." A clear-cut connection in Latino history between blacks and Hispanics is Arthur Alfonso Schomburg, the famous black bibliophile. A respected member of the Prince Hall Masons, he headed the Negro Collection at Fisk University and became curator of his own collection at the New York Public Library—a collection that is the core of the library's present-day Schomburg Center for Research in Black Culture. A close friend of W. E. B. Du Bois and Carter G. Woodson, he spent his life gathering evidence to prove "Negroes have history." (Elinor Des Verney Sinnette, at Howard University, wrote an exciting biography about the man and his oeuvre.) Few know that Schomburg was born, by most accounts, in Puerto Rico in 1874 or that, when he came to New York, he was a militantly active young man involved in the Caribbean revolutionary struggles. Although he reached high positions within the black intellectual world, his written English was, in the words of a friend, the philosopher and educator Alain LeRoy Locke, "impossible." Bernardo Vega described Schomburg's style as reflecting "the Hispanic, Latin quality of his spirit and culture." Locke occasionally edited Schomburg's writing and, as Des Verney Sinnette quoted, described his effort as "a labor of love—for Schomburg is a loyal old friend who isn't to blame for his flamboyant English because he was born in Puerto Rico and educated in Spanish."

Schomburg frequently delivered papers and lectures on black issues. Closely tied to figures in the Harlem Renaissance, including Langston Hughes, Claude McKay, and Marcus Garvey, he contributed an essay, "The Negro Digs Up His Past," to Locke's 1925 anthology *The New Negro,* which began as a special issue of the journal *Survey Graphic,* and about which I shall say more in Chapter 7. Although he never wrote a book-length manuscript, his writings include a 1910 tract on the Cuban poet Plácido and a couple of articles in Martí's newspaper, *Patria.* In one essay Schomburg discussed Francisco Xavier Luna y Victoria, the first native-born bishop of the Catholic church in Panama, whose mother was black. And for Du Bois's magazine *Crisis,* he wrote several pieces: "The Fight for Liberty in St. Lucia," about Haiti's revolt for independence, as well as "the desperate struggle that took place about the same time on the [West Indian] island of St. Lucia"; a study of Evaristo Estenoz, a black Cuban general who fought for the rights of people of African descent and founded the Independent Colored Party in Cuba; an appraisal of the Spanish mulatto artist Sebastián Gómez, a slave owned by white artist Bartolomé Esteban Murillo; a piece on Juan de Pareja, another black Spanish painter; and a biographical sketch of General Antonio Maceo, an African-Cuban hero. Indeed, Schomburg's discussion of issues of race and racism in Latin America and the Caribbean, especially the refusal by leaders to grant political representation to blacks, "save that which was bestowed to them as a charity," is essential. Aside from plantations, blacks were employed, especially in Brazil and Cuba, as field workers, domestic servants, and cowboys. Although slavery prevailed until late in the nineteenth century, sometimes blacks were permitted to wander around easily, and soon blacks became crucial agents of acculturation, transmitting African symbols and motifs to the general population, changing the fashion in which society perceived itself. (In Cuba, in particular, between the sixteenth and nineteenth centuries the folklore of the black community was easily tolerated.) As was mentioned earlier, on *Día de Reyes* in Havana, blacks were set free for one day, something unheard of elsewhere in the region. Associations known as *cabildos,* devoted to the different African origins of Cuban blacks, encouraged each slave to find the particular clothes that were part of his or her African background and to wear them in the street to dance and sing. As a result, although few know it, the Cuban army that fought for independence during the Spanish-American War was mainly black and mulatto. Since Chinese contract laborers from the south of China constituted 3 percent of the population by the second half of the nineteenth century, the Cuban army also included many Chinese, an ethnic group that even fewer Hispanics are willing to acknowledge. The Chinese had arrived in Cuba as workers in miserable conditions. In one historical chronicle, a white Cuban soldier captured by the enemy was asked what on earth he was doing among Negroes and Asians. This incident illustrates the racial texture at the time, often unknown to those who are unfamiliar with Caribbean history. Antonio Maceo, the Cuban army's chief of staff, was a mulatto who was surrounded by a large number of black colonels, lieutenants, and generals.

The *indio* also remains powerless in vast regions of Hispanic America: persecuted, exploited, silenced, forgotten, or ignored. Although both blacks and Indians are an integral part of the Hispanic culture, their link is a chain of mishaps. As Borges put it bluntly and sarcastically in his *Universal History of Infamy*: "In 1517, Fray Bartolomé de Las Casas took much pity on those Indians who wasted away in the grueling infernos of Caribbean gold mines, and he proposed to the emperor Charles V the importation of blacks, who would waste away in the grueling infernos of Caribbean gold mines."

The very term *indio,* to begin with, is a historical misunderstanding that resulted from Columbus thinking that he had set foot in India during his first voyage. Today the word is derogatory, an offense: *No seas indio*; Don't be stupid! The word *indio* symbolizes rural, non-European life, a link to the instinct, a witness of an ancestry Latin America feels uncomfortable about. As independence became an issue in the early nineteenth century, politicians and diplomats discussed ways to annihilate Indians, to destroy them so they could impose "civilization" on their lands. As can be seen in Domingo Faustino Sarmiento's *Facundo* and in scores of Argentinian works like José Hernández's *El Gaucho Martín Fierro,* the Europeanized peoples of the Río de la Plata fought to eradicate gauchos, while *indios,* a symbol of barbarism, a reminder of an undesirable past, were attacked in Mexico, the Andes, and Central America. The gaucho, a cowboy or horseman, was often a figure of fun for the Argentinian intelligentsia. He was seen as bestial, a brutal instrument of a type of dictatorship that pushed society far from Europe. In either case, the indio and the gaucho were pastoral creatures that had to be sacrificed to achieve modernity.

At the beginning of the twentieth century, an aesthetic and political movement known as *indigenismo* fought to return to the source, to give Indians their well-deserved status. Governmental agencies were created to rescue and nurture almost extinct tribes, and the Indian was treated as an animal species about to disappear, a scientific object of curiosity to be discussed in panels and introduced as a good savage in novels and plays. As modernity set in, Indians were used as reminders of the collective past and, tragically, as producers of tourist souvenirs. Indeed, Hispanic America turned its aboriginal population into a frozen postcard image: serapes and sombreros, dolls and embroidery sold by poor indios in government-sponsored markets: memory for sale, the Teotihuacan pyramid as a set for a perfect photograph. In Andean countries like Peru and Bolivia, on the other hand, the indios always lived totally marginalized, denied a history and treated as ghosts, as slave laborers whose lands were stolen, as nonentities; their presence remains unrecognized in the dynamic of the official culture; they have no access to their countries' constitutions and, despite a number of legal amendments, probably never will. Hispanic America remains uncomfortable when it comes to accepting its pre-Columbian heritage; it would rather look northward and across the Atlantic than inside.

Homosexuality is another repressed ghost in our closet, also to be understood in the light of the schism dividing our collective soul. Since ours is a galaxy of brute macho types and virginal and devoted women, gays, although fatally crushed in the battles between the sexes, represent another facet of what I refer to as "translated identities." Repressed, silenced—shouldn't we also reconsider our dogmatic, villainous approach to sex? And if we do, what will happen to our virile Latin phallus, two-fisted, broad-shouldered, hairy-chested? We nurture an obsessive, almost religious devotion to the maternal figure: La Mamá Grande—*Madre, sólo hay una . . . Y como tú ninguna.* Mamá controls and regulates affection. She generates guilt and compensates suffering. Home is her terrain, an altar. We adore her, revere her, and worship her. She is the family's vertebral column, an aleph in which everything begins and converges. Among Hispanics, most verbal curses attack the mother as the ultimate source of dignity: *chinga tu madre,* fuck your mother; *puta madre,* your mother's a whore. Indeed, at the center of the Hispanic faith is the adoration to the Virgin—Coatlicue, Yemayá, and Vírgen María. We are awash with virgins: Vírgen de Guadalupe, Vírgen de La Caridad del Cobre, Vírgen del Rocío, Vírgen de la Macarena, Vírgen de Triana, Vírgen de Coromoto. "The virginal figure that has presided over the life of Spain and Spanish America with such power and for so long," argues Carlos Fuentes, "is not a stranger to [the] ancient maternal symbols of both Europe and the New World. In Spain during the great Easter celebration, and in Spanish America through a reimposed link with the pagan religions, this figure of veneration becomes a troubling, ambiguous mother too, directly linked to the original earth goddess." As in Chicana painter Yolanda M. López's *Portrait of the Artist as the Virgin of Guadalupe,* a self-portrait with modern intonations, the Virgin is depicted as a mestiza, ethnically linked to her people.

We are victims of an inferiority complex based on sex and race. "A Latin lover," says Luis Valdez in his play *Zoot Suit,* "is *nothing* but a foking Mexican." Whenever I arrive in Mexico City, someone ready to carry my luggage always says: *"¿Adónde le llevo las maletas, patrón?"* I have yet to open my mouth, but they are already addressing me as their master. A normal response in Spanish is *a sus órdenes,* at your command, or *mande usted,* at your disposal, denoting a lack of self-esteem. But machismo is rampant. The Papá symbolizes abstract power. A *deus absconditus,* silent and noncommitted, he dictates his wishes from afar. His frequent absence, his inadequacy, is linked to the Iberian conquistadors' arrival as bachelors or entangled husbands, knights who were more than ready to abuse and rape Indian women, leaving them alone and pregnant.

I recall an occasion at the Guadalajara Book Fair when the director of Editorial Planeta sat with me and a gay friend of mine from Venezuela, a New York City resident, and in a disgusting display of macho pyrotechnics, talked for almost an hour about the size of his penis. Every time he referred to homosexuals, he would use such terms as "perverted," "kinky," "twisted," and "depraved." The fact that next to him was a self-described "queer writer" only fueled his attack. He glorified the United States as the greatest nation on earth but claimed sexual abnormality would ultimately force its decline. Days later my Venezuelan friend told me the publisher surreptitiously made an advance to him that very night. They shared a hotel room.

In school, boys are requested to constantly test their stamina and muscular strength, *ser muy macho.* Girls can cry, express their inner emotions, but men are encouraged to remain silent instead of sharing their psychological ups and downs. To open up, *abrirse,* is a sign of feminine weakness, whereas to penetrate, *meter,* means superiority. To fuck is to prove the male self, to subdue one's own feminine half. Physical appearance is fundamental: Obesity, limping, even baldness denote incompleteness, an effeminate characteristic. Role models are still the movie stars of the black-and-white Golden Age era of Mexican cinema such as Pedro Armendariz, Jorge Negrete, and Pedro Infante: an ultra-masculine Emiliano Zapata mustache, short, dark hair, a mysterious Mona Lisa smile, vigorously thin, well-built bodies, and an unconquerable sense of primordial pride symbolized by a never-to-leave-behind pistol. Fearlessness is at the core of the macho character: better to kill than to live on your knees. Cowardice means vulnerability. Deformity was not only an evidence of weakness but a sign of unreadiness to face the tough world. In spite of his verbal bravura, Cantinflas was antimacho: poorly dressed, bad-mouthed, short, unhandsome, and without a gun. Mexican films of the forties and fifties are about revolutionaries and *charros*, rural custom-dressed machos ready to capture their beloved's trust through a show of strength—the male aspect of the Hispanic collective soul incarnate.

As a nuclear stronghold, the family perpetuates the sense that female virginity is a requisite, to arrive pure at the wedding canopy, while men are encouraged to fool around, to test the waters of copulation and love-making. A prostitute is always an easy triumph and consented sex isn't the macho's idea of challenge. Courting women with serenades and flowers, laying them in bed, undressing them, fucking them—no better term applies: *cojer, chingar, mancillar*—only to throw them out the door, that's every Hispanic male's hidden dream. The *piropos*, street tongue-twisters expressed spontaneously less to enhance a woman's beauty and more to prove, through languid reveries, our sexual control, are an extreme display of the violent eroticism that invades us. The size and strength of his penis are a man's only passport in the universe. Take the example of Oscar "Zeta" Acosta, the Chicano lawyer and novelist who was an admirer of Benny Goodman and Dylan Thomas, and a close friend of Hunter S. Thompson. He wrote two intriguing novels about the civil rights upheaval in the Southwest, *The Autobiography of a Brown Buffalo* and *The Revolt of the Cockroach People*, which can be read as a man's rite to passage from adolescence to boastful machismo. On their covers, a photograph by Annie Leibovitz shows Acosta as a Tennessee Williams type, a perfectly insecure macho showing off muscles, with a facial expression denoting spiritual desperation: in his undershirt and elegant suit pants, excited but worried, fat, with ulcers, the lines in his forehead quite pronounced. He is thirty-nine and a bit worn out. Acosta lived his life thinking his penis was too small, which, in his words, would automatically turn him into a fag. His whole oeuvre is invaded by remarks on a shameful psychological complex. Acosta recurrently perceived himself as a freak, a virile metastasis.

If it hadn't been for my fatness, I'd probably have been able to do those fancyassed jackknifes and swandives as well as the rest of you. But when my mother had me conceived I was obese, ugly as a pig and without any redeeming qualities whatsoever. How then could I run around with just my Jockey shorts? V-8's don't hide fat, you know. That's why I finally started wearing boxers. But by then it was too late. Everyone knew I had the smallest prick in the world. With the girls watching and giggling, the guys used to sing my private song to the tune of "Little Bo Peep": "Oh, where, oh where can my little boy be? Oh, where, oh where can he be? He's so chubby, *pansón,* that he can't move along. Oh, where, oh where can he be?"

Machismo and *caudillaje:* A *caudillo* is a man whose superiority makes him lead and command others, a dictator who rules by sheer will and controls by force—*Yo, el Supremo.* His control of other people's lives is not meant to be an egotistic endeavor, however. Rather, the caudillo often finds a way to make himself look like a public servant, presenting himself as a martyr to a collective cause. Common folk hardly feel a sense of humiliation in being overpowered, simply because every man is a ruler, a macho, in his own home, and every woman is used to being controlled. Bernal Díaz del Castillo, a chronicler of the Conquest of Mexico, claims that when Cortés was given the power to direct his army, he immediately assumed the manners of a lord. He began to adorn himself and to take much more care of his appearance than before. He wore a plume of feathers, a medallion and a gold chain, and a velvet cloak trimmed with loops of gold. In fact, Díaz del Castillo observes, he looked like a bold and gallant captain. Augusto Pinochet, Fulgencio Batista, Fidel Castro, Porfirio Díaz, Francisco Franco, Anastasio Somoza, Doctor Francia (idealized by Thomas Carlyle)—we have plenty.

Education, politics, cuisine, eroticism—echoes of machismo can be found everywhere. From Pamplona to Guadalajara, the Mexican-style rodeo, and *la tauromaquia,* and the sophisticated art of bullfighting that hypnotized Ernest Hemingway are macho expressions. Dressed in sensual costumes, the bull-fighter, the embodiment of honor, dances around the arena making erotic gestures. Parodied in *Matador,* a film by the Spanish director Pedro Almodóvar, style and ritual are of ultimate importance. The matador's manipulation of the animal is a sign of human control over instinct. Mercy and animal rights are seldom an issue, as in Munro Leaf's 1936 children's tale, an Anglo softy, *The Story of Ferdinand,* with sweet drawings by Robert Lawson, about a sensible and sentimental bull with a delicate ego that loves to smell flowers and refuses to participate in a corrida in Madrid. In reality, bulls are raised to die in the arena in a huge business throughout the Hispanic world.

Similarly, the *charro,* brother of the Argentine gaucho and the American cowboy, his uniform—a large sombrero and a cloak to capture a horse or a bull—dating back to the 1910 Revolution, figuring prominently in Tex-Mex music and ranchera songs by Banda Machos and other groups, is asked to dominate wild horses through stamina. A *charreada,* which involves huge numbers of participants and spectators, takes place in a plaza. As folklorist John O. West, who devotes part of his book *Mexican-American Folklore* to describing its features, claims, during a typical competition, horse and rider, acting as one, gallop up to the fence, stopping just in time to avoid a smashup. After the horse is at a complete stop, a signal from the judges tells the rider to maneuver the horse in a 90-degree angle with its hind legs in a fixed place. A second signal requires a 360-degree turn, after which the rider dismounts and remounts again without movement from the animal and then backs out of the arena in a straight line of at least sixty yards. The slightest wavering and hesitation on the horse's part results in penalty points.

The *coleadero,* among the most popular events in the Southwest, takes place in a key-shaped alley in which steers are "tailed" in a dust-producing and lively event. As a wild steer is released from a pen at one end of the alley-way, a cowboy rides alongside, salutes the judges, slaps the steer on the rump three times, and slides his hand along the steer's back until he can grab the tail. He must wrap the tail around his boot and then speed up his horse. This forward motion flips the steer off balance, and the harder he falls, the better the score.

In its Mediterranean roots, romance Latin style is directed toward a first impression and a first encounter. Whatever comes next is secondary. Courting becomes a prologue to love, often accompanied by serenades and a bouquet of flowers (however, customs are slowly evaporating as technology and fast relationships become the norm). Possessed by doubt and insecurity, the macho spirit finds recreation in challenge: testing its romantic strategies, pondering its physical presence, counting its victims. *Aguantar,* to show stamina, to endure, as Samuel Ramos points out in his seminal *Profile of Men and Culture in Mexico,* is rooted in our behavior. Our nuclear family, often quite large because of the religious opposition to birth control, is at once a stronghold and a springboard for achieving success. Self-interest and loyalty are the glue that keeps it together. The family bestows a person with a sense of dignity, responsibility for perpetrating such a sense and for protecting the pride of other family members. A family's secrets are abstruse, locked in a high-power security box. Without *dignidad,* which safeguards the family's honor and perpetuates an artificial view of morality, a person is pushed to desperation and solitude: Nothing works, no doors open, no success ever comes. *Es gente bien educada*: dignity means education, a sense of order, and maintenance of the status quo. Everybody can taste its delicate flavor; all it needs is mere restraint.

Sex in the Hispanic family constitutes a spiderweb, and gays are absurdly perceived as sick and disgraceful. Although monogamy and chastity are extolled, daughters who are sexually abused by their fathers are omnipresent, especially among the lower class (most victims keep their secret buried forever). Incest and promiscuity are recurring phenomena, and extramarital affairs, often tacitly agreed on by husband and wife, are also pervasive. Although such rules of conduct may not differ drastically from those in other societies, among Hispanics a proud sense of morality and dignity and the compulsive need to safeguard the honor of the family, constantly nurtured by the Catholic church, make our codes considerably more hypocritical. As Judith Ortíz Cofer wrote in her volume of prose and poetry *The Latin Deli*:

The book of dreams in Spanish
says the tree is my father.
The fruit that disappears
stands for words not spoken,
hopes and wishes left unfulfilled.
But it does not tell me
why I still feel starved
after I eat.

Compadres, sort of godparents, loyal family friends who take responsibility for a child if the parents are indisposed, are a facet of the extended family, which often includes numerous cousins, uncles, and distant relatives. Even among those on the periphery, the code of honor prevails. *Dignidad* and *honor*: Rodrigo Díaz de Bivar, known as El Cid through Guillén de Castro y Belvis's epic poem and Pierre Corneille's tragedy, who fought for and against the Moors in Spain, struggled to avenge his daughters' dignity and his own honor after his sons-in-law beat and abandoned them.

Dignity precludes intimacy, introspection, and a disdain for negative publicity. Consequently, the Hispanic world, as Luis Buñuel was prone to show, is populated by masked evils and generational sins. Such behavior, once again, is embedded in our history. Since 1492 was also the year of the triumph of ethnic cleansing in Spain, the Iberian conquistadors carried to the New World the concept of *pureza de sangre*. As seen in Lope de Vega's *comedias* and Francisco de Quevedo's conceptual poetry, a man's honor was grounded in a pure Christian background, never degraded by Jewish and Muslim traces. Among Hispanics, religion promotes xenophobia, intolerance, and a disdain for differences. Intolerance, indeed, is an important trademark of the Hispanic soul. With few exceptions, missionaries in the New World did not defend Indians. Instead, they mistreated them, forcing the Indians to convert to Christianity by means of torture and abuse. It is not surprising, therefore, that our rebellions are akin to outbursts against the Catholic church. Photographer Andres Serrano's famous image of a cheap plastic crucifix submerged in a liquid with bubbles, called *Piss Christ*, which, as Robert Hughes stated, was influenced by Max Ernst's painting of the Virgin Mary spanking the Infant Jesus, is symptomatic of the anger within the Hispanic psyche.

Sex is power. Paz contends in *The Labyrinth of Solitude* that for men, to make love is to possess, to control, and to dominate. Women open up, which means that they are broken, incomplete, whereas men penetrate, invade, conquer, and capture. *Coger,* the Spanish verb for fornicate, also means to take over and away. (Other verbal alternatives are *linchar* and *chingar.*) Although our folklore is full of androgynous types, gender distinctions prevail in society. Ours is an openly phallocentric culture, full of latent eroticism, behind-doors physical pleasure, and sexual abuse. Lacking dignity, honor, and completeness, gays are scorned, abused, and ridiculed without end. A broken macho, often referred to as *puto* and *marica,* homosexuals, as ghosts in the collective mirror, personify physical pleasure. Open about their sexuality, they receive the social scorn with an admirable sense of pride, a different type of *aguante* throughout what seems an infernal existence. Gay behavior is ubiquitous in the Hispanic world. During the plantation period in the Caribbean and the cacique system in Latin America, erotic encounters between classes were never strictly heterosexual. Numerous homosexual relations took place regularly, incited by *plantadores* and *mayorales.* Young females, Indians and slaves alike, turned into objects of desire, were used to satisfy landowners, as were adolescent men, although perhaps to a lesser extent, in an Epicurean fiesta of frantic liaisons. Many army officials in the Communist government in Cuba, for instance, and many revolutionaries close to Fidel Castro during the Sierra Maestra uprising, were gay, although they hid their encounters from the public simply because phallocentrism is inherent in the Hispanic psyche. Perfect inhabitants of the hyphen, targets of intolerance forced to bargain for room where they can expose their inner selves, numerous homosexual Hispanics are writers and artists, from José Lezama Lima to Manuel Puig. Gay and lesbian Latino writers in the United

States, sharing the pathos, are also at the forefront of an aesthetic and ideological battle. From Pat Mora to Cherríe Moraga (who formulated the concept of "Queer Aztlán") and Gloria Anzaldúa, from Reinaldo Arenas to Jaime Manrique, from John Rechy to Elías Miguel Muñóz and Arturo Islas, whose literature, metaphorically speaking, is written on their own epidermis, are the living proof of the painful encounter between body and intellect. Rechy's novel *City of Night,* considered the first openly gay Latino novel, is a raw document of the neon-lit world of hustlers, drag queens, lonely stigmatized men looking for casual sex. Muñóz's *The Greatest Performance* is arguably the first Latino novel to deal with AIDS, and Richard Rodríquez, in his second book, *Days of Obligation,* includes an essay, "Late Victorians," about his own homosexuality and AIDS in general. He ponders the impact of the epidemic. "We have become accustomed to figures disappearing from our landscape. Does this not lead us to interrogate the landscape?" he asks.

Author of *Farewell to the Sea* and *The Ill-Fated Peregrinations of Fray Servando,* Arenas lived and wrote the latter part of his oeuvre in Manhattan, until his suicide. He is also responsible for the memoir *Before Night Falls,* a devastating document by all accounts, describing his plight as a gay writer in Fidel Castro's Cuba, his escape during the Mariel boat lift, his underground life in the United States as a writer and cause célèbre, and his suffering with AIDS. He died in 1990, after leaving an open letter blaming Castro for his tragic fate. His work is characteristic of Cuban-American literature in having an air of nostalgia and an almost destructive political pathos. In 1968, at twenty-five, Arenas claimed that he had fornicated with more than 5,000 men, in addition to a number of women, animals, and natural objects (trees, holes in the ground, supermarket bags, and so forth). If he had not died at forty-seven, the number could have reached about 8,500. What's remarkable about *Before Night Falls,* aside from Arenas's honesty, is the fact that the book comes from the Spanish-speaking world, where erotic confessions are scarce and seldom so political.

In [Cuba], I think, it is a rare man who has not had sexual relations with another man. Physical desire overpowers whatever feelings of machismo our fathers take upon themselves to instill in us.

An example of this is my uncle Rigoberto, the oldest of my uncles, a married, serious man. Sometimes I would go to town with him. I was just about eight years old and we would ride on the same saddle. As soon as we were both on the saddle, he would begin to have an erection. Perhaps in some way my uncle did not want this to happen, but he could not help it. He would put me in place, lift me up and set my butt on his penis, and during that ride, which would take an hour or so, I was bouncing on that huge penis, riding, as it were, on two animals at the same time. I think eventually Rigoberto would ejaculate. The same thing happened on the way back from town. Both of us, of course, acted as if we were not aware of what was happening. He would whistle or breathe hard while the horse trotted on. When he got back, Carolina, his wife, would welcome him with open arms and a kiss. At that moment we were all very happy.

Arenas portrayed Hispanic society as being obsessed with homosexual sex and, throughout his autobiography, intellectuals like Antonio Benítez-Rojo, José Lezama Lima, Lydia Cabrera, Virgilio Piñera, and Heberto Padilla are treated either as objects of adoration or as targets of ridicule. A window to an undisclosed chamber of the Latino psyche, Arenas's autobiography is a showcase of Hispanic life as an everlasting carnival. Guillermo Cabrera Infante wrote in an obituary: "Three passions ruled the life and death of Reinaldo Arenas: literature (not as a game, but as a consuming fire), passive sex, and active politics. Of the three, the dominant passion was, evidently, sex. Not only in his life, but in his work. He was the chronicler of a country ruled not by the already impotent Fidel Castro, but by sex. . . . Blessed with a raw talent that almost reaches genius in [his autobiography], he lived a life whose beginning and end were indeed the same: from the start, one long, sustained, sexual act."

If Arenas symbolizes concrete nonentities in Hispanic society, we also have other types of ghosts: ghosts of memory. Rather than death, earthly life, made of unforeseen twists, is in our eyes mysterious, enigmatic, esoteric, mystical, and laughable. In a Mexican-American legend retold by John O. West, a woman, María, dies leaving her poor husband José alone. After a while, his neighbor, Donanciana, taking pity on him, brings food and flowers and begins regularly looking after José. After a while he falls in love with her and they marry. One night, when Donanciana stays with her sister in a neighboring village, José sleeps outside on a cot, under the cottonwood trees. At midnight he awakes suddenly, something cold pressing his feet. In the dim moonlight he sees María's ghost. Terrified, he yells and runs into the house, barring the door. The next day he goes to see a priest, who reassures him that María was a kindly soul. José must ask her ghost, when she comes back, what she wants. José again sleeps outside the following night. María awakes him and he says: "What do you wish of me?" She answers: "I'm glad you're happy with Donanciana, but I cannot rest because I owe the grocer, Xavier, *seis pesos*. Please give him the money." José is Xavier's first customer the next day, covers the debt, and María never returns.

These types are our amiable, sympathetic ghosts. Ambrose Bierce's outstanding definition of a ghost is "the outward and visible sign of an inward fear." As he wrote in *Devil's Dictionary*:

> He saw a ghost.
> It occupied—that dismal thing!—
> The path that he was following.
> Before he'd time to stop and fly,
> An earthquake trifled with the eye
>   That saw a ghost.
> He fell as fall the early good;
> Unmoved that awful thing stood.
> The stars that danced before his ken
> He wildly brushed away, and then
>   He saw a post.

Outward and inward fears. We have a closet full of shadows and apparitions, concrete and abstract, that helps us to deal with the obstacles displayed by destiny. As Ernest Hemingway showed in *The Old Man and the Sea*, a tale of courage about a fisherman at war with an oceanic behemoth, we defy death, approaching it not as a fearful, final, desperate event but, rather, as a continuation of earthly existence by other means, an encounter with nothingness deserving a grain of sugar. Indeed, the *calavera*, a sugar-made skeleton displayed in the Rio Grande area, a skeleton turned into candy, fear metamorphosing into sweetness, is a feature of folklore that is ubiquitous in pictorial art. In Chicana artist Santa Berraza's 1980–1984 *El descando final o la entrada*, for example, which was also recently part of the touring "CARA" exhibition, calaveras decorate the margins of portraits of young and old men as the ghost of Emiliano Zapata resonates in the background. Death surrounds the living. And in Ester Hernández's famous 1982 poster *Sun Mad Raisins*, a ghost replaces the ordinary maiden used by Sun Dry Raisins.

The dead, in Hispanic eyes, are never distanced from the living. During the *Día de Muertos*, mistakenly understood as the south-of-the-Rio-Grande response to Halloween and vividly depicted in Malcolm Lowry's *Under the Volcano* (about an alcoholic British consul spiritually lost in Cuernavaca), entire peasant and lower middle-class urban families in Mexico and Central America spend a night in cemeteries next to their beloved deceased, offering them food and a chance to be reunited, at least for one day. The decoration of graves is an essential; flowers, candles, crepe paper, images of saints, and photographs make the tombs festive, and a special type of sweet bread is baked: *pan de muertos.* Rather than nurturing fear, through folklore lower-class Latinos look at the dead as advisers and companions. John Nichols, a New Mexican author, has a dead old man in *The Milagro Beanfield War,* part of his Nirvana Trilogy, constantly communicating with the living. The character brings to mind Meliquíades, the ghostlike gypsy in Gabriel García Márquez's *One Hundred Years of Solitude,* the carrier of the Buendía family's memory. It is also reminiscent of a dazzling story by Enrique Anderson Imbert, an Argentine writer and professor at Harvard, about a scholar who is invited to deliver an ill-fated lecture at Brown University. On his arrival, the protagonist is placed in an old mansion, not far from where horror-story writer H. P. Lovecraft once lived. He is shown to his room by an obese innkeeper, but not before noticing a portrait hanging in the entrance hall, an oil painting of a gentleman who turns out to be the last member of the family that originally owned the house. Jeremiah Tecumseh Chase, as the innkeeper says his name was, stands proud in his army uniform, a rifle at his side, and has a noticeably toothless smile. Curious about this bizarre feature, the scholar asks the innkeeper, who answers with a tale of lust and betrayal. A heroic Civil War sergeant, Chase had married a celestial beauty. One morning, while his business partner from Connecticut was staying over, Chase woke up early and decided to go bird-hunting. He invited his partner to go along, but the partner declined. Chase got dressed, prepared his guns and other equipment, and kissed his wife good-bye. Halfway through his hunting trip, he realized he had forgotten his watch and decided to return home. As he reentered his room, he found his partner and wife in bed together. The two men began to fight. The partner injured Chase on the chin with a sword, and Chase's teeth went flying. Then the men pulled guns; the ensuing duel left both men dead and the woman a widow.

To this day, the innkeeper concludes, Sergeant Chase, in pain, wanders in darkness through the mansion. A few minutes later, the scholar, in his sixties, exhausted after the long trip, gets towels and soap and locks himself in his room. He undresses, rereads parts of the lecture, puts his false teeth in a half-full glass of water on a bed table, and thinks of the sergeant's portrait in the hall. It must have been painted after Chase's death, he thinks. He then falls quietly asleep. At around midnight he hears a strange sequence of noises—a door opening, a loud conversation, a gunshot, laughter, a lady whining. When he looks around, he sees Chase's ghost angrily approaching him. He closes his eyes thinking it is all a dream. After a while the sounds cease and things go back to normal. The next morning, however, he realizes his false teeth have disappeared from the glass, and without them, he is too embarrassed to deliver the lecture. What is striking is that instead of quickly returning home, the scholar stays one more night in the mansion. He wants to meet Sergeant Chase again and ask Chase to return his false teeth. He gets them after he and the ghost have a friendly chat.

Death as communion. Whereas Halloween is a holiday of comic horror, All Saints' Day, celebrated on November 2 in Mexico and some Central American countries, as well as by segments of the Chicano population in the Southwest, is a pastoral occasion for the masses, a social event in which sadness plays only a small role and the fragile separation between life and death disappears. We believe that death is a geography, a Leibnitz monad, a parallel universe. Consequently, a male spirit, a dybbuk of sorts, could have an affair with a woman. Transcendentalism is a mundane act. Every believer is a *spiritista*, trusting the soul to pre-Columbian deities. Among our most memorable ghost stories, recycled by every generation, is *La Llorona*, the weeping lady, who, according to some folklorists, is the ghost of Hernán Cortés's lover and interpreter in disguise. La Malinche, a legend claims, was pregnant with the conquistador's child. Replaced by a high-brow Iberian wife, she decided to avenge her honor by hunting him to death. The urban intellectual elite, on the other hand, never quite distant from the plain folk, nurtures cosmopolitan fears. In Rubén Darío's words and a rough translation:

> *Dichoso el árbol que es apenas sensitivo,*
> *y más la piedra dura porque esa ya no siente,*
> *pues no hay temor más grande que el temor de ser vivo,*
> *ni mayor pesadumbre que la vida consciente.*
>
> *Ser y no saber nada y ser sin rumbo cierto,*
> *y el temor de haber sido y un futuro terror . . .*
> *Y el espanto seguro de estar mañana muerto,*
> *y sufrir por la vida y por la sombra y por*

Lo que no conocemos y apenas sospechamos
Y la carne que tienta con sus frescos racimos,
Y la tumba que aguarda con sus fúnebres ramos
¡Y no saber adónde vamos,
ni de dónde venimos! . . .

———

Happy the tree, that scarcely feels,
And happier the hard stone not to feel at all,
For there is no pain greater than the pain of being alive,
Nor burden as heavy as conscious existence.

To be, and to know nothing, and to have no certain path,
And the fear of having been and a dread future . . .
And the hideous sureness of being dead tomorrow,
And suffering for life and from darkness and for

That which we do not know of and barely suspect,
And the flesh tempting with its cool grapes,
And the tomb that waits with its funeral wreaths,
And to know not whither we go,
Neither whence we come! . . .

Whereas Halloween, a display of gothic motifs, mocks death, Día de Muertos is marriage with the afterlife. Used to refer to poems and cartoon-like skeletons written and drawn especially for All Saints' Day, calaveras are a sort of valentine that are sent to people in which politicians, historical events, and public figures are made fun of in a friendly manner. Seen from a European perspective, they derive from the medieval imagery of the dance macabre. The art critic Peter Wollen dated the tradition to fresco paintings of the fifteenth century and to *The Dance of Death*, a series of woodcuts by Hans Holbein the Younger first published in 1538. Very much a part of the Chicano popular tradition, the character is a creation of the Mexican lampooner and engraver José Guadalupe Posada, considered a precursor of the artists Diego Rivera, David Alfaro Siqueiros, and José Clemente Orozco, and a major influence on modern Chicano art. Because he lived in a crucial historical moment, his art is directly linked to his life and thus needs to be seen as interrelated.

A man of humble background, Posada was born in 1851 in the city of

Aguascalientes, Mexico.* His parents were of Indian descent and illiterate. Germán Posada, his father, was a baker who owned a small shop; Petra Aguilar, his mother, was a housewife. As an adolescent, Posada studied with Antonio Varela at the Municipal Academy of Drawing in Aguascalientes. In 1867 he began practicing "the trade of the painter," and the following year he apprenticed in the lithography workshop of a well-known figure of the time, Trinidad Pedroza. Years later he traveled to Mexico City and met the artist and engraver Manuel Manilla, who introduced him to Antonio Vanegas Arroyo, an editor and publisher of street gazettes and a true pioneer of modern journalism. Arroyo recognized not only Posada's artistic talent but his prodigious drive; he offered to hire him, with a promise of complete artistic freedom. Working for Arroyo, Posada produced hundreds of thousands of cartoons, love letters, schoolbooks, card games, penny dreadfuls, and commercial advertisements like posters for circus performances and bullfights.

Although Manuel Manilla was the first to draw some skulls in newspapers and street gazettes, it is commonly thought that Posada, during his association with Arroyo, created these humorous, vivid drawings of dressed-up skulls or skeletons engaged in such activities as dancing, cycling, guitar playing, drinking, and masquerading. Because he popularized them, he is often mistakenly credited with inventing them. Indeed, he so personalized the imagery that his calaveras have become metaphors of his homeland: They are to Mexico what Uncle Sam is to the United States. Originally, he only intended to commemorate the country's Day of the Dead, when the poor and illiterate picnic and sleep in cemeteries to be close to their beloved dead. But the calaveras were immensely popular. They captivated audiences by poking fun at literary works from *Don Quixote* to José Zorilla's play *Don Juan Tenorio*. Scores of artists were influenced by them, many part of the Chicano movement of the 1960s. Rivera's mural *Dream of a Sunday Afternoon in the Central Alameda,* in Mexico City's Hotel del Prado until the 1985 earthquake, depicts the skeleton of a society belle wearing a scarf and hat. Posada stands arm in arm with the skeleton on the skeleton's left, and to her right is Frida Kahlo and a childish self-portrait of Rivera himself. Many of Posada's calaveras bear no signature, and over the years the works of countless imitators and forgers have been falsely attributed to him. Dead in

*See my essay "José Guadalupe Posada, Lampooner," *Journal of Decorative and Propaganda Art* 16 (Summer 1990): 55–71.

1913 when the revolution was talking place, he had lived penniless in a neighborhood near the Tepito marketplace and was buried in a pauper's grave in the Dolores cemetery.

Posada made death amusing, ludicrous, and less frightening. Faith in the unproved and unscientific, alternative modes of belief, folk wisdom, and superstition are a Latino trademark, proof that paganism and idolatry still pervade our unconscious. Our syncretism, which often involves mystical and idolatrous practices like Santería and voodoo, is, no doubt, a symptom of our cultural density. Whereas Protestantism found a new land in North America with the arrival of the British colonialists, Catholicism was established in the Hispanic world through a chain of painful attacks and interruptions. But the missionaries who forced Indians in the Americas to convert achieved only a partial success. We continue to believe in the supernatural. Diego de Torres, a viceroy of Peru, expressed to his European peers the disenchanted attitude with which natives approached Catholicism. "They express doubt and difficulty about certain aspects of the faith," he wrote, "principally the mystery of the Holy Trinity, the unity of God, the passion and death of Jesus Christ, the virginity of Our Lady, the Holy Communion, and resurrection." Doubt, our alibi. Through superstition, we journey back to a pre-Columbian past. As is clear in Rudolfo A. Anaya's *Bless Me, Ultima,* about a folk healer with supernatural powers who strikes up a friendship with a little boy in New Mexico, an ever-important figure among Latinos is the *curandero,* which indicates that in spite of the availability of modern scientific medicine many are loyal to alternative approaches to cure, often based on herbs. As John O. West shows, we are ruled by *mal de ojo,* as well as *el susto,* cured by invoking the names of saints in Nahuatl while stroking a patient with corn kernels, and by *empacho,* a dangerous condition that causes the soul to leave the body—the equivalent of depression and anxiety. From Miami and New York City to Los Angeles, the *botánicas,* folk pharmacies, play an important role in barrio life. Citizens come to buy nonscientific medicines to cure physical and psychological ailments. In addition, various rituals, known in Peru as *chamico* and in Mexico as *toloache,* are suggested to wives to control husbands and to prevent them from running away with other women. Our parade of superstitious artifacts and faith healers also includes *graniceros,* people struck by lightning who have the power to control the weather.

Multiple identities, dense culture: Our collective psyche is a labyrinth of passion and power, a carnival of sex, race, and death. Can the United States incorporate in its multifarious metabolism such a display of irrationality—an ancestral legacy of which it is impossible to dispossess Hispanics? While embracing us in its protective arms, while making room for Latinos, should Anglo culture expand, revamp, its overall approach to faith and reason? As a Spanish proverb states, *"El que adelante no mira, atrás se queda,"* "not to look ahead is to stay behind." And ahead means miscegenation.

5

◆ ◆ ◆

Sanavabiche

(OR, THE ART OF *CANTINFLEAR*)

Our tongue, our self.

Alburquerque, a family saga by Chicano writer Rudolfo A. Anaya, is about a young man of illegitimate birth, a boxing champ who fights his way to success, and opens with the following statement: "In April of 1880 the railroad reached la villa de Alburquerque in New Mexico. Legend says the Anglo stationmaster couldn't pronounce the first *r* in *Albur,* so he dropped it as he painted the station sign for the city. . . ." By attempting to restore the original Spanish spelling, Anaya hoped to reclaim the Latino heritage not only of the bicultural, bilingual metropolis but, indirectly, of the whole country. Pronounce *Nuevo México* and *Tejas*—cross out Albuquerque! Will tomorrow's spelling of the United States, in Spanish, be *los yunaited estates?* The unifying theme of this chapter is our devotion to the mother tongue, which creates dividing linguistic loyalties.

Unlike other ethnic groups, we Latinos are amazingly loyal to our mother tongue. Because of the geographic closeness of the countries of origin and the diversity in the composition of their communities, Spanish remains a unifying force, used at home, in school, and on the streets. Thirty-four percent of native-born Chicanos, 50 percent of mainland Puerto Ricans, and 40 percent of native-born Cuban-Americans have participated in bilingual education programs. To be or *ser*: that's the real question: Spanish and English, a native tongue and an adopted tongue, a foot here, another across the border and the Caribbean—a home at home and abroad. A rooster in the United States sings "cock-a-doodle-doo"; another in Guatemala says *qui-qui-ri-qui;* and a third one, a Latino, cock-a-doodle-doos and *qui-qui-ri-quis* simultaneously.

Spanish or English: Which is the true Latino mother tongue? They both are, plus a third option: Spanglish—a hybrid. We inhabit a linguistic abyss: *Entre Lucas y Juan Mejía* claims a Dominican saying: between two mentalities and lost in translation. Gustavo Pérez-Firmat wrote in his poem "Dedication":

The fact that I
am writing to you
in English
already falsifies what I
want to tell you.
My subject:
how to explain to you
that I
don't belong to English
though I belong nowhere else,
if not here
in English.

Or consider a segment of his "Bilingual Blues":

I have mixed feelings about everything.
Soy un ajiaco de contradicciones.
Vexed, hexed, complexed,
hyphenated, oxygenated, illegally alienated,
psycho soy, cantando voy:
You say tomato,
I say tu madre;
You say potato,
I say Pototo.
Let's call the hole,
un hueco, the thing
a cosa, and if the cosa goes into the hueco,
consider yourself at home,
consider yourself part of the family.
Soy un ajiaco de contradicciones,
un potaje de paradojas,
a little square from Rubik's Cuba

que nadie nunca acomplará
(Cha-cha-cha.)

Loyalty to either Spanish or English depends on which generation you're addressing. Since Spanish was for many decades a domestic tongue forbidden in schools and public places in the Southwest, Florida, and parts of New England, the community saw it as a sign of resistance. Tomás Rivera deals with the dilemma in his work: *Yo hablo español* meant I will not surrender to Anglo values and ways of life. "Dogs and Mexicans not allowed!" read a sign in the South when, in the late 1960s, Gabriel García Márquez traveled with his wife and child in an old car throughout the South, looking for traces of William Faulkner's art. It was not until the late 1960s that Latinos opened a door to a new awakening—the knowledge that, although they were Spanish, proficiency in English could only be an asset. From the 1970s on, bilingualism became the fashion.

The bilingual education movement originated in 1960, in Dade County, Florida, where public schools were unexpectedly inundated with Cuban immigrants escaping the Castro regime. Mainly because they were sure to return to their home island, the prerogative of these new exiles was to keep their native tongue, Spanish, as an integral part of their children's pedagogical environment. Consequently, they fought for intelligent laws to allow their children to be taught both languages in public schools. Thus, bilingual education was not the result of poor academic performance by Latino children, but an attempt to remain loyal to ethnic roots. It emerged among Cubans as a solution to their life in exile, not as a reality of lower-class Mexican or Puerto Rican children in California or New York. By the mid-1970s and during the 1980s, the program expanded to states like Texas, Massachusetts, and New Jersey, and its scope was truly enormous. Schools could apply for federal funds to implement the bilingual method and, because of legal intricacies and as a result of political battles by astute leaders, governmental money given to them for other educational purposes was often contingent on their implementation of Spanish courses. The irony became clear. At some point, the state not only favored but compelled schools to develop bilingual education programs, thus granting Hispanic culture a legitimate academic status no other group had ever had.

No doubt a pattern had been set even before the early 1960s. The National Conference of Spanish-speaking People, led by Luisa Moreno and Josefina

Fierro de Bright, formed in 1938, was one of the earliest Chicano civil rights organizations to equate freedom of speech with freedom of language usage. And almost a decade and a half later, another organization, the American Council of Spanish-speaking People, held its founding convention in El Paso. By the time the Dade County activities were germinating, the Political Association of Spanish-speaking Organizations, known as PASSO, evolved from the Viva Kennedy Clubs in Texas in 1960 and acquired political force in the Southeast. The result was evident: Spanish was here to stay, and laws had to accommodate it. In 1974, in *Lau v. Nichols,* the Supreme Court ruled that English-only curricula in public schools were discriminatory.

To be sure, the word *English* is found nowhere in the U.S. Constitution nor in any subsequent amendment. As Theodore H. White wrote in 1986, Americans are a nation born of an idea; the idea, not the place, created the United States government. Place or locus, of course, also includes language; after all, one is born into a tongue. The issue of codifying a national tongue was never even raised at the Constitutional Convention in Philadelphia in 1787. Social diversity was not then an issue: England was the mother country, and English, the mother tongue. But 194 years later, in 1981, the English Language amendment, promoted by the English Only movement, was introduced in Congress. English, under fire as the only cohesive force to keep the country together, was bleeding. The attempt to turn English into the nation's official tongue was the medicine. Congress had passed the Bilingual Education Act in 1968 and, seven years later, the Bilingual Voting Rights amendment. By the early 1980s, demographics had altered the population's racial composition. A growing number of non-European immigrants were making their homes in the West Coast and New England. Many arrived from Asia, south of the Rio Grande, or the Caribbean, endangering traditional white supremacy.

Quarreling over the national language is certainly nothing new. Ever since the British colonists first settled in New England, and especially during the waves of German, Jewish, and Italian migrations, many Americans have defended English as a national language. For example, after the Mexican-American War, politicians north and south of the Rio Grande agreed that Spanish, together with English, would become the language of government in the newly acquired lands—that there would be not one, but two tongues. The promise was left unfulfilled, and language rights for Spanish speakers, then a slight majority in the region, were ignored. Thus, although the English

Language amendment may never become law, the issues surrounding it divide the nation.

Spanish and English: *SEpnagnlisshh*. Language is a most useful tool to contrast both worldviews: that of the United States and that of Hispanic America. Spanish, labyrinthine in nature, has at least four conjugations to address the past, and the one future tense is rarely used. One can portray a past event in multiple ways, but when it comes to a future event, a speaker in Buenos Aires, Mexico City, or Caracas has little choice. A symptomatic fact: Hispanics, unable to recover from history, are obsessed with memory. English, on the other hand, is exact, matter-of-fact, almost mathematical, a tongue with plenty of room for conditionals, ready to seize destiny. Spanish makes objects male and female, whereas in English, the same objects lack gender. As if one was not enough, Spanish has two verbs for *to be*: one used to describe permanence, another to refer to location and temporality. Thus, a single sentence, say Hamlet's famous dilemma, *to be or not to be,* when translated into Spanish has a double, never self-negating, clear-cut meaning: to be or not to be alive; to be or to be here. *Ser o no ser; estar o no estar.* (And, consequently, *estar y no ser, ser y no estar*). English simplifies: to be, period—here and now. Again, Spanish has two verbs for *to know*: one used to characterize knowledge through experience, the other to designate memorized information. *Conocer o Saber.* To know Prague is not the same thing as to know the content of the Declaration of Independence. Much less baroque, English rejects complications.

At the dawn of Hispanic American history, something was lost in the translation: a sense of belonging, a crystalline identity. Bernal Díaz del Castillo, in his chronicle of the conquest of Mexico, stated that after Motecuhzoma II gave Hernán Cortés gifts of gold and other precious objects, he offered Cortés twenty slave girls, among whom was La Malinche, also known by her Indian name, Malinzin, and her Spanish appellation, Marina. La Malinche soon became the conquistador's mistress; an Aztec traitress; and, more than anything else, a translator and an interpreter. Love and language: How accurate was she? Through her, Cortés discovered his enemy's real power and strategy. Consequently, *malinchista,* south of the Rio Grande, in its wide range of meanings, refers to a coward, an apostate, a deserter: a *traduttore traditore.* As Alejo Carpentier wrote about discovering one's own vehicle of communication after a long journey away: "I felt imprisoned, kidnapped, an accomplice in something execrable, locked up in the plane, with the oscillation three-step rhythm of the fuselage battling a head wind that, at times, bathed the aluminum wings with a light rain. But now, a strange voluptuousness lulls my scruples. Here a force penetrates me slowly through the ears, my pores: language. Here it is, then, the language that I spoke as a child; the language in which I learned to read and to sol-fa; the language grown moldy in my mind, cast aside like a useless tool in a country where it could not help me."

With its Romance roots, Spanish is capable of amazing pyrotechnics. A favorite among Hispanics is the genial comedian Cantinflas, a linguistic genius. Although Mario Moreno Reyes, his Mexican creator, died in 1993 at age eighty-one, Cantinflas, a mischief maker, Moreno's sublime 1936 creation and the protagonist of forty-nine films, survives simultaneously as an archetype and as a symbol of the Hispanic psyche: An archetype of the urban Hispanic *lépero,* an irreverent rascal with semirural traditions, disoriented yet astute, who confounds others by means of an unconcerned verbosity and enjoys reinventing himself in the social labyrinth; he is also a symbol of the pros and cons of modernizing Latin America after World War II. Cantinflas was a master of confusing people through chaotic speeches and indirect reports. He constantly played with words and gambled with meanings.*

Born in 1911 in a poor neighborhood in Mexico City, Moreno, the son of a mailman and the sixth of thirteen children, was a charming boy capable of enchanting bystanders, who would attentively watch his pirouettes on the sidewalk and listen to his linguistic tricks, throwing him a couple of centavos as sign of appreciation. As an adolescent he was a bullfighter, shoe shiner, taxi driver, and boxing champ before joining the itinerant *carpa*—a Mexican-style circus that intertwines standup comedy and sketches with acrobatics. Young Moreno was happiest when impersonating scoundrels and clowns on stage. One night, the legend goes, forced to replace an indisposed announcer, he made the audience laugh. Nervous and almost peeing, his words were incoherent, his sentences intricate and ridiculous. No tomatoes were thrown, though. Instead, his exaggerations and talkativeness automatically turned him into a *peladito*—everybody's favorite pal. His routine became a repertoire.

As a well-rounded fictional character, Cantinflas materialized when somebody, between smiles and tears, shouted from a balcony: *¡En la cantina tu inflas!* The expression hypnotized Moreno: he adapted it, turning it into a nom de guerre. The character's development was not unlike that of Charlie Chaplin, although it emerged from a different film mecca—Mexico City—

---

*See my obituary in *Review: Latin American Literature and Arts* 49 (Fall 1994): 94–95.

which, during the 1930s, was incubating what would shortly be known as the Golden Age of national cinema. Moreno began his career as a supporting actor in a 1937 film. He then married Valentina Zubareff, the daughter of a *carpa* owner who employed him. Valentina suggested that Cantinflas be used in ads for domestic products, and after the commercials were well received, Moreno, excited and ambitious, created Posa Films to produce films that had his fictional creation as the protagonist. Around 1939 the company distributed two shorts: *Siempre listo en las tinieblas* and *Jenjibre contra dinamita,* which were followed by the internationally renowned *Ahí está el detalle* and *Ni sangre ni arena,* made in 1940 and 1941, respectively, the first directed by Juan Bustillo Oro, the second by Alejandro Galindo. Charlie Chaplin, after watching several Cantinflas films, is believed to have declared: "He's the greatest comedian alive. . . . Far better than me!"

During World War II, Moreno was introduced to Miguel M. Delgado, who would direct innumerable hits, such as *Romeo y Julieta, Grand Hotel,* and *El analfabeta.* Perhaps the best, most solid sign of Moreno's immortality is the colorful 1951 mural by Diego Rivera about national heroes in the entranceway of Teatro Insurgentes in Mexico City, in which Cantinflas is the spinal column, as well as Rufino Tamayo's abstract portrait. Although in Europe and among Anglos in the United States, Moreno (not his *peladito*) is recognized—as Passepartout in *Around the World in Eighty Days,* a 1956 film with David Niven and Shirley MacLaine, and as the protagonist in *Pepe*—his Hollywood life was ill-fated. The word *Cantinflas* entered the Spanish dictionary: as a verb, *cantinflear* means to talk too much and to say nothing; as a noun, *cantinflada* describes an adorable clown; and as an adjective, *cantinfleado* means dumb. *Cantinflas, cantinflea, cantinfladas*: To confuse, to evade reality, to use language as a weapon.

Cervantes's tongue is the glue that keeps Hispanics together, the point of encounter for Latinos north of the border. People and the media keep it alive. In the United States, Spanish dailies began circulating immediately after the Treaty of Guadalupe Hidalgo. The mandate of *El Clamor Público,* for instance, founded in 1866 in Los Angeles, was to create a sense of unity against the new status quo. Newspapers multiplied quickly. By 1900 more than 125 Spanish-language newspapers were in circulation throughout the United States. *La Voz Pública* was founded in 1932 in Santa Fe, and *El Malcriado,* the United Farm Worker's Association's newspaper, which began publication in 1964, has had a substantial readership. Capitalizing on the growing importance of Hispanics across the Rio Grande, a number of Mexican newspapers, including *El Heraldo de México,* established offices in Arizona, California, New Mexico, Texas, and other states, hugely expanding their readership. One of the most important Spanish-speaking newspapers is *La Opinión,* which began publication in Los Angeles in 1926. At first, it was a family business, but it soon expanded to become a major political and intellectual force. Read daily by several million people, it is the major forum on Latino life in the Southwest. A couple of other powerful dailies—*El Diario* in New York City and *El Nuevo Herald,* the Spanish edition of the *Miami Herald*—together reach several million readers. Acting as a bridge between Hispanics and the system, the papers print supplements about immigration laws and quotas, street and institutional discrimination, job opportunities, and civil rights.

Magazines for Latinos also have expanded. In 1989, Univisión, the television network, launched *Más,* a quarterly magazine about stars, music, cuisine, and traditions, that had the largest circulation among this ethnic minority until its closing in 1993. Edited by Enrique Fernández, a Cuban columnist for the *Village Voice* with an academic past, the journal began to fail when it went from being a quarterly to a bimonthly. Other commercial journals like *Canales, Vanidades,* and the Spanish edition of *Cosmopolitan,* dealing with soap operas, merengue, and women's fashion, are printed in Florida and the West Coast and influence public opinion.

Throughout the Hispanic experience in the United States, radio and theater have served as promoters of the Spanish language. By the time the citizens of Mexico found themselves part of another reality after the Treaty of Guadalupe Hidalgo, cultural manifestations began to flourish. Some professional theaters begun by Mexicans and Mexican-Americans appeared in Arizona, California, and Texas. During the Mexican Revolution, to escape the bloodshed, native Mexican artists, intellectuals, and theater people took up permanent residence in the United States. These theaters became quite popular as street spectacles and broadcasters of news: Around 1912, the troupe Telegram Theater, for instance, screened news events from Mexico, developing the form into an art. In the 1920s, a huge expansion of dramatic performances took place: Mexican theater companies toured Chicago, Cleveland, Detroit, New York, and Philadelphia. But these companies declined in popularity and importance after the Great Depression because many of the expatriates went back to Mexico and movies became the more popular medium.

So who speaks Spanish in the United States? Or, rather, who speaks what kind of Spanish? People who walk through the streets of Miami, Los Angeles, or New York and have a sense of things Hispanic know that there is no one

Spanish in North America but many—at least four: the ones used by Puerto Ricans, by Chicanos, by Cubans, and by the other subgroups. Although Latinos share a common cultural heritage and use the same grammar and syntax, the various idioms—or, should I say, quasi-dialects—they use daily make for hilarious misunderstandings.

In the early 1980s, for instance, when the Latino consumer began to be taken seriously by major marketing corporations, an insecticide company decided to launch a product on Spanish-speaking television and radio. The company hired an advertising agent with little expertise and an incomplete knowledge of Hispanic linguistic idiosyncrasies. The result was a commercial that stated that the product was infallible in killing *bichos*. When the ad went on the air, almost a third of the audience roared with laughter every time they saw or listened to it. The word, you should know, means bug or insect in Mexico, but in San Juan, it is used to refer to the penis. Ready for the penis killer? And another infamous ad, which illustrates the ignorance of Spanish in general, was that for the Chevy Nova, which also was received with hilarity in the Hispanic community. "No va" means "it goes nowhere." Just as a British commercial would have to be reshaped to be used in the United States, words within the Hispanic community in this country depend on the various contexts in which they are used. Of course, a common understanding can be found, yet communication is the art not just of imparting, conveying, and exchanging ideas and information, but of knowing how to do so.

The only way to distinguish between one linguistic Spanish-speaking group and another is through its unique national past: The vocabulary used by the four groups depends on particular historical circumstances. Argentines are less the product of an interracial mixture between the Spanish conquistadors and the native Indians and therefore have a more Europeanized Spanish than that of, say, Mexicans, who have integrated pre-Columbian terms and names (Aztec, Mayan, for example) in their day-to-day language. Dominicans use expressions like *macutear* (to ask for money), *rebú* (dispute, quarrel), and *de apaga y vámonos* (something extraordinary), which other Spanish-speakers would not understand. In general, Latinos in Chicago or Los Angeles or New Jersey, no longer say *mercado* for supermarket, but *marketa*; in addition, they say *voy a parquear el auto,* rather than *voy a estacionar el automovil,* and *aplicar a la universidad* instead of *solicitar entrada a la universidad.* In 1990 I attended a conference at the University of Southern California whose topic was Spanish and the United States media. In attendance were linguists, as well as advertising agents, journalists, writers, educators, editors, and independent scholars, all professionals from the various fields that shape the daily language. While debating, some showed signs of distress after realizing how "sick" Spanish really is. All the participants had different origins: Peruvians, Guatemalans, you name it. What was interesting was that the panelists had to refrain from using neologisms—and for that they were often ridiculed. It was a revealing symptom: It showed how Spanish-speaking media workers, although conscious of their social and educational role, don't speak an unaffected language; they are part of the sickness they seek to cure. Add to this the fact that because of the money and attention placed on Hispanic media in this country, people in Caracas, Venezuela, or in Santiago de Chile, who watch Hispanic television from the United States on cable channels are beginning to use the same malapropisms, transforming the Spanish language in their individual countries. That the changes here have a strong echo worldwide reminds me of a curious linguistic reverie that my wife once noted. When the English term *supermarket* began to be used, Latin Americans quickly imitated it; the result was *supermercado*. The Spanish word was then shortened to *super,* and as I was growing up in the early 1970s, that was the name applied to large grocery stories. Soon another adaptation emerged— an oxymoron if there was ever one: *mini-super,* to describe a small *mercado* with ambitions.

For as much as I bet that Spanish will survive as a language in this country, it will not and cannot do so in its purest, orthodox, Castilian form. Yiddish, I believe, is again a parallel example. For almost two hundred years, educated Jews in Eastern Europe, often referred to as *maskilim,* refused to grant Yiddish the status of a legitimate language of communication, although during the eighteenth century thousands of poor *shtetl* inhabitants used it in their everyday lives. Yiddish is part Hebrew; part German; and part a sum of Slovak, Czech, Russian, Polish, and other Indo-European idioms. Only after a forceful and long struggle was the dialect finally elevated to the level of language, and before the Holocaust, it was spoken by more than 11 million people. Granted, the comparison between Spanish and Yiddish may seem to be simplistic, yet, it is also enlightening. Spanish is in the process of revamping its own roots in the United States, and if Hispanics refuse to give it up, as they have in the past few decades, the result may be a perplexing mixture that belongs nowhere and is the product of linguistic Darwinism.

Literature by Latinos written in Spanish, it ought to be said, has flourished in the United States since 1848. The works of Reinaldo Arenas, Marjorie Agosín, Rosario Ferré, Eugenio Florit, Julia de Burgos, José Kozer, Fernando

Alegría, and Herberto Padilla serve as examples. Among the recent practition-
ers is Isaac Goldemberg, a Peruvian Jew, who, after a long sojourn that took
him to Europe and the Middle East, landed in Manhattan, where he wrote *La
vida a plazos de Don Jacobo Lerner,* published by a small bilingual press in
New Hampshire, Ediciones del Norte, which specializes in publishing the
work of Latin American exiles. Other transitional figures are Ariel Dorfman,
who after the coup d'etat in his native Chile in 1973 that overthrew Salvador
Allende, finally settled, for six months a year, in North Carolina. Originally a
Spanish-language writer, he switched to English to gain a larger audience.
Death and the Maiden, his Broadway drama, describes the suffering of torture
victims in an unspecified South American country. Elena Castedo, author of
Paradise, also switched to English and then translated her own work into her
mother tongue, Spanish. The Colombian Jaime Manrique, author of *Latin
Moon in Manhattan,* began writing in Spanish and then finally settled for
Shakespeare's tongue. The Guatemalan Victor Perera, author of *Rites: A
Guatemalan Boyhood,* switched from English into Spanish. Guillermo Cabrera
Infante, who chose English to create *Holy Smoke,* a hilarious semihistorical
essay on the development and importance of cigars and the act of smoking
in the Western World, used literature to recover a joyful reality left behind in
Havana.

Jorge Luis Borges, Manuel Puig, João Ubaldo Ribeiro, and Carlos Fuentes
are other writers who ought to be added to the list. Borges's "Autobiographical Essay," written in English in collaboration with Norman Thomas Di Giovanni and published in *The New Yorker* in 1976 (and later part of *The Aleph
and Other Writings*), never appeared in the Argentine author's native tongue
during his lifetime. Puig translated his own work *Eternal Curse on the Reader
of These Pages,* about the relationship between a sick patient and a Hispanic
caretaker in New York, into English, as Ribeiro did with his encyclopedic
Brazilian novels *Sergeant Getúlio* and *An Invincible Memory*, known in Portuguese as *Viva o povo brasiliero*.

Native-born Latino writers like Oscar Hijuelos and Sandra Cisneros are presented with a curious, if somewhat disingenuous dilemma. To be read in the
countries their parents left behind, they have to be translated into Spanish;
that is, as Hispanics they have to "return" to their own linguistic territory by
losing something they have already gained. Which one is their mother
tongue? English, no doubt. But if their goal is to reflect the barrio life they
came from and if their need is to reach those who come from the barrio,
these writers would have to write in Spanglish—although, of course, no pub-

lisher would print their books, simply because it would be commercially unfeasible.

The story of Spanish is the story of its various pasts, but also of its intriguing futures. And one of those futures is being shaped right now around us—as we speak. The result may be an affront to Quevedo and Borges: a bastardized yet authentic version of the same language used by Christopher Columbus, who, by the way, didn't know how to write and spoke a terrible Spanish. (Ramón Menéndez Pidal, the Spanish linguist, wrote in 1942, to commemorate the Genoese's so-called discovery, an enlightening study of *su lengua,* his spoken language.) The first American and already with a linguistic handicap: Columbus, a man lost in the intricacies of words.

Even though *el español* is very much a U.S. tongue and its increasing political power is unquestionable, entrance into the American Dream requires a fluency, however limited, in Shakespeare's language, which brings me back to the topic of bilingual education. Should Spanish be taught at school? Why have Hispanics taken so long (some sixty years) to learn Shakespeare's tongue and to reject Cervantes's? Should Hispanics be treated differently, linguistically speaking, from other minorities? Are students in bilingual programs better off? Are Hispanics who take bilingual education more likely to go to college than those who don't? As a movement and a program, is bilingual education unique to Hispanics?

It is a well-known fact that a large number of Chicanos, Puerto Ricans, and Cubans use Spanish and English at home. *Hablar español* is to reclaim one's past. Because of the widespread need for bilingual professionals, those fluent in both oral and written Spanish and English are far better off than their unilingual counterparts. Their chance of making it in college increases by almost 80 percent, and once they are fully conscious of their professional possibilities, they often tend to improve their bilingual skills. Felipe Alfau, an Iberian novelist, begins his novel *Chromos: A Parody* (published in 1990, but written in the 1940s, when Spanish was not ubiquitous north of the Rio Grande), with the following paragraph:

> The moment one learns English, complications set in. Try as one may, one cannot elude this conclusion, one must inevitably come back to it. This applies to all persons, including those born to the language and, at times, even more so to Latins. . . . It manifests itself in the awareness of implications and intricacies to which one had never given a thought; it afflicts one with that officiousness of philosophy which, having no busi-

ness of its own, gets in everybody's way and, in the case of Latins, they lose that racial characteristic of taking things for granted and leaving them to their own devices without inquiring into causes, motives or ends, to meddle indiscreetly into reasons which are none of one's affair and to become not only self-conscious, but conscious of other things which never gave a damn for one's existence.

Modernity, as Steven G. Kellman argues, is largely a reality of exile, a project of psychic, if not geographic, dislocation. Alternative tongues open up doors to other worlds. Translation is a way to get around the problem that is like a Tower of Babel; the lack of understanding can be resolved by asking a specialist to bring one language to another. But translation, at least in the literary sense, is an impossible art. Words and phrases are not just descriptions of the objects and circumstances involved, but more often than not denote the spirit as well. One can replace a word in Spanish with its equivalent in English; in fact, there are computer programs for doing so. A cultural translation, on the other hand, requires human imput. To translate is to adapt, to find a replacement for a particular word by understanding its idiosyncratic meaning. For example, try to put a Beatles song to Quechuas isolated in the northern Peruvian jungle, alienated from Western civilization. Regardless of the fact that the record player will itself be a curious, quasi-divine object when they first see it, the noises heard, "Like the fool on the hill . . ." or "I love you yeah, yeah, yeah . . . ," will seem inharmonious, incoherent—a sheer aberration. To translate word by word, even to explain what is meant by love in our society, will not do. Indeed, the Quechuas might run away terrified after hearing the first sounds. Borges once told a translator to write not what he said, but what he wanted to say. In Spanish, the expression *quiero decir* literally means "I want to say" or "I am trying to say," although it has come to be understood as "I mean." Looking for an English equivalent of *quiero decir,* we must remember how often we use that phrase to correct or reword what we are "trying to say." When it comes to curses and oaths, the linguistic chasm is insurmountable: Although the meaning may be different, the spirit is universal. In English, for example, to insult your mother, one would call you, regardless of your gender, a son of a bitch; in Spanish you would be called *un hijo de puta*—son of a whore. As Gregory Rabassa notes, the closest word to *whore* in Shakespeare's tongue is the archaic *worsen,* which nowadays would cause little fury. Or think of *cabrón,* cuckold, without an exact equivalent in English. A distance, a loss. In other words, we are always wanting to say what we can never say. George Santayana, raised in Spanish, wrote his poetry in English. He claimed:

> Of impassioned tenderness or Dionysian frenzy I have nothing, nor even of that magic and pregnancy of phrase—really the creation of a fresh idiom—which marks the highlights of poetry. Even if my temperament had been naturally warmer, the fact that the English language (and I can write no other with assurance) was not my mother-tongue would of itself preclude any inspired use of it on my part; its roots do not quite reach to my center. I never drank in childhood the homely cadences and ditties which in pure spontaneous poetry set the essential key. I know no words redolent of the wonder-world, fairy-tale, or the cradle.

In her enchanting essay "Mother Tongue," the Chinese-American novelist Amy Tan, author of *The Joy Luck Club,* discusses her plight as the daughter of a Chinese woman who spoke broken English. Listening to her mother, she often thought that not only her mother's language, but her reasoning, was broken. In fact, the term *broken English* is already a misnomer: it suggests imperfection, incompleteness. But the alternatives aren't better: "nonstandard English," "simple English." "When I was growing up," Tan stated, "my mother's 'limited' English limited *my* perception of her. I was ashamed of her English. I believed that her English reflected the quality of what she had to say. That is, because she expressed them imperfectly her thoughts were imperfect. And I had plenty of empirical evidence to support me: the fact that people in department stores, at banks, and at restaurants did not take her seriously, did not give her good service, pretended not to understand her, or even acted as if they did not hear."

One of the most puzzling questions about the Bible is why diversity of language doesn't appear until Genesis 11, with the Tower of Babel. When Adam, to identify objects around him, names what he sees with his human eyes, in which language does he do it? According to a Talmudic interpretation, he does it in Hebrew, *lashon ha-kodesh*—the sacred tongue, God's language. All other tongues are vox populi, human vehicles of communication, not profane but mundane. Why then doesn't the Bible state it? Is it self-evident? Could one imagine a proto-language, the linguistic source of source, the first tongue after which all Babel-like variants emerged? Or else, could Adam have been a polyglot, speaking at least two tongues: his and the Almighty's? When the Spanish conquistadors first came to the New World, they shared something only the biblical Adam had: the naming of things. The Mexican writer Andrés Iduarte went around saying that he would give anything to be the first, or among the first, persons on the moon, simply to be able to name things. To name is to acquire, to control, to possess. In ancient times, when the people of Israel shaped their spiritual identity, idolatry prevailed. By knowing the name of a god, the worshiper could easily manipulate its powers. Thus, the rabbis decided to hide God's name. Today we have variants: Adonai, Elohim, Yaweh (a syllabication of YHWH), and so on; none is accurate, they are all approximations. As Rabassa claimes, the Iberian newcomers had recourse to three different methods in their nomenclature: They could accept the Indian name, in a version usually colored by their own tongue; they could assign a name that identified the creature or object as one approaching a known animal or thing in the Old World; or they could apply an entirely new and descriptive name to the things and living creatures they saw. We have many examples of all three methods. Woodchuck, quetzal, and jaguar are examples of the first, but some Spaniards, as Rabassa claims, when they spied the jaguar for the first time baptized it *tigre,* even though they had never been to India or seen a tiger. Or take the case of lemon and lime: in Spanish, *limón* is lime, and *lima* is lemon. Why, I don't know; actually, nobody seems to know: The Iberian conquistadors named the objects at random, upside down.

Richard Rodríguez expresses a similar fascination with language switching and snatching. An early product of affirmative action and ethnic quotas, *Road-ree-guess* became a "scholarship boy" and devoted his early adulthood to completing a Ph.D. dissertation on John Milton at Berkeley and the British Museum. But he changed his mind and became an essayist. He rebelled against bilingual education because, from his perspective, it encourages minorities (especially Latinos, whom he calls Mexicans and Hispanic-Americans) to remain loyal to their background and legacy, thus delaying their full assimilation into the American Dream. Rodríguez grew up in Sacramento. "An accident of geography sent me to a school where all my classmates were white, many the children of doctors and lawyers and business executives," he claims. "All my classmates certainly must have been uneasy on that first day of school—as most children are uneasy—to find themselves apart from their families in the first institution of their lives. But I was astonished." He continues:

> The nun said, in a friendly but oddly impersonal voice, "Boys and girls, this is Richard Rodriguez. . . ." It was the first time I had heard anyone

name me in English. "Richard," the nun repeated more slowly, writing my name down in her black leather book. Quickly I turned to see my mother's face dissolve in a watery blur behind the pebbled glass door.

Many years later there is something called bilingual education—a scheme proposed in the late 1960s by Hispanic-American social activists, later endorsed by a congressional vote. It is a program that seeks to permit non-English-speaking children, many from lower-class homes, to use their family language as the language of school. (Such is the goal its supporters announce.) I hear them and am forced to say no: It is not possible for a child—any child—ever to use his family's language in school. Not to understand this is to misunderstand the public uses of schooling and to trivialize the nature of intimate life—a family's "language."

If bilingualism can be condemned, life with an accent was, until recently, a condemnation. *I no spik englich, ¿comprende?* Not anymore, though: In the age of multiculturalism, an accent is as exotic as a piña colada or a margarita, or perhaps not even as exotic. Furthermore, Rodríguez's argument, set forth with a weight and a solid narrative style unparalleled in modern U.S. literature, is nearsighted. My reaction: He is right! Bilingual education is wrong. One's own family's language is private, personal, intimate; English is plural, communal, collective. Amy Tan's plight—the embarrassment over her mother's second language—is typical of second-generation immigrants: They improve on their parent's idiomatic skills and thus distance themselves from their parents' universe. Generations come and go; the wise men in Ecclesiastes knew it: There is a place and time for everything under the sun. And yet, what Rodríguez ignored is the nation's cultural climate. It's too late to change! The damage has been done. Bilingual education has formed the minds of women and men who understand both languages and believe both, Spanish and English, English and Spanish, to be legitimate and authoritative. These tongues may fight, they might hate each other—but they must coexist. Today the United States lives partially *en español*. Why sacrifice the benefits of a mistake? Latinos feel close to their roots through language, and Spanish is slowly becoming ubiquitous.

The struggle to overcome discrimination based on partial knowledge of English is as old as the country. The best, and most tragic, early example of a life lost in translation is described in the corrido of Gregorio Cortez Lira, studied in detail by Américo Paredes, a pivotal figure in the history of Hispanic letters in the United States. Paredes was born in 1915 in Brownsville, on the

Texas-Mexico border, and became interested in border traditions. In 1934 one of his early poems won first place in the Texas state contest sponsored by Trinity College in San Antonio. The following year he began publishing poetry in *La Prensa*, the newspaper there. Paredes's interest in border folklore led to the 1958 publication of his doctoral thesis at the University of Texas at Austin, *With His Pistol in His Hand,* one of the first studies of the Mexican corrido. Today, Paredes is professor emeritus of English at the University of Texas at Austin. In 1989 he was awarded the Charles Frankel Prize by the National Endowment for the Humanities "for outstanding contributions to the public's understanding of the texts, themes, and ideas of the humanities."

The year was 1901 and Cortez was a brave vaquero from either Hidalgo or Matamoros, who could shoot a .44 and a .33 with equal talent. But he was not an aggressive man, at least not according to the legend. He had a brother, Román, loudmouthed and discontented, with whom he traveled north to make some money. The two brothers picked cotton and cleared land for the Germans. They finally settled in a place called El Carmen, in Texas. Román owned two beautiful sorrels; they looked alike, except that one was lame. According to Paredes, an American who owned a little sorrel mare was dying to get one of Román's horses. He offered to swap the mare for one of Román's horses, but the Mexican refused. One day, however, Román was in the mood for a joke. He met the gringo on the road, they talked, and he decided to exchange his horse for the mare. He promised to deliver it a while later. But instead of giving him the right sorrel, he gave him the lame one. When the American realized what he got, he asked the sheriff of El Carmen to accompany him to where Gregorio and Román lived. When he and the sheriff arrived, Gregorio, who had foreseen something strange for that day, was shaving. The brothers exchanged some words, and the gringos misunderstood what they said, so the sheriff took out a gun and killed Román. Furious, Gregorio got his pistol ready. The sheriff shot three times and missed; Gregorio shot three times and killed his enemy. He did not kill the other American out of pity, but his tragedy had begun. He had to escape, to run away from the law. The linguistic misunderstanding between the Mexicans and the gringos is described by Paredes in the following way: The Americans had come into the Cortezes' yard and up to where Román was leaning over the door, looking out.

The American had a very serious face. "I came for the mare you stole yesterday morning," he said.

Román laughed a big-mouthed laugh. "What did I tell you, Gregorio?" he said. "The Gringo Sanavabiche has backed down on me."

Now there are three saints that the Americans are specially fond of—Santa Anna, San Jacinto, and Sanavabiche—and of the three it is Sanavabiche that they pray to the most. Just listen to an American any time. You may not understand anything else he says, but you are sure to hear him say, "Sanavabiche! Sanavabiche! Sanavabiche!" Every hour of the day. But they'll get very angry if you say it too, perhaps because it is a saint that belongs to them alone.

And so it was with the Major Sheriff of the county of El Carmen. Just as the words "Gringo Sanavabiche" came out of Román's mouth, the sheriff whipped out his pistol and shot Román.

As discussed in Chapter 4, a fundamental component of Hispanic culture—from the cult of Santería to Enriquillo (the Dominican runaway slave who is featured in Fray Bartolomé de Las Casas's *History of the Indies*) onward, from the Cuban ethnographer Fernando Ortíz's concept of point counterpoint to novelist Reinaldo Arenas's *pentagonía*—is our baroque self-consciousness, mirrors reflecting other mirrors time and again. Our architecture, music, pictorial art, and letters are filled with self-references: novels that refer to themselves and to other novels that refer to themselves, paintings about paintings, and so forth. Recalling one of Fidel Castro's slogans, included in a speech at the Fifty-third Plenary National Congress of Cuban Workers and published in 1987 in *Cuba Socialista*: "We must correct the errors we made in correcting our errors." Our collective soul is based on foreign, exogenous components. Gustavo Pérez-Firmat stressed this fact in discussing Cuban culture in particular, but his analysis, without disregarding national differences, applies to the Hispanic galaxy as a whole:

Because of the island's peculiar history, the Cuban writer or artist is specially sensitive to opportunities for translation, in both geographical and linguistic senses of the word. Not having a native store of cultural goods, and conditioned by history to the ways of the transient rather than the settler, the Cuban writer has the habit of looking onward, of being on the lookout for opportunities for displacement, graphic and topographic. In my opinion, this onward glance, this "outlook," underlies translational (and, in this case, transnational) performances. . . . Cuban culture subsists in and through translation.

By incorporating and activating African, Indian, and European symbols and motifs, we translate, adapt, reinvent, and bargain. What's original in us? The act of translation itself. The fact that we communicate in Spanish, Portuguese, or French (and now English) already makes us copies, reproductions, reflections of somebody else's linguistic code.

In any case, Gregorio Cortez took his best horse and rode five hundred miles to the border. By then, the incident had become a scandal. The president of the United States offered $1,000 for his head, and all the sheriffs of the region were out to get him. Every time he faced a death threat from a sheriff, he shot in self-defense and ran. He ended up killing many people. By then, in retaliation, his whole family was put in jail. Cortez's mother, wife, and daughters were held in jail until the so-called criminal gave himself up. And after running away like a desperado, he finally turned himself in. When he was put on trial, it soon became clear that there were two laws: one for Texas Americans and the other for Texas Mexicans. But Cortez was found not guilty: He had killed in self-defense because his brother's blood had been spilled. Numerous times he was put on trial, but he was never found guilty. So, when he was about to be set free, one of his enemies came up with the solution: They would put him on trial for having stolen a sorrel mare. They asked him if the horse that had helped him escape was his, and he had to answer no. So he was found guilty, and his punishment was 99 years and a day in prison—99 years and a day!

Things unexpectedly turned in his favor in less than a year, when President Abraham Lincoln's daughter requested the governor to grant Gregorio Cortez clemency and set him free before Christmas. The governor had promised that he would grant any request she made, and although the prisoner had a highly publicized trial, he was set free. However, Cortez's enemies couldn't stand the leniency, so they collected a large sum of money and paid a man who was in Cortez's prison to poison him. And he did. Gregorio Cortez's body is buried somewhere in Matamoros, Brownsville, or Laredo. According to Paredes, the legend became such a symbol of resistance that the singing of the corrido about it was forbidden for a number of years: Its existence and spontaneous spreading throughout the Southwest were considered dangerous.

In the outstanding 1983 television film by Robert M. Young, starring Edward James Olmos, Gregorio Cortez is a bandido who doesn't understand the sheriff's English and mistakenly kills him. The death has far-reaching consequences: Cortez runs away, is persecuted by a brigade of angry

Anglos, and ultimately gives up. The following is one of the many variants of the ballad:

En el condado del Carmen	In the county of El Carmen
miren lo que ha sucedido	Look what has happened;
murió el Cherife Mayor,	The Major Sheriff died,
quedando Román herido.	Leaving Román badly wounded.
Otro día por la mañana	The next day, in the morning,
cuando la gente llegó	When people arrived,
unos a los otros dicen:	They said to one another,
—No saben quién lo mató.	"It is known who killed him."
Se anduvieron informando.	They went around asking questions,
Como tres horas después,	About three hours afterward;
supieron que el malhechor	They found that the wrongdoer
era Gregorio Cortez	Has been Gregorio Cortez.
Ya insortaron a Cortez	Now they have outlawed Cortez,
por toditito el estado	Throughout the whole state;
que vivo o muerto lo aprehendan	Let him be taken, dead or alive;
porque a varios ha matado.	He has killed several men.
Decía Gregorio Cortez	Then said Gregorio Cortez,
con su pistola en la mano:	With his pistol in his hand,
—No siento haberlo matado,	"I don't regret that I killed him;
al que siento es a mi hermano.	I regret my brother's death."
Decía Gregorio Cortez	Then said Gregorio Cortez,
con su alma muy encendida:	And his soul was all aflame,
—No siento haberlo matado,	"I don't regret that I killed him;
la defensa es permitida.	A man must defend himself."
Venían los americanos	The Americans were coming;
que por el viento volaban	They seemed to fly through the air;
porque se iban a ganar	Because they were going to get
tres mil pesos que les daban.	Three thousand dollars they were offered.
Tiró con rumbo a Gonzalez.	He struck out for Gonzalez;
varios cherifes lo vieron,	Several sheriffs saw him;
no lo quisieron seguir	They decided not to follow
porque le tuvieron miedo.	Because they were afraid of him.

Venían los perros jaunes,	The bloodhounds were coming,
venían sobre la huella,	They were coming on the trail,
pero alcanzar a Cortez	But overtaking Cortez
era seguir a una estrella.	Was like following a star.
Decía Gregorio Cortez:	Then said Gregorio Cortez,
—¿Pa'qué se valen de planes?	"What is the use of your scheming?
Si no pueden agarrarme	You cannot catch me,
ni con esos perros jaunes.	Even with those bloodhounds."
Decían los americanos:	Then the Americans said,
—Si lo alcanzamos, ¿qué havemos?	"If we catch up with him, what shall we do?
Si le entramos por derecho	If we fight him man to man,
muy poquitos volveremos.	Very few of us will return."
Se fue de Brownsville al rancho.	From Brownsville he went to the ranch,
Lo alcanzaron a rodear,	They succeeded in surrounding him;
poquitos más de trescientos,	Quite a few more than three hundred.
y allí les brincó el corral.	But there he jumped their corral.
Allá por El Encinal,	Over by El Encinal,
según lo que aquí se dice,	According to what we hear,
se agarraron a balazos	They got into a gunfight,
y les mató otro cherife.	And he killed them another sheriff.
Decía Gregorio Cortez	Then said Gregorio Cortez,
con su pistola en la mano:	With his pistol in his hand,
—No corrían, rinches cobardes	"Don't run, you cowardly rangers,
con un solo mexicano.	From just one Mexican."
Tiró con rumbo a Laredo	He struck out for Laredo
sin ninguna timidez:	Without showing any fear,
—Síganme, rinches cobardes,	"Follow me, cowardly rangers,
yo soy Gregorio Cortez.	I am Gregorio Cortez."
Gregorio le dice a Juan	Gregorio says to Juan,
en el rancho del Ciprés:	At the Cypress Ranch,
—Platícame qué hay de nuevo,	"Tell me the news;
yo soy Gregorio Cortez.	I am Gregorio Cortez."
Gregorio le dice a Juan:	Gregorio says to Juan,
—Muy pronto lo vas a ver,	"You will see it happen soon;

anda y dile a los cherifes	Go call the sheriffs
que me vengan a aprehender.	So they can come and arrest me."
Cuando llegan los cherifes	When the sheriffs arrived,
Gregorio se presentó:	Gregorio gave himself up,
—Por la buena sí me llevan,	"You take me because I'm willing,
porque de otro modo no.	but not any other way."
Ya agarraron a Cortez	Now they have taken Cortez,
ya terminó la cuestión	Now matters are at an end;
la pobre de su familia	His poor family
la lleva en el corazón.	Are suffering in their hearts.
Ya con esta me despido	Now with this I say farewell,
a la sombra de un ciprés,	In the shade of a cypress,
aquí se acaba cantando	This is the end of the singing,
la tragedia de Cortez.	Of the ballad about Cortez.

Time has turned Gregorio Cortez into a myth. He is the ultimate tragic American hero. Intellectuals oscillate between a loyalty to English and a longing for Spanish. Perhaps the life and work of Oscar "Zeta" Acosta, the modern counterpart to the Gregorio Cortez legend whom I mentioned in Chapter 4, more than anyone else exemplifies the reverse linguistic odyssey of the Latino writer. Although Acosta's works are considered underground classics in the ethnic literary tradition, his name is little known among non-Hispanics. A lawyer and activist during the Chicano movement of the 1960s in Los Angeles, his was a relentless hunt for an evanescent personal identity. Acosta spent his short existence trying to make sense of whomever he saw reflected in the mirror, looking for a home, and examining his roots and psychological chemistry. He believed he was a descendant of Aztlán. Acquiring a new persona was a useful device for portraying himself as a Robin Hood— neither Chicano nor Anglo but something else, a hybrid: a misfit, indeed, but one with a dream.

Acosta wrote the account of his existential pilgrimage in his two books, *The Autobiography of a Brown Buffalo* and *The Revolt of the Cockroach People*, both masterly narratives in the tradition of Ken Kesey's *One Flew over the Cuckoo's Nest*. At once surrealistic and belligerent, they describe his spiritual reality beyond the mundane. Acosta suffered from a dogmatic Catholic education, and his work expressed his profound hope for an individual redefinition and an ultimate liberation. Originally published by a small press in San Francisco called Straight Arrow (directly linked to *Rolling Stone* magazine), *The Autobiography of a Brown Buffalo* describes his adventures after he quit his job at an Oakland legal clinic and became a marijuana-smoking hippie. His innermost need was to understand himself, to sense his roots as legitimate. But after a long, nightmarish ordeal, the struggle leaves him empty-headed. The book ends with his return to El Paso. *The Revolt of the Cockroach People,* the sequel, begins the moment Acosta leaves his birthplace for California. The two volumes are authentic gems. The prose is candid and hypnotizing, and the style unique and typical of the epoch. Acosta keeps going back and forth among certain key issues: his identity, the Chicano struggle for self-determination, sexuality, and his Catholicism. The reader is bombarded with images, yet never feels lost. The investigation into the essence of the Chicano minority couldn't be more humorous and Rabelaisian. In 1974, shortly before he disappeared mysteriously, Acosta claimed his goal was to master the Spanish language and write for a Mexican newspaper. He even thought of writing a full book in Spanish. Consequently, if Gregorio Cortez was lost in translation, Oscar "Zeta" Acosta, in reverse, hoped to find himself in a new linguistic fit; he wanted to translate himself, to reinvent his own image. He wanted to return to the uterus.

Loss and return: *El español,* rather than fading away, will flourish in the United States. According to some conservatives, *inglés* is fading away because of the overwhelming number of newcomers who are incapable of learning the language at the speed of previous minorities—even though Latinos and Asians are doing it faster than at any time before. Unity, the English-only advocates argue, has been replaced by chaotic multiplicity: Each minority is now an isolated, autonomous entity, and the entire country has become not a whole, but a sum of belligerent, mutually exclusive parts. Consequently, they say, the United States is slowly dismembering, returning to the Tower of Babel. Multiculturalists, on the other hand, argue that our racial reality today is unlike that of any period in the past, that Eurocentrism will be replaced by a truly global culture, and that bilingualism should be welcomed insofar as it helps the assimilation process.

The argument put forth by the guardians of English follows five easily understood points: (1) English has been the United States' strongest common bond, the "social glue" that holds the nation together; (2) linguistic diversity inevitably leads to political disunity; (3) state-sponsored bilingual services remove incentives to learning English and keep immigrants out of the mainstream; (4) the hegemony of English in the United States is threatened by swelling populations of minority-language speakers; and (5) ethnic conflict will endure unless strong measures are taken to reinforce unilingualism. But in today's fragmented world, it is hard not to be an advocate of multilingualism: Rather than banning or stigmatizing the languages of immigrants and native Americans, we should treat them as resources that could benefit the country both culturally and economically. The most intelligent solution is to favor bilingual education programs that develop children's ability to speak their mother tongues, rather than discard them through a single-minded emphasis on English, as the supporters of the English-Only movement intend to do. If adopted as the sole official language of the United States, English must be used in governmental papers and offices, which means it will jeopardize a wide range of rights and services available to non-English speakers. Furthermore, it is certain to spread fear among newcomers. In fact, one may argue that the English-Only movement is a blunt attack against free speech and a showcase of the country's xenophobia. "Oh, say, can you see, by the dawn's early light, What so proudly we hailed at the twilight's last gleaming. . . ." The folklorist John O. West tells a joke about a bilingual parrot for sale in a pet store. A gringa walked in and asked:

"How much is the parrot?"

"Wow, ma'am," uttered the owner. "This is a very expensive parrot, because he speaks both Spanish and English."

"Oh really? Can you get him to speak in both languages?"

"You sure can. Look, it's quite simple: If you pull the left leg, he speaks English." And he pulled the parrot's leg. "Good morning!" said the bird.

"And if you pull the right leg like this, he speaks Spanish." And the parrot said: "¡Buenas días!"

At which point the gringa asked: "What happens if you pull both of his legs, will he speak Tex-Mex?"

"No," answered the parrot. "I'd fall on my ass, you stupid gringa."

6

◆ ◆ ◆

Toward a Self-definition

Latinos as *incivilizados* and cannibals! Hispanics as chimpanzees!

Is there such thing as a Latino identity? Where to find it? On the street? In mass media images? In art and letters? What do others make of us? What's our self-definition? Herbert A. Giles, in 1926, translated a Chinese tale by and about the Taoist philosopher Chuangtzu, who lived circa 369–286 B.C. One night Chuangtzu dreamed he was a butterfly; when he woke up, he did not know if he was Chuangtzu who had dreamed he was a butterfly or a butterfly now dreaming that it was Chuangtzu. Similarly, as double-faceted creations, Latinos get lost somewhere in the entanglement between reality and the dream. Anarchic, irresponsible, lazy, untrustworthy, treacherous—these stereotypes reach way back to Columbus's diaries, in which Indians are described as naive, peaceful idolaters, ignorant of the paths to Christian salvation. Edmundo O'Gorman suggests that the distortion may go even further back, since America, the continent, was surely "invented" by the European imagination decades before the *Niña*, *Pinta*, and *Santa María* finally sailed to the Bahamas. At any rate, distorted views portraying New World indigenous people as uncivilized, as chimpanzees, quickly spread throughout the Old Continent, and by the time Shakespeare's last play, *The Tempest*, premiered in London in 1611, as England embarked on expanding its terrain toward Ireland and as settlers like Sir Walter Raleigh, Sir Humphrey Gilbert, and Lord De la Warr began the colonization of North America, these views had become intrinsic to common sense. In *The Tempest*, with its underscored imperialist message that has been analyzed by historians and critics (including Stephen

Greenblatt, Roberto Fernández Retamar, Aimé Césaire, George Lamming, and Ronald Takaki), Prospero is exiled with his daughter on an island in Bermuda (*Bermoothes*). The island is inhabited by Caliban—an anagram for cannibal—a savage creature who has learned to speak thanks to Prospero: "You taught me language, and my profit on't / Is, I know how to curse. The red plague rid you / For learning me your language!" Caliban's counterpart is Ariel: The first represents instinct, disorder, aggression, bestiality and the second, hope, a dreamlike existence. The fact that Shakespeare sets the whole adventure across the Atlantic helps one to understand how Great Britain and Europe as a whole saw itself reflected in the mirage of the New World. To redeem himself, Prospero will marry his daughter Miranda to the king's son. He sees Caliban as a sexual threat to her. "I have used thee (filth as you art) with humane care," he tells Caliban, "and lodged thee in mine own cell till thou didst seek to violate the honor of my child." Prospero is the voice of wisdom and the intellect who perceives his relationship with Caliban as that of master and servant: One controls, educates, enlightens, mandates; the other is controlled and educated and becomes a servant of the master. Indians in *The Tempest* are not always bestial, though. Gonzalo, for example, says: "I saw such islanders . . . who, though they are of monstrous shape, yet, note, their manners are more gentle, kind, than of our human generation you shall find many—nay, almost any." Just like Amleth, a Viking prince, became Hamlet, Caliban, in Shakespeare's hands, is derived from Caribbean. *Carib,* as Francis Jennings once showed, a name of an Indian tribe, soon came to be understood as a savage in America, a New World populated by semihuman idolaters.

Distortion, (re) invention: Although Montaigne tried to dispel the twisting of meaning ("there is nothing foreign in these nations . . . what happens is that everyone calls what is foreign to his own nation *barbarian*"), in *Caliban: Suite de La Tempête,* Ernest Renan's 1878 drama, the offensive portrait continues, as it does in an infinite number of European cultural artifacts. The Hispanic geography is a larger-than-life map that is constantly being redrawn by foreigners, a region where fantasy and reality collide. This chapter centers on the clashing ways in which Hispanics, and Latinos as well, perceive and are perceived. It is easy to find a beginning: Latin America can be seen as a design, an invention of conquistadors, explorers, scientists, chroniclers, geographers, archaeologists, naturalists, missionaries, merchants, corsairs, soldiers, journalists, novelists, poets, scholars, artists, adventurers, and travel writers, women and men alike, from Columbus and Fray Ramón Pané,

Alonso de Ojeda, Gonzalo Fernández de Oviedo, Diego de Landa, Hernán Cortés, Bernal Díaz del Castillo, Fray Toribio de Benavente, Fray Bernardino de Sahagún, Pedro Ciesa de León, Gaspar de Carvajal, Sir Walter Raleigh, José Gumilla, Sir Francis Drake, John Hawkins, Antonio Pigaffeta, Alvar Núñez Cabeza de Vaca, W. H. Hudson (author of the now-forgotten *The Purple Land*), Herman Melville, Helen Hunt Jackson (whose naturalistic novel *Ramona*, set in California, describes the fading Spanish order and displays an annoyingly wooden Hispanic cast of characters, even while the author, much like Harriet Beecher Stowe and, later, Gertrude Atherton, was a passionate defender of the rights of American Indians), Flora Tristán, H. M. Tomlinson, John Reed, Michael Gold, Paul Morand, Blair Niles, Rudyard Kipling, D. H. Lawrence, Stefan Zweig, Aldous Huxley, John Kenneth Turner, John Steinbeck, Harriet Doerr, the Beat Generation, Ambrose Bierce, Waldo Frank, Katherine Anne Porter (whose *Flowering Judas* abounds with peasants and talented Russian filmmakers in an Aztec landscape), Ernest Hemingway, Graham Greene, V. S. Naipaul, James Michener, Peter Matthiessen, Salman Rushdie, Bruce Chatwin, and Paul Theroux. The list is endless and excludes anthropologists, creative researchers equipped with tape recorders, ready to seize the Hispanic psyche, wander through its labyrinths, making its penurious mysteries palatable. Take Oscar Lewis's *The Children of Sanchez,* about a lower-middle-class family in Mexico City, an instant best-seller, in which the researcher detailed the incestuous relationship between fathers and daughters; analyzed machismo; and discussed, in condescending ways, the culture of poverty, conceived as a self-inflicting condition. A pastiche of interviews turned into first-person accounts, Lewis's volume is simultaneously fiction and nonfiction, just as *La Vida,* about a Puerto Rican family in New York, penetrates our idiosyncratic paths. Dissecting the Hispanic minutiae, such portraits from strangers, some more than others, are often patronizing, a view from victimizers, and thus hurt. Foreign views *cum* character. Love, gastronomy, sex, work, thoughts—everything is included, and the creatures portrayed, *los hispanos,* look bizarre, awesome, fanciful, humorous, barbaric. Our customs are enchanting because they are different, are scientific items. Victor Hernández Cruz wrote:

> You can't leave your house
> these days without finding
> Something new
> I found Oscar Lewis'
> Tape recorder

Behind a pizza shop in the Bronx
And they wouldn't give me
Ten dollars for it
At the pawnshop

What happens when Caliban comes home with the researcher? In Columbus's second voyage, the Genoese mariner brought back to Spain caged
Indians (James Fenimore Cooper used them in his 1840 "dime" novel *Mercedes of Castile: or, The Voyage to Cathay**), a present that frightened many
Iberians. Imagine Martians brought back to Earth by astronauts: How would
one approach them? As Fray Toribio de Benavente, aka Motolinía, chronicled,
a debate erupted in Europe. Were they human? How could one distinguish
them from monkeys? Heated arguments ran back and forth until somebody
proved that Aztec, Maya, and other native Americans, unlike chimpanzees,
could cry. Tears, clear saline liquid in lachrymal glands, were a sign of humanity. Since then, Eurocentrism has continued to turn Hispanics into carriers of
an unfair amount of distortion.

We Hispanics and Latinos also have carried on a solid, ongoing search for
an authentic collective identity, an attempt, less known around the globe
than the multifarious views of colonizers, to decipher Caliban's secrets. Our
self-definitions are everywhere: Luis Buñuel's *Los Olvidados*; Francisco José
Goya y Lucientes's *The Dressed Maja* and *Las Meninas*; Juan Domingo Perón's
descamisados; Brazilian *quilombos*; Cantinflas's verbosity; the macho click of
actors Jorge Negrete and Pedro Infante; María Félix's "celestial" beauty in
films by Emilio "El Indio" Fernández; Mozart's *Don Giovanni*; the Jesuits'
monopoly on education in the Spanish colonies, which resulted in the so-
called Squillance riots of 1766; Jorge Luis Borges's amazing aleph; outstanding soccer players; Fernando Botero's and Abel Quezada's cartoons and
obese creatures; television personalities Raúl Velazco, Paul Rodriguez, and
Johnny Canales; and corny ballad-singer Julio Iglesias. Since independence,
we have been busy figuring out our metabolism. Our task is to understand
what Ortega y Gasset referred to as *yo y mi circunstancia*: a tête-à-tête with the
ghosts of history, a rendezvous with -ises and -isms—Marxism, psychoanalysis, deconstructionism. To be acquainted with these cornerstones of the
Hispanic intelligentsia south of the Rio Grande, to be enlightened by them,

*See my book *Imagining Columbus: The Literary Voyage*, 67–71

must be an assignment of every Latino, no matter what his or her individual background.

The year 1900: Any study of the Hispanic psyche ought to start (and perhaps end) with the groundbreaking volume *Ariel,* a compass, a book-long letter, what Richard Rodríguez called "an argument," addressed to Latin America's youths. José Enrique Rodó, its author, a late-nineteenth-century Uruguayan critic, took issue with Shakespeare's *The Tempest,* forcefully arguing that Ariel, a dreamer, an idealist, symbolizes Hispanics, while Caliban, a materialist interested in profits and success, personifies the United States. Angered by the Spanish-American War, Rodó in his message encouraged young people in Buenos Aires, Montevideo, Mexico City, and other major capitals to defy the tempting U.S. model of behavior: to be authentic, original, un(North)American. *Ariel,* together with José Martí's anti-imperialist rhetoric, opened up the road taken by the Hispanic intelligentsia in portraying the Anglo-Saxon civilization, and the U.S. government, in particular, as the devil incarnate: Any disaster, any tragedy, whether natural or human, is caused by our merciless imperialist neighbor. (I once read a statement by Ernesto Cardenal, a Nicaraguan poet and a Sandinista minister of the interior, accusing the U.S. government of masterminding a violent hurricane that swept Central America.)

Rodó wasn't the first to embark on such an ambitious study of the Hispanic psyche. First Fray Bartolomé de Las Casas, who transcribed Columbus's diaries and composed a friendly history of the holocaust of natives in the Americas, was responsible for the so-called black legend, accusing Spanish conquistadors of abuse, rape, and torture. Then came Alonso de Ercilla y Zúñiga; Garcilaso de la Vega, aka El Inca; Juan del Valle Caviedes; Sor Juana Inés de La Cruz; Alfonso Carrió de la Vandera; José Joaquín Fernández de Lizardi; Andrés Bello; José María Heredia; Juan Montalvo; Ricardo Palma; José Hernández; Eugenio María de Hostos; and Domingo Faustino Sarmiento, among others. The desire to understand the New World is directly linked to the search for a collective identity this side of the Atlantic that finds its difference, its uniqueness when compared to Europe. Consequently, to trace the very first attempts to define what Alfonso Reyes called *la inteligencia americana,* one needs to go back to colonial times, when the first writers faced the challenge of describing what they saw and to report on the conquest and colonization they had witnessed.

At times the Spanish used was inadequate. Immediately authors, some *criollos* and other native Indians, began to use a variety of forms (letters, chronicles, historical accounts, etc.), mixing styles and injecting doses of magic and exotic, framed by a baroque approach, that today are unavoidable in the literature produced south of the Rio Grande. Up until the nineteenth century, a desire to analyze, to decipher the American self, to ponder its qualities and limitations, occupied the intelligentsia from Buenos Aires to Mexico City. And since Latinos are direct successors of those founding explorers, it is impossible to discuss their craft without first tracing their intellectual roots.

The continual investigation of the Hispanic psyche in the Americas reached a high tone between 1825 and 1882, when the southern hemisphere was plagued by what one historian called "the independence fever," an atmosphere of sheer cultural emancipation. Works by Descartes and later on the French encyclopædists Diderot, d'Alembert, Montesquieu, Rosseau, and Voltaire, although illegal for a while, circulated in educated Hispanic circles, inspiring a sense of self-determination and a wish to overcome the heavy influence of the Church over society. Simultaneously, the influence of liberal ideas coming from the 1776 Declaration of Independence in the United States, and the embrace of public figures such as Thomas Jefferson and Benjamin Franklin, promoted an openness and a desire for freedom and autonomy. It was a time of the formation of the national spirit in Latin America, a romantic period which placed an emphasis on originality, heroic individualism, and liberal thought, a time when nature and the primitive and indigenous were glorified.

Domingo Faustino Sarmiento was an engaging educator and intellectual and one of Argentina's early presidents (1868–74). He wrote *Facundo: Civilization and Barbarism: Life in the Argentine Republic in the Days of the Tyrants*, a biography of Juan Facundo Quiroga, a zealous and ruthless advocate of federalism who participated in civil strifes and was assassinated in 1835. Sarmiento fervently wanted his native country to repress gaucho and other aboriginal manifestations, to renounce Argentina's bucolic past, and to follow Europe and the United States on the road to modernity. His Facundo Quiroga was a symbol of darkness, a mixture of cruelty and passion, a vivid incarnation of the forces threatening Argentina's stability. An admirer of Benjamin Franklin's *Autobiography* and a devoted reader of James Fenimore Cooper, Sarmiento billed his book, published in 1845, as a semifictional novel, part geosociological description, part ideological essay, and part imaginative invention: a mirror of the country's innermost struggles. Deeply concerned by Argentina's ambiguous commitment to a cosmopolitan, technological future, Sarmiento wrote in favor of unity, viewing Buenos Aires as a central civilizing force and attacking federalism as a supporter of fragmentation and chaos.

Over the decades, *Facundo: Civilization and Barbarism* became a founding text in Latin American culture. Its opening contains an examination of the Pampas, the region where Quiroga spent his adolescence, but since Sarmiento was never in the area, he based his knowledge on accounts by English tourists, proving, once again, the impact of foreigners' views on our intellectual habitat. Studying his protagonist's heroism and criticizing the dictator Juan Manuel de Rosas, who instituted a regime of terror, Sarmiento's book, incredibly influential, is a voyage to our collective heart, and has been celebrated by Ezequiel Martínez Estrada, Enrique Anderson Imbert, and Ernesto Sábato, among many others.

Along the same stylistic lines is Euclides da Cunha's *Os Sertões,* published in Brazil in 1902 and known in English as *Rebellion in the Backlands.* A correspondent for *O Estado de São Paulo,* the author was assigned around 1897 to cover a peasant revolt in the northeast hinterland, led by a mystic, Antônio Conselheiro, who opposed the recently proclaimed republic. His followers, outlaws and hooligans, practiced free love and settled in small communities in Canudos, refusing to pay taxes or to respect the local authorities. (Mario Vargas Llosa based *The War of the End of the World* on the tragic events of Canudos and on da Cunha's account.) Much like Sarmiento's analysis of Argentina, the journalistic narrative of da Cunha is an epic study of the battles between civilization and barbarism, the forces of light and darkness, in Brazil's society at the turn of the century. It offers insights into the nation's psyche and a thorough examination of the collective weltanshauung. Again, the text is a hybrid, part truth and part fable. Indeed, it is a mistake to use da Cunha as a primary historical source. He is unreliable as a chronicler. Yet, his volume serves a fundamental purpose: It is a window into Brazil's attitude toward its multiethnic background, its difficult road to progress, its labyrinthine identity.

José Vasconcelos's *La raza cósmica,* an outspoken philosophical treatise published in 1925, is particularly important because it articulates, in what now seems like Nietzschean terms, a theory about a sort of Hispanic supremacy in the international arena. Vasconcelos speculated about the ethnic mix in Mexico's society, and, although he accepted the superiority of whites but not their arrogance, believed that until Mexicans, and Hispanics at large, accept and feel comfortable with their Iberian past, their road to the future will remain bumpy. Typical of the discourse about miscegenation prevailing in the 1920s and onward, Vasconcelos's treatise stated that the only alternative for the Indian population was their adaptation to "Latin civilization." The writer saw himself as a Creole Ulysses, a Mexican version of the ancient Greek mythical hero. He championed democracy while promoting the idea of the aristocracy as the main source of learning. A traditional moralist, as a minister of education he got the federal government to create a national system of primary schools. He idealized Domingo Faustino Sarmiento, himself a promoter of the slow annihilation of gauchos to bring health to Argentine society. What's puzzling is his view that the Mexican people would ultimately triumph by digesting what he considered "the classics" (Dante, Homer, Cervantes, Tolstoy, Romain Rolland, and Benito Pérez Galdós), never questioning how the thoughts of these men would fit the intellectual needs of Hispanic campesinos. The cosmic race, he thought, could become a world power if properly guided.

Other insiders' views of Latin America include José Carlos Mariátegui's *Seven Interpretative Essays on Peruvian Reality,* which served as an inspiration for Abimael Guzmán's Shining Path movement, and attempted to explain in Marxist terms, in 1928, why the native Indians were an eternal reminder of the country's non-European metabolism. Other Peruvians, such as Manuel González Prada, Luis Alberto Sánchez, and Sebastián Salazar Bondy, have devoted their attention to examining their collective identity. Pedro Henríquez Ureña's *Essays in Search of Our Expression,* perhaps the most outstanding nonfiction book by anyone from the Dominican Republic (he delivered the Charles Eliot Norton Lectures at Harvard in 1940–41), is among the most fascinating in its claim, repeated incessantly since then, that Hispanic culture at its core is derivative and unoriginal. The fact that Spanish is our communicating vehicle, Ureña claims, already points to the sense of replication that prevails. As an ethnic hybrid, part African, part Catholic, part Jewish, part Arabic, and part native (Aztec, Quechua, Zapotec, Maya, Inca, and the like), ours is the language of the colonizers, not of the colonized. As Juan Marinello put it, we become real through an idiom that is ours by virtue of its foreignness. Our art will oscillate *ad infinitum* between belonging to this and the other side of the Atlantic. A hyphenated self, neither here nor there.

In Cuba, Fernando Ortíz, known as the island's third discoverer—after Columbus and Alexander von Humboldt—devoted his oeuvre to analyzing the Cuban soul: *la cubanidad.* Ortíz's *Cuban Counterpoint: Tobacco and Sugar,* translated into English by Harriet de Onís in 1947, is a study of Cuban Creole culture (*el criollismo*) by means of analyzing the actual and symbolic value of the island's two main products: tobacco and sugar. In the introduction, Ortíz begins by comparing them. Read the following quote from his 1923 volume *Un catauro de cubanismos*:

> *Guayabo*—The tree that produces the *guayaba*, according to the Dictionary of the Academy. Why does it add: "In French: *goyavier*"? Does it mean to suggest that it is a gallicism? Really? Well, does the Dictionary by any chance provide the French translation of every word? No? Then out with the *goyavier!* The etymology, if that is what it is being proposed, is not worth a *guayaba* [*no vale una guayaba*], as we say. Let's call, instead, some of the twenty-two acceptions and derivatives of *guayaba*, cited by Suárez, that, like *guayabal, guayabera, guayabito,* would look better in the Castilian dictionary than that inexplicable Frenchified etymology. This *guayaba* is just too hard to swallow! [*¡Que no nos venga la academia con guayabas!*], and let us thus note, in passing, another Cubanism.

Ortíz openly accused the official language academy in Spain of kidnapping Cuba's soil. To name is to possess. No quote, I believe, can better describe the desire to find things authentic in the region. If the *guayabo* isn't Caribbean, what is? Why then use a French term to describe it? Cuban speculative essays have also been written by Alejo Carpentier, Guillermo Cabrera Infante, and José Lezama Lima.

Mexico stands as an infinite well of similar interpretative essays, most of which were written in the twentieth century as a result of the impact of Freud's psychoanalysis, together with the theories of Carl G. Jung and Alfred Adler on the collective unconscious. To list them, I would need to start with Julio Guerrero's studies on crime and Ezequiel A. Chávez's groundbreaking discussion of the Mexican sensibility and character, both published in 1901, as well as José Vasconcelos's idea of the mestizo as *la raza cósmica*. But the most outstanding examinations are Samuel Ramos's *Profile of Man and Culture in Mexico* and Octavio Paz's perceptive and discerning *The Labyrinth of Solitude*. By dissecting social types like a Cantinflas-type hoodlum known as *el pelado* and the bourgeoisie, Ramos suggests that by imitating Europe, Mexico suffers from a strong inferiority complex and that the Creole national culture is a mask, a facade hiding the true Mexican self. A larger-than-life intellectual given to temper tantrums,* in his volume, Paz uses, and abuses,

---

*I discuss his contribution in "Of Arms and the Essayist," *Transition* 60:102–17.

the image of the mask. His influential volume, published in serial form in *Cuadernos Americanos* and subsequently collected in book form, was written, in part, at the end of the 1940s in Los Angeles; in it Paz discusses religion, death, and the traumas of history in Mexico and, by extension, in the vast Hispanic world.

Other insightful contributions to the never-ending search for a Hispanic identity include essays by Carlos Monsiváis, Gabriel Zaid, and Roberto Fernández Retamar, whose "Caliban: Notes Toward a Discussion of Culture in Our America" is a Marxist response to Rodó. When it comes to Latinos, the soul-searching process, until recently attached to each different subgroup, ought to be divided into two major stages: before and after the Chicano movement and its aftershocks. Compared to the south-of-the-border tradition of self-defining studies, our production—given the heterogeneity of Hispanics in the United States, the linguistic dilemma, and the slow process of empowerment—has been smaller, scattered, and less consistent. Only occasionally has an essay penetrated the heart of the matter, and when it does, it seldom addresses issues shared by Cubans, Puerto Ricans, Chicanos, and others. Until recently, each collectivity produced a fragile, exclusive, self-contained body of psychological and anthropological essays. Thus, the emergence of a coherent identity is still in the making. Still, a few instances are worth noting. I am thinking, for instance, of Juan Gómez-Quiñones's important though poorly written text, "On Culture," in which, using obtuse academic jargon and offering statements that, when isolated, sound pompous and ridiculous, he examines the character of Chicano life from a theoretical perspective and argues that resistance is, no doubt, a minority trademark. Among his main arguments is that the Mexican culture in the United States is divided into three sectors or subcultures: (1) those committed to assimilation, for the most part, people who are outside the Chicano cultural context; (2) a transitional group, living in the hyphen; and (3) those referred to as *mexicanos,* closer in spirit to the reality south of the border than to Anglo life. "Academic writers," Gómez-Quiñones suggested, "have not contributed much to clarifying the problem of culture [among Mexican-Americans]. . . ." Their writings often stress assumptions based on the perception of minority culture as static and homogeneous, pointing to its backwardness and championing acculturation to Anglo middle-class values. He stresses resistance as a collective signature and, since ethnic culture in his view is an essential expression of class relations, the belief that Chicano culture can thrive only by rejecting foreign domination and refusing to assimilate. "The legacy of war, as well as other factors, means the Mexicans are viewed and treated as a subject people by Anglo individuals and institutions. Across class lines racism in a particular form, a pervasive rationalized anti-Mexicanism, has been experienced by and directed at Mexican people. Coexistence, the economy and subjugation have caused a continual cultural syncretic process, a culture of adaptation, of survival, of change which welds the people together. Historically, continuous resistance and conflict [are] the result of continuous oppression which can unite." Aside from his other work on history and politics, Gómez-Quiñones's 1977 essay is fundamental to the search for a Hispanic identity across the Rio Grande because it articulates for post–Vietnam War readers a clear ideological attitude: to revolt, to rebel, to secede. It also focused on border culture, Aristeo Brito's fictional town Presidio, as something unique, a hyphenated reality that writers and scholars in the late 1980s became deeply attracted to. A highlight of such interest, actually preceding Gómez-Quiñones by almost two decades, is Américo Paredes's *With His Pistol in His Hand,* a study of Gregorio Cortez discussed in Chapter 5, in which Chicanos are genetically viewed as mestizos, whereas culturally they are perceived as a tentacle of Mexico in the United States.

Other fragmentary studies on Latino culture include Edna Acosta Belen's *The Puerto Rican Woman* and Rodolfo Acuña's *A Mexican-American Chronicle.* Richard Rodríguez's controversial first book, *Hunger of Memory,* detailing his humble beginnings in Sacramento, California, and how he became a graduate student at the University of California at Berkeley, writing a dissertation on John Milton, is a landmark in the Latino search for self-definition. Composed of five autonomous essays, the volume contains an engagingly uniform analysis of the writer's journey from anonymity to celebrity. To paraphrase Virginia Woolf, Rodríguez deserves a room of his own among the Latino intelligentsia. Thinking that Spanish should not be encouraged among Hispanic children in public schools, his reactionary views are at odds with those of the rest. An accomplished stylist with a prose at once mathematically built and deeply felt, he believes that by allowing Spanish-speaking students to use their native tongue, the government will promote a sense of duality, an identity conflict in them. Minority quotas, in his opinion, are unfair and undemocratic simply because, as in the jungle, the most apt should prevail (get a job or a fellowship or be accepted to colleges, for instance). Obviously, this conservative agenda has turned him into an agent provocateur of sorts. Yet, ironically enough, his book has become something of a minor American classic, required reading in universities and high schools.

Hunger of Memory is an engaging analysis of the writer's journey from silence to voice, a transformation as dramatic as Martín Ramírez's, and his successful pilgrimage from a psychiatric hospital to art galleries in New York, Sweden, Denmark, and elsewhere. Before Linda Chavez and other neoconservatives, he attacked liberals for rejoicing in the promotion of blacks and Latinos as victims and for allowing their guilt to shape affirmative-action programs. He argues vehemently, for example, that requiring Spanish instruction in the classroom is dangerous because it creates an abyss—a sense of separateness between the student and mainstream America. The book became a favorite target of attack by student activists and politically correct university professors, who sometimes seemed eager to demonize the writer. But as Rubén Martínez and other critics have perceived, Rodríguez is not any sort of right-winger. Political analysis is neither his interest nor his strength. Rather, he is offended when his writing is used for the partisan endorsement of governmental programs and responds accordingly. And he gets even angrier when his work is exploited for ideological reasons. In interviews and articles, he has described his book as another *Labyrinth of Solitude*. But I find this characterization incomplete. Rodríguez's voice is alienated, anti-Romantic, often profoundly sad. Whereas Paz embarks on an archaeological examination of the Hispanic cultural idiosyncrasy, Rodríguez is strictly personal. He does not offer a historical analysis as much as a meditative and speculative autobiography—a Whitmanesque "song of myself," a celebration of individuality and valor in which, against all stereotypes, a Mexican-American becomes a winner.

In his second collection of essays, *Days of Obligation,* Rodríguez claims that his Mexican father perceived the world to be a sad place, whereas as a child, he saw it as a fiesta. Adulthood, however, taught Rodríguez to reverse his childhood view. He grew up to see California as a culture of comedy and Mexico as the embodiment of tragedy: In California the present lives, while in Mexico history continues to count. The recurring themes—AIDS, barbarism versus civilization among Hispanics, and religion—although developed independently, ought to be seen as the vertebral column through which we Latinos are struggling to understand ourselves. "Late Victorians," the third essay, examines Rodríguez's circumspect homosexuality. "The Latin American Novel," although its title is misleading, is a study of the impact and value of both Catholicism and Protestantism south of the Rio Grande and among the Chicano population in California. Rodríguez talked to a number of Anglos and South Americans who considered Jesus Christ the embodiment of the centuries-old suffering collectively endured since the arrival of the conquistadors. Yet he ponders the impact of Protestant missionaries who have succeeded in converting poor, Spanish-speaking believers—some 50 million of them, from Mexico to Argentina—seeing in it a sign of Catholicism's lack of adaptive strategies and fragile standing in modern times. As a believer who regularly attends Sunday Mass, his analysis offers powerful insights into traditional Catholic symbols. "Catholicism," according to Rodríguez, "may be administered by embarrassed, celibate men, but the institution of Catholicism is voluptuous, feminine, sure. The church is our mother; the church is our bride." He thanks the church for the schooling he received— his views of life, death, sex, and happiness—and yet, throughout the years not only has he lost the strength of his faith, but he foresees an immediate crisis for the church. "Should a Mass in San Francisco be performed in Spanish?" he wonders. English, after all, is this nation's "unofficial" official language. Will multilingualism eventually divide the church?

Just as Gómez-Quiñones stimulated many Chicano historians and scholars to enter the field, Rodríguez, an extraordinary writer, a man of polarities, a chameleon, a Dr. Jekyll and Mr. Hyde of sorts, who considers himself first a gringo and then a Mexican, is a leading literary voice, accessible to a wide readership, on the road to Latino self-consciousness. His craftsmanship as an essayist, the artful playing of ideas and incidents, although in the spirit of Montaigne and John Stuart Mill, fits well the American tradition of transcendentalists like Thoreau and Emerson and twentieth-century masters like Mary McCarthy. His contribution is akin to that of James Baldwin, perhaps because the two have so much in common: their homosexuality, their deeply felt voyage from the periphery of culture to center stage, and their strong religiosity and sense of sacredness. Without sentimentality or fear, Rodríguez, an outstanding actor, plays the part with great subtlety and intelligence: He is the embodiment of that complex fate shared by those born twice American: hybrids always living in the hyphen, with one leg here and the other across the Rio Grande.

Autobiography is a favorite genre of immigrants, and Latinos are certainly not an exception. Before Rodríguez, a different sort of autobiography, exemplified by Piri Thomas's *Down These Mean Streets,* also attempted to unravel the mysteries of the Hispanic psyche. Born John Peter Thomas in New York City in 1928, the Puerto Rican author grew up in a poor family in El Barrio during the Great Depression. After the U.S. involvement in World War II, his father, employed in an airplane factory, invested in a little house in Babylon,

Long Island, to provide "opportunities, trees, grass and nice schools" for his children. Thomas's memoir deals with the family's early life and his experience in alien turf in a middle-class suburb, where he was shaken by racism and eventually was estranged from his father and siblings. Thomas then moved to Spanish Harlem, met a girl named Trina, pushed dope for a living, and wondered about his identity: Was he Puerto Rican even if he didn't speak Spanish? Should he consider himself part of the black community because of his skin color? He traveled to the Deep South, where he experienced segregation, and then to the West Indies, South America, and Europe. He returned to New York hating everything white, became a criminal and a drug addict, and was imprisoned. In prison, he became a Black Muslim, found self-respect, and began writing his autobiography. He was introduced to Angus Cameron, an editor at Alfred A. Knopf, and after receiving a grant, finished his memoir. The publication of *Down These Mean Streets* was followed by other books of prose and poetry, as well as a life as a speaker and activist helping young people. Thomas's own redemption led him to help others.

Similarly, Luis J. Rodríguez's *Always Running: La Vida Loca* is an autobiographical account of gang life in Los Angeles and the struggle to overcome a difficult existential journey in the slums. At age twelve, the author was already a veteran gang member surrounded by shootings, arrests, killings, and the slow death of family and friends. He managed to find light, became an award-winning poet in Chicago, and believed he had left urban violence behind when he realized that his young son had become a member of a gang. Recalling James Joyce's *Ulysses*, the volume is structured around the search the father undertakes to find and rescue his son.

Scholar Ernesto Galarza's insightful *Barrio Boy*, written from a sociologist's perspective, is also about Americanization. Little Ernie, the protagonist, journeys from a Mexican mountain village, Jalcocotán, to a barrio in Sacramento, undergoing swift changes in character and beliefs. Nevertheless, Richard Rodríguez is the one who set the tone for what can be described as affirmative-action memoirs. After his, other so-called affirmative-action volumes appeared, including Ruben Navarrette, Jr.'s, *A Darker Shade of Crimson: Odyssey of a Harvard Chicano,* about deception among Latinos in privileged colleges, a topic I will discuss in Chapter 7, and *When I Was Puerto Rican,* by Esmeralda Santiago, a success story structured as an individual victory over social determinism. Santiago, a jíbara born in a zinc shack in rural Puerto Rico and the oldest of eleven children of a welfare mother who moved the family to Brooklyn, went on to graduate from Harvard and Sarah Lawrence and today owns a film production company in Boston.

Also important is anthropology by Latinos, our response to Oscar Lewis. Among the most disturbing examples, often perpetuating obnoxious stereotypes, is the oeuvre of Carlos Castaneda, highly popular in the 1960s among hippies. It continued to fascinate throughout the 1970s, until, because of the cultural climate of the times, his later titles were ignored. Castaneda, whose citizenship at one point was rumored to be Chilean, Peruvian, or American of Mexican descent, started with the *Teachings of Don Juan,* a book that resulted from field research for a master's thesis. The author turned scientific objectivity upside down by getting involved with his subject: Don Juan, a Oaxaca native and a shaman who introduced Castaneda to what the writer called "an alternative reality." It was followed by *Journey to Ixtlán* and *Tales of Power*—the result, a Yoknapatawpha-like map of Oaxaca's aboriginal beliefs.

Octavio Paz wrote an introduction to Castaneda's first title, published in Spanish by Fondo de Cultura Económica, in which he compares Castaneda's work to Claude Lévi-Strauss's *Tristes tropiques,* part anthropological autobiography and part ethnographic testimony. One of the topics of discussion in the book is the use of herbs to create hallucinatory states of consciousness. At the end Paz refers to Don Juan and Don Genaro as a Don Quijote and a Sancho Panza of wandering witchcraft and attempts to establish Castaneda's contribution as a nondogmatic, poetical approach to anthropology. "Bertrand Russell once said that 'the *criminal* class is included in the human class,'" Paz says. "One could say: 'The *anthropologist* class is not included in the *poet* class, with rare cases.' One of those cases is Carlos Castaneda."

The volume's publication coincided with the apex of the hippie generation and the explosion of an anti-establishment movement north of the Rio Grande and in Europe. The book quickly became popular among rebellious students in Paris, California, Mexico, and even Eastern Europe and was used as a pivotal instrument to promote what came to be known as the "counterculture," alternative ways of understanding reality through a rediscovery of ancient pre-Columbian cultures. But as Castaneda's career progressed, he moved further along the lines of anthropological studies and became a peculiar case of best-selling celebrity, a ghost, an enigma: Few have seen his photograph or met him in person. He never goes on tour or gives readings. In the fashion of Thomas Pynchon, his manuscripts are delivered mysteriously to their editors through an agent, and his permanent address and phone number are unknown. His first book was followed by at least seven more. Castaneda's work has become more and more impressionistic and has turned into a caricature of itself. Lewis and Castaneda opened the door to a number of anthropological and history works addressing the ethnic and cultural differences between both sides of the Rio Grande.

Do these works amount to a definition of Latino identity? Who shall articulate, once and for all, an all-encompassing definition of our translating identity? Gloria Anzaldúa describes the reason for our situation: "Because I, a mestiza, continually walk out of one culture and into another, because I am in all cultures at the same time." In the final count, it's no doubt a sign of nearsightedness to mourn the absence of a solid tradition of soul-searching studies by Latinos about our collective psyche in our flamboyant age of technology and communication superhighways. After all, Latinos today know more about what is expected from us because of television. Spanish-language television north of the Rio Grande is indeed a major cultural force. An analysis of its impact and messages is thus needed. Since 1946, when KCOR in San Francisco become the first full-time Spanish-language television station owned and operated by a Chicano, the growth of this medium has been tremendous. With more than 250 hours of programming per week, Latino television reaches 93 percent of all Latino households in the United States, is incredibly popular in the Caribbean and South America, and is watched by curious non-Spanish-speaking viewers. Where do the programs come from? What do they deal with? What kind of material do they transmit? Do they have a political agenda? What do they understand is the Latino identity? Are they in favor of total assimilation? Do they perceive the Latinos of the future as a powerful non-English-speaking community?

Telemundo, with programs produced in this country, south of the Rio Grande, and in Spain, operates, together with CNN and MTV, to offer a schedule targeted to both young and mature audiences. Some thirty years ago, John Blair & Co., its predecessor, owned television stations in Puerto Rico and Florida. Reliance Capital Group, an investment partnership, bought the business, and between 1985 and 1986 acquired stations in Los Angeles and New York. Within a year, Telemundo was born, and although growth continued in other markets, Reliance still controls some 78 percent of the outstanding stock. Although the current management is mostly Cuban, the network focuses on the heterogeneity of Latinos. The collective roots of this ethnic minority, traced to Latin America and the Caribbean, are exploited through folklore and stereotypes. Take the case of the now-canceled *La feria de la alegría,* a spirited game show always full of color, expensive prizes, and simpatico hosts, or *A la cama con Porcel,* a late-night variety show with an obese Argentine star and a set of vulgar female hoofers that make the June Taylor Dancers' costumes look simple. These programs find their success in the idea of life as a masquerade, an ongoing fiesta, a colorful carnival complete with clowns and childish contests, and in macho jokes and sexual innuendo. Hardly alone, the social types parading before the cameras of Telemundo personify the sexual and racial concerns addressed in Chapter 4: polygamous husbands and handsome Latin lovers, hardworking wives with the desire to have fun, and defenseless Latinos abused by Anglos.

The competitor, Univisión, with a round-the-clock schedule transmitted nationwide, is less frivolous, more serious in tone. Its target audience seems to be the Chicano and Central American population in California, Texas, and New Mexico. While Telemundo, in its evening CNN news, has anchors from Chile and Puerto Rico, *Noticiero Univisión* has Mexicans with accents identifiable to viewers in, say, East Los Angeles and Houston. Emilio Azcárraga, for a while the company's sole commanding leader, is a Mexican tycoon and one of the world's richest men, with as great an understanding of telecommunications and its role in the future as Ted Turner. Azcárraga is a major shareholder of Televisa, a media emporium based in Mexico City with markets all over Latin America and Europe. He converted SIN, the first Spanish network in the United States, created in 1961, into a huge international system. Rich with global connections, the company became a subsidiary of Hallmark Cards in the late 1980s. Hallmark paid $286 million to acquire five Spanish-language stations and another $265 million for the rest of Univisión. After that, A. Jerrold Perrenchio—a Hollywood producer who leads a group that owns Venevisión, Venezuela's largest broadcaster, as well as Televisa in Mexico—agreed to buy Univisión for $550 million, which means that Emilio Azcárraga is again its major owner.

The two networks value the low- and middle-income household as their genuine authentic customer. Intellectual matters are frequently set aside, replaced by interviews with Hollywood stars and broadcasts of second-rate movies. Ads are from major corporations like Coca-Cola, medium-size companies like Goya, and small businesses like cosmetic clinics; their quality ranges from sophisticated commercials to slides. The two networks have also silently declared an open war against Anglos. Hispanics are portrayed as naive but brave Robin Hoods and Latino lovers disgraced by the merciless system. Their goal is to create a sense of unity and mutual understanding of the various subgroups within the ethnic minority, to build a force ready to fight back. Some time ago, for instance, Univisión sent a reporter to examine complaints by Hispanics of suspiciously rejected bank loans. The journalist discovered that, indeed, racist quotas and unfair dealings had occurred and, as a result, some Spanish speakers had been denied loans to start small businesses or to buy homes. But instead of explaining how to fight discrimination within the framework of institutionalized banking, the network prepared a piece on *las tandas*, a spontaneous method of banking common in the Mediterranean and Latin America through which people in need can get money by receiving a community loan and then rotating the payments. The program endorsed the extra-banking activities, ignoring their legal implications, and indirectly invited viewers to engage in such practices. Such rebellious, nonconformist messages go even further. Programs on Telemundo and Univisión are often anti-Semitic. In a recent documentary, for example, a Santería *brujo* explained the existence of two types of evil, the benign and the Jewish, without the producer ever offering a contextual comment. Also, during the Crown Heights racial fighting in 1991, the newscasts often portrayed Jews negatively and identified blacks as the only victims. Latino television too often encourages viewers to find scapegoats for their plights.

On the other hand, viewers cannot but admire the high-quality news that they frequently get from *Noticiero Univisión,* no doubt superior to that of English-speaking channels. The focus given to the different Latin American countries, their monetary troubles and political instability, surpasses anything offered by Peter Jennings, Tom Brokaw, or Dan Rather. Correspondents stationed in Lima, Mexico City, Buenos Aires, Bogotá, and other big urban centers follow the daily events and keep Latinos well informed about the homelands they left behind. The sense of unity among us and the war against Anglos reached its highest levels in 1988, when Univisión conducted *Destino '88,* a thorough report of the presidential campaign that was motivated by the desire to understand the true impact of Latino votes at the national level. The programming covered both the Democratic and the Republican conventions and concluded with the election. The political agenda was evident. How powerful are Latinos when acting together, when supporting only one candidate? Reporters forced Michael Dukakis to use his college Spanish to attract sympathizers (he did so quite well) and George Bush to promote his Mexican daughter-in-law as actual proof of his love for this ethnic community. Similar coverage for the 1992 election took place: The views and opinions of Bush, Bill Clinton, and H. Ross Perot were thoroughly discussed. If they were totally united, Univisión and Telemundo claimed, Latinos could decide who the next president of the United States would be.

The mere existence of Telemundo and Univisión is a headache to supporters of the English-Only movement and to critics of bilingual education. As the fastest-growing segment of the television industry in the United States, these networks serve some thirty-five markets, including Los Angeles, New York, San Francisco, Miami, and San Antonio. In 1990, Telemundo alone had revenues of nearly $128 million, higher than ever before. Almost all of the network's programming is conducted not in Spanglish, but in a standardized, proper form of Spanish. Its overwhelming power to reach more than four-fifths of the Latino households is not only creating media superstars— such as the talk show celebrity hosts Paul Rodríguez and Cristina and the Chilean-Jewish host of *Sábado Gigante,* Don Franciso—but is making new generations feel attached to their ancestral tongue. Meanwhile, the Spanish spoken in this nation, in a state of degeneration by its daily contact with the English language, as I claimed in Chapter 5, is spreading in Latin America, thanks to cable transmissions. Although the free-market competition of Univisión and Telemundo has resulted in a dramatic improvement of style and quality, the networks remain unoriginal, their derivative programming often imitating the content and techniques of English-language television. Take, for example, the failure of *En Vivo,* a news show by Univisión with highly professional journalists and interviews with specialists invited to discuss important news of the day, a model so similar to *Nightline* that it was bound to fail. Sources close to the program also blamed the show's demise on the impossibility of getting attractive specialists within reachable distance to analyze the current news. Be that as it may, the program's main problem, and that of Spanish-language television in general, is its insurmountable lack of originality.

So down with the written word? We are hooked to television and its ever-changing images for an explanation to our mysteries. While Latino culture and identity remain in constant change, to paraphrase Juan Gómez-Quiñoness, a set of fixed motifs, emanating from high-brow art, literature, popular culture, and the mass media, can be distilled. Are we chimpanzees? Will Caliban discern the difference between Chuangtzu and a butterfly? How are we?

7

◆ ◆ ◆

Culture and Democracy

Ethnicity, rather than class, is behind the proliferation of multiple constituencies in United States society today. We are no longer Americans as such but hyphenated identities: Hispanic-Americans, Asian-Americans, African-Americans, and so forth—a divided people. Weren't we always? We live as citizens of the hyphen, a sign of the abyss that separates us. Everybody has a loyalty, everybody has a political agenda. Fortunately, little can be done at this point to retrieve the effect of this multiple fracture. The seeds of chaos are already spread out and a tragic outcome might be waiting in the near future. Although thanks to multiculturalism we are more enlightened today and the American mind has happily opened up at least a bit, we are also profoundly fragmented. I am hyphenated, *ergo sum*. A land of immigrants that began as a microcosm of the world, a sum of Others, where is America heading? Perhaps the only possible way to understand, and even digest, our collective shortcomings is by debunking the absurd idea of the United States as a promised land. "Paradise anew shall flourish, by no second Adam lost. . . . Another Canaan shall excel the old," wrote the trader and journalist Philip Freneau in his 1788 poem "The Pictures of Columbus." He was of course describing the origin of a new biblical nation that, in the hands of the Puritan pilgrims of the *Mayflower*, was hoped to be a clear improvement over Europe in terms of justice and liberty, a territory where barbarism would be replaced by order and democracy. Until a couple of decades ago, Freneau's vision, his messianic view, was accepted unchallenged as the official story. But since the late 1960s, another vision, rebellious in tone, has been put forth by militant historians, artists, and intellectual activists, one that sees America as an invention, the crossroads of hope and violence, democracy and intolerance; America the beautiful and America the ugly. Unlike Mao Zedong's mass campaign in China, which began in 1966, multiculturalism as a humane cultural revolution is a battle that hopes to renew the country's basic institutions and to revitalize the popular trust by means of a peaceful exchange of ideas. But is it possible? The enemy, it seems, is everywhere and nowhere, a ghost of history. We align ourselves under an invisible flag and, one way or another, the battle will inevitably leave a deep scar. Is it possible that in the near future we the people might reject unity and seek diversity, breaking the union into numerous pieces along ethnic borders—the United Others of America? Wasn't this country, shouting the battle-cry of freedom, supposed to be paradise on Earth? Could Whitman have foreseen the future implications of a nation of varied carols?

What is the United States if not a magisterial Dickensian novel, an ambitious narrative with an incredibly varied cast? Cultural climates change and heroes become villains. A land of shifting frontiers: the conquest of the Old West, the war against Mexico before 1848, the idea of Manifest Destiny, the military incursion in World War II, in Vietnam, and Cambodia. America the ugly and the beautiful is inhabited by a divided self. Today the Land of Opportunity runs the risk of becoming the Land of Otherness. Often dreams are deferred. And what happens to a dream deferred? asked Langston Hughes in a poem. Does it dry up like a raisin in the sun? Or does it explode? Otherness is a cancer without redeeming medicine. In his volume *Orientalism*, where anthropology and literary criticism collide, the post-colonial critic Edward W. Said shows that Europe's idea of the Orient has less to do with actual geography than with Chateaubriand, Nerval, Ernest Renan, and Edward William Lane, devoted to shape its mystique, an otherness of insurmountable exotism. Others are bizarre, awesome, fanciful, foolish, humorous, abnormal, unreal. As I have show in the previous chapters, we Latinos often fall into such categories. Since men and women make their own history—what they know is what they have made—the idea of Hispanic culture is man-made, carefully costumed to fit a set of values and habits Western civilization has come to understand as typical to Spain and the Spanish-, Portuguese-, and French-speaking Americas. Myopic, undiscerning, the United States has carefully built a comfortable view of us as second-rate: lazy, disorganized, unintelligent, politically unstable, rebellious, deceiving. Similarly, we approach Anglos as cold, unconcerned, money-driven. W. E. B. Du Bois said, "Between me and the world there is ever an unasked question, unasked by some because of sensitive feelings others through the difficulty in finding the right words—How does it feel to be a problem? Or better, how does it feel to be ignored?" Latinos are and always have been perceived by the gringos, in their obsessively repetitive Eurocentrism, as inferior neighbors, an unwelcome guest, a simpleton, queer and unappealing. Many north of the border still think of Latin America as a composite sum of banana republics with corrupt government officials and an exotic stage of drugs, prostitution, and violent love.

Within the United States the culture war knows no trench. Sometime ago, while walking through downtown New York City, a black teenager approached me. "Hello, Mr. White Man!" he said. "You're the Devil, you know." Trying to remain calm, I decided the best thing to do was to continue walking. Although my aggressor kept shouting at me, the incident didn't turn violent. It was, nonetheless, deeply troubling to me. What incited this young man to verbally attack me, obviously, had more to do with the country's past, with slavery, racism, intolerance, and oppression, than with our mutual present. After all, it was the first time we accidentally saw each other. (But perhaps he would disagree: The present, he would claim, his and mine, is as oppressive as anything in the past.) In any case, we alone in the darkness of the night had automatically become enemies: My whiteness was his problem; his explosive attitude was mine. In a matter of seconds we saw hatred in each other's face. Hatred, maliciousness, and hostility. I was his Other and he was mine—and to be the Other, everybody knows, is to offend, to transgress. "Hello, Mr. White Man!" To hell with *e pluribus unum,* I thought afterward. Latino, Jewish, who cares: I was simply the Other. Curiously, together my aggressor and I, a black and a Latino, represent a threat for mainstream America.

Caliban's Utopia: the United States. How then to understand the hyphen, the encounter between Anglos and Hispanics north of the Rio Grande, the mix between George Washington and Simón Bolívar? To what extent is the battle between two conflicting worldviews inside the Latino heart, one obsessed with immedi. e satisfaction and success, the other traumatized by a painful, unresolved pas, evident in our art and letters? Should the opposition to the English-Only movement, Chicano activism, the politics of Cuban exiles, and the Nuyorican existential dilemma be approached as manifestations of a collective, more or less homogeneous psyche? As I hope is clear at this point, Hispanics, after almost a century and a half, with an abundance of history, are still traveling from marginality to acceptance in the United States, from opposition to the mainstream culture to a place on the center stage. A new consciousness is emerging, a new Latino. Alain Locke, one of the founders and supporters of the Harlem Renaissance, published in 1925 an anthology of current work, *The New Negro: An Interpretation*. Alongside texts by the most outstanding members of the group, from Arthur Alfonso Schomburg and Langston Hughes to Jean Toomer, Countee Cullen, Richard Wright, and Zora Neale Hurston, among others, the volume contained an introduction by Locke, in which he forcefully outlined the new trends in black writing: the discovery by the educated, urbanized blacks of the beauty, vigor, and honesty of life in this most alienated neighborhood of the Big Apple. Although they stood at some distance from their own people, Locke and his colleagues also felt strongly alienated from mainstream American society: They wanted to speak out, to be heard and read in their own aesthetic terms. Their collective vision, which is as clear today as it was at the time, stood against the understanding of blackness by precursors like Paul Laurence Dunbar and Charles W. Chesnutt, whose work they thought conformed to white standards. A similar phenomenon, beyond city borders, is sweeping Latino culture today. Latino actors and comedians, such as Magda Gomez, Luis Valdez, Andy Garcia, and Rosie Perez, are sought after by Hollywood moguls, and some like Edward James Olmos continue to combine art and activism. Linda Rondstadt, in a search for her Mexican ancestral identity, is recycling ranchero songs and corridos. Tex-Mex banda melodies are extremely popular throughout the Southwest, and Spanish-language *telenovelas*, filmed in Miami, are watched around the globe. Such trends (the trend in literature is the best example) are forcing the old-fashioned concerns and obsessions of the founding fathers—José Antonio Villarreal, José Yglesias, and the like—to give place to values and voices that are more appropriate for the times. The transformation of culture in the United States today, no question about it, is accomplished not through guerrilla warfare, but from within the marketplace. *Abajo la revolución! Viva lo comercial!*

In 1993, together with Harold Augenbraum, director of the Mercantile Library of New York, I edited an anthology, *Growing Up Latino: Memoirs and Stories,* whose goal was to achieve what Locke had done almost seventy years ago. The anthology offers a selection of the best fiction by Cubans, Dominicans, Puerto Ricans, Mexicans, and other subgroups and opens with a prologue explaining how the new are attempting to replace the old—another renaissance of ideological and commercial proportions. The book could have been titled *The New Latino: An Interpretation,* except that, unlike Locke's, ours was a display of the whole spectrum, the trendy and the established, a view of dusk and dawn, a testimony of renewal. As is felt on every page through-out the volume, what is at stake in the new Latino consciousness, more than anything else, is democratization, a journey from regions of political upheaval and corruption to a land of civil liberty and respect. "We hold these truths to be self-evident," wrote Thomas Jefferson, "that all men are created equal; that they are endowed by their creator with certain unalienable rights; that among these are life, liberty, and the pursuit of happiness." To return to the question pondered earlier in these pages: Life in the hyphen—what do we, as Latinos, want from the United States, and what do Anglos expect from us? How do we fit in the American Dream? In this chapter I conclude my medi-tation by directly confronting the question of our cultural assimilation.

A comparison with the artistic literary odyssey south of the Rio Grande is appropriate here. While dictatorial governments stumble, refusing to incorpo-rate everyone in their policies, numerous works of remarkable quality have appeared in Latin America since the late eighteenth century, often opposing the regime in vogue, most of them with a single objective in mind: modern-ization, to bring Hispanic society to the banquet table of Western civilization, to introduce people to and to subscribe to the trends and goals of industrial-ization and collective freedom. Similar to the role that letters played in Eastern Europe throughout the Communist period and even earlier, among us Hispanics, literature in its embodiment of a subversive spirit has been synony-mous with rebelliousness: It has denounced, condemned, accused, and even threatened. Fiction versus dogma: During colonial times the Catholic church, for instance, thinking it could make people believe in "the unreal," portrayed the novel as "a hazardous object," "an invitation to blasphemy," and thus for-bade its distribution. Thank God and dictatorship, nothing was better than censorship to promote Hispanic literature. Prohibition generated a huge black market. Enlightened readers would import "illegal" books by Rousseau, Diderot, and other French encyclopedists; Samuel Richardson; Henry Fielding; and Lawrence Sterne, which then circulated underground. People would acquire trashy Iberian novels only to enjoy the forbidden fruit and because fic-tion and the imagination, regardless of time and space, are essential compo-nents of human behavior. Without them, without dreams, life equals death. Censorship, omnipresent in Hispanic societies, always backfires. Literature, by pushing to open windows to promote progress and debate, has traditionally been seen as the sister of politics. Thus, a work of fiction is often perceived as an aesthetic artifact of dangerously ideological caliber.

It is not surprising, then, that when the Hispanic American novel finally emerged as an artistic genre during the nineteenth century, the countries in which it first appeared and quickly became popular were Argentina and Mexico, after which a long period of silence followed until other nations awakened to the same literary fever. Independence from the Old World was a hot issue, and literature served to promote change. A sign of free-thinking modernization, a struggle against colonial obscurantism, the novel struggled to introduce European ideas and aesthetic trends, from naturalism to regionalism. Nevertheless, the bridge between literature and nationalism depended on particular circumstances. Lizardi, for instance, the first Hispanic novelist, whose book *The Itching Parrot* appeared in 1816 and was partly translated into English more than a century later by Katherine Anne Porter, had little to do with Mexico's nationalist movement (which developed some fifty to sixty years later as a platform for Father Miguel Hidalgo y Costilla's independence movement). Lizardi juxtaposed political, economic, and sociological themes in his narrative, but never cultural ones, simply because he had no quibbles with Mexican culture. The anti-Rosas intelligentsia in the Río de la Plata, on the other hand, especially the group to which Esteban Echeverría, author of *The Slaughterhouse,* belonged, created purely political literature. And in Cuba, culture became the sole engine behind the nation's literature, whose first novels had a strong antislavery worldview. Gertrudis Gómez de Avellaneda's 1841 novel *Sab* describes the nature and customs of her native Cuba while exposing the tragic consequences of slavery. The book appeared ten years before Harriet Beecher Stowe's *Uncle Tom's Cabin* and it certainly wasn't the first of its kind in the Caribbean.

The old, bloody crossroads where literature and politics meet are a thermometer measuring freedom and the intellectual climate in Latin America. Anastasio Somoza tried to erase Ernesto Cardenal's poetry from the face of Nicaragua; during Augusto Pinochet's dictatorship in Chile, the works of Pablo Neruda, Ariel Dorfman, and Isabel Allende were forbidden; books by Oswaldo Soriano, Manuel Puig, Julio Cortázar, and numerous other émigrés were not allowed in Argentina in the so-called dirty war. And when Castro came to power, unlike in the Soviet Union and countries in the Eastern Bloc (with the probable exception of Poland), novels ceased to be produced for a couple of years. Writers were put on a blacklist and were not published. Beginning in 1968, a special army committee that was part of the Comintern was in charge of Cuban culture, and derivative, uninteresting novels, such as *The Last Woman and the Next Combat* by Manuel Cofiño, that imitated the patterns of Soviet "socialist realism" began to be published.

Social realism ought to be opposed to something, and in the case of Cuba it was the "dark, retrograde forces" personified by santeros and other social types taken from the voodoo tradition. To make his characters believable, Cofiño referred to Santería, which was forbidden at that time by Castro's regime, describing Orishas in negative terms. Ironically, such descriptions, not the narrative as a whole, attracted readers. And even while José Antonio Portuoso, an opportunist Marxist critic, claimed in his prologue to Cofiño's novel that the book was "the first, truly revolutionary novel" to be written under communism, people actually paid little attention to the hero, a protagonist who ends up sacrificing his life for the good of the society. The Cuban government was eventually forced to change its policy, creating the Ministry of Culture at the end of 1975, and under the leadership of Armando Hart, a member of the old guard, married to Haidée Santa María, a policy of limited openness was set.

We nurture a long-standing habit of perceiving the writer as a spokesperson for the masses, a symbol of freedom of speech. The closing down of dailies like Jacobo Timmerman's *La Opinión* in Buenos Aires, the attacks against *La Prensa* and the assassination of Pedro Joaquín Chamorro in Nicaragua, and the incarceration and death of many others, are attempts to suppress openness and independence, and yet, such adulation of writers has both an attractive and a noxious side. Simply by virtue of their vociferousness, we naively glorify those who speak out. We view poets and novelists as alternative politicians, as if their fantasy was far more appealing than the repetitious reality with which we cope. Antimodels are always at hand: Neruda's Stalinist inclinations, Leopoldo Lugones's fascism, Jorge Luis Borges's rightwing opinions in spite of his friction with Juan Domingo Perón, and Gabriel García Márquez's long friendship with the tyrant Castro. In the end, Carlos Fuentes, a sympathizer of the oppressed, and Julio Cortázar, seen by many of his followers as as exemplary for his commitment to the Cuban and Sandinista revolutions, represent only themselves; they are simply disoriented intellectuals whose politics are useful only for understanding their own dilemmas.

The Heberto Padilla affair—which reached its height in 1971 and was described by the victim in his autobiography *Self-Portrait of the Other* and also by scores of scholars, novelists, and participants in the events—ought to be viewed as a catalyst, the birth of a different attitude toward intellectuals in Latin America. Hypocrisy, nationalism, treason, and the role of art and literature were at issue. A favorite idol of writers of the so-called Third World, Fidel Castro, helped by apparatchiks, forced a celebrated dissident poet and former diplomat, after sessions of intimidation, to confess publicly to crimes he never committed. An international uproar followed. Scores of writers and editors worldwide, from Susan Sontag to *New York Review of Books* editor Robert Silvers, eventually forced Cuba's Communist regime to allow Padilla to go into exile, first at Princeton University and then in Miami. Castro's rapprochement with the Hispanic intelligentsia came to an end. *El Líder* furiously attacked Latin America's narrative writers of the 1960s with his customary rhetoric: "Why should we elevate to the category of problems of this country problems which are not the problems of this country? Why, my dear bourgeois liberal gentlemen? Can you not feel and touch the opinions expressed by millions of students, millions of families, millions of professors and teachers, who know only too well what are their true and fundamental problems?" After the harassment of Padilla and with the end of the Cold War, the equating of writers with intellectual freedom and honesty has to be looked at under a different light. The debt crisis of the 1980s brought changes in the region's cultural climate that are still being played out. Rather than nationalizing huge private properties and corporations, contemporary Latin American leaders, led by the neo-Perónist Carlos Saúl Menem in Argentina and Carlos Salinas de Gortari in Mexico, tried to emulate the U.S. model of a free-market economy. Simultaneously, the Soviet Union and the Eastern European Communist bloc crumbled and Castro's Cuba lost strategic and historical importance. Abimael Guzmán, the leader of Peru's Shining Path, symbolized the extreme course of incorporating the Maoist system to the Inca milieu, to follow a different pattern than that of Fidel in the Caribbean.* And the Zapatista army in Chiapas once again fought to legitimize the rights of the Indian population in the Hispanic world. In sum, the Cold War that brought an end to a form of utopia in Latin America—colored by terrorism and guerrilla groups, and by governments oscillating toward the state-run Soviet idea of internal policy—challenged the intelligentsia to find a new role in the social system.

A lack of openness, debate, and respect for other people's opinions no doubt pervades the Latino psyche. We Latino intellectuals and artists perceive ourselves as repositories of ancient images to be protected against extinction in a milieu that is linguistically and culturally alien to our ancestors. When seen from a distance, as Richard Rodríguez says in *Days of*

---

*I've speculated on this challenge in "Two Peruvians," *Transition* 61:18–39; and "Gabo in Decline," *Transition* 62:58–78.

Obligation, such rivalry offers an insightful view of the way in which we Latinos conceive ourselves in the United States: Latin America is seen as being devoted to eternal truths, to the act of recalling, to continuity through oral tradition; Anglos, on the other hand, are viewed as nurturing an obsession with artificiality and the ephemeral. Thus, one is enchanted with the past and the other is enchanted with the future; one safeguards what is gone, and the other is constantly reinventing itself. Are we fit for democracy? In general, is the Hispanic population in the United States comfortable with freedom? I often hear complaints, on television and in the print media, of Latinos failing to vote in federal, state, and local elections. Adjectives like *uninvolved, antisocial,* and even *apolitical,* are invoked. But can someone who has been raised never to trust abusive politicos suddenly become a champion of democracy? Isn't a new set of values and beliefs needed to reactivate a trust that hardly existed in the place once called home? And what role are Latino intellectuals and artists called on to play vis-à-vis the community? A paradigm of an antihero in Latino literature is the writer Felipe Alfau, a mysterious Spaniard whose creative journey indirectly forces us, like no one else, to confront our democratic, political, and racial fears and beliefs. His fame and current standing as an exemplary Spanish writer in English have no doubt benefited from his more-than-seventy-year life in the United States. And yet, until the end he remained a monarchist and saw racial diversity as the cancer eating up the heart of the American Dream. Like Richard Rodríguez, he is trapped in the contradictions of a system he thoroughly dislikes, from which he has emerged with applause and recognition. He is an anti-Leftist resurrected thanks, in part at least, to a review by Mary McCarthy in *The Nation.* He is also an anti-Semite whose revival has been pushed forward by Jewish criticism.

Born in Barcelona in 1902, Alfau was the child of an itinerant couple with addresses in the Iberian peninsula, the Philippines, New York City, and later Mexico.* His father, Antonio Alfau, a multifaceted journalist from a humble background, a naturalist, a congressman, and criminal lawyer who died when Felipe was seventeen, counted among his ancestors a vice president of the Dominican Republic in 1859, who fought against Haiti, helped in the annexation of Santo Domingo, and later became governor of Seville. Felipe's upbringing would later turn him against Hispanics from humble beginnings.

---

*See the special issue devoted to Alfau, *Review of Contemporary Fiction* 13, no. 1 (Spring 1993): 142–252.

The Alfau family (Catalan and Arabic roots can be found in the name) had strong ties to the military: Antonio's father and a couple of Felipe's brothers were army officers, and one even fought during the Spanish Civil War in Franco's battalions (he was kidnapped and shot by the insurgents in 1936). Eugenia Galván, Felipe's mother, a stereotypical bourgeois woman who spent long hours reading romantic novels and playing the piano, came from a prosperous family with properties in Santo Domingo. Among the couple's six other children are Jesusa, also a writer (she published a novel, *Los débiles,* before she turned twenty), who later married Antonio Solalinde, a famous Wisconsin linguist, and Monserrat, who worked for Mexico's publishing house Editorial Porrúa.

Felipe's father, a passionate traveler, aside from long stays in the Philippines, moved to the Dominican Republic around 1898 and to the United States, where he founded *Novedades,* a Spanish-language weekly for the emerging Latino population, which was at the time composed mainly of Spaniards and well-off South American nationals. He brought the family along. By then Felipe had lived in Cataluña, Madrid, and Guernica, the latter famous for the tragic German bombing that inspired Pablo Picasso to paint a black-and-white fresco about death and the human condition. It was in Guernica that the future writer saw his older sister Pilar, whom he loved, die at age eighteen of a strange illness. The death had a tremendous impact on him. He would return time and again to its tragic images in his memory and would invoke his sister's spirit in his poetry and fiction.

Never a champion of assimilation and democracy, Felipe Alfau ought to be considered the first Latino writer who *consciously* switched to English and did so for commercial and avant-garde artistic reasons. At an early age he decided to write in Shakespeare's tongue because Spanish seemed provincial, bucolic, for his innovative, experimental aspirations. Later, the Spanish Civil War gave a political undertone to his decision: He wanted to run away from ideology.

When talking about his linguistic transformation, the figure of Alberto Gerchunoff, the grandfather of Jewish–Latin American letters, comes to mind.* Before him, one can find sketches, poems, vignettes, and chronicles of immigrant life, written by Jewish refugees in Russian, Polish, Hebrew, Yiddish, and at times in a rudimentary Spanish. But Gerchunoff's beautiful and meticulously measured Castilian prose in *The Jewish Gauchos of the*

*See my introduction to *Tropical Synagogues: Short Stories by Jewish-Latin American Writers* (New York: Holmes & Meier, 1994).

Pampas, translated into English in 1955 by Prudencio de Pereda and influenced by Cervantes, opened up the road to other writers to switch to the national language. In 1891, when the boy was seven, Gerchunoff's father traveled from Russia to the Pampas, and the family followed him. Agriculture and cattle raising were the jobs designated for the former shtetl dwellers, and hard labor was their lot. As expressed in his 1914 autobiography *Entre Ríos, My Country,* published posthumously in 1950, Gerchunoff admired his fellow Argentines' capacity for work. His family first lived in the colony of Moisés Ville, but when his father was brutally killed by a cowboy, they moved to the Rajil colony.

Gerchunoff's translingualism is as admirable as is Alfau's. Language, after all, is the basic vehicle by which any newcomer must begin to adapt to a new country. Most immigrants to Latin America improvised a "survival" Spanish during their first decade, but in Gerchunoff's case, he not only learned to speak perfect Spanish as a child, but by 1910, at age twenty-six, his prose was setting a linguistic and narrative standard. Reading him today, one can discover in his writing stylistic forms that were later developed by his followers, among them Borges. Simultaneously, Gerchunoff's brief biographical sketches of such writers as Sholem Aleichem, Miguel de Unamuno, James Joyce, Max Nordau, and Isaac Loeb Peretz, which appeared in newspapers and magazines, and his deep and careful readings of British writers, such as G. K. Chesterton, H. G. Wells, and Rudyard Kipling, influenced future artistic generations on the Río de la Plata. Even if he did not fully belong to the popular *modernista* movement budding at the turn of the century in Latin America, many welcomed his writings. His political objective was to help Jews become Argentines: to be like everyone else. Following Gerchunoff's death, after some two dozen books and innumerable articles, Borges praised him as "the writer of *le mot juste.*" Such a distinction, one should add, is seldom awarded to an immigrant.

The moment Gerchunoff switched to Spanish, he became a cultural mentor and a compass for later Jewish writers in Argentina. By writing in Cervantes's tongue, he became a part of the chain of Spanish and South American letters; Yiddish, the language of most of the immigrants, was left behind after he began publishing, exchanged for Spanish, a cosmopolitan, secular vehicle. Mendele Mojer Sforim, the grandfather of Yiddish literature, found in Yiddish his vehicle for communicating with his people; for Gerchunoff, it was Spanish. The two were equally celebrated as speakers of the collective soul. A bucolic tone is to be found in the twenty-six stories collected by Gerchunoff in *The Jewish Gauchos,* the book to which he owes his fame, a parade of Spanish-speaking but stereotypical men and women from Eastern Europe adapting to the linguistic and cultural reality of the southern hemisphere. The autonomous narratives that make up every chapter, some better than others, re-create life, tradition, and hard labor in this "new shtetl" across the Atlantic. The focus is on the relationship of Jews and gentiles and the Jewish immigrants' passion both for maintaining their religion and for understanding and assimilating new habits.

Unlike Gerchunoff, Alfau did not set the tone for future generations. After a welcoming critical reception, his oeuvre was lost to oblivion until the late 1980s, when a small publisher in Illinois, Dalkey Archive Press, revived it. Thus, although today he is considered a cornerstone, a conservative, even reactionary founding parent of Latino letters, he was a writer without readers. As was Martín Ramírez, the Chicano schizophrenic painter who was isolated in a psychiatric hospital almost his entire life, Alfau is the epitome of the Latino artist who is surrounded by and relegated to silence.

Alfau's importance lies precisely in his obscurity. His intellectual and existential odyssey were in shadow for many decades. Nobody knew who he was, what the motivations behind his work where, who he had been influenced by. He was unknown and unread—a phantom. And because of this absence he has become a symbol. Now that the cultural climate has changed, to find out more about him and to understand his plight has become a sort of mandate. What were his links to Iberian culture? What role did his family play in his journey through literature? Scattered data is beginning to emerge. Alfau isn't the only Iberian link in the Latino cultural progression. Other Spaniards have written in the United States: George Santayana; Juan Ramón Jiménez; Eduardo Mendoza, and Federico García Lorca, who studied English at Columbia University, where he wrote *The Poet in New York,* a reversal of Whitman's universalism, about the individual immersed in a mass society.

Like Henry Roth's masterpiece *Call It Sleep,* the fate of Alfau's *Locos: A Comedy of Gestures* was remarkably curious. Written in 1928, it was published in 1936 by Farrar & Rinehart. Part of a series, "Discoverers," it was one of those failed editorial projects sold only to subscribers that never reached bookstores and hence had a marginal sale. Almost nobody read it. Alfau ended up being a writer without readers, without followers. In spite of his pessimism and misanthropy, Alfau kept writing for himself and his friends. He finished a second novel, *Chromos: A Parody,* during the 1940s, but again could not find a publisher for it. The novel would remain unpublished for forty years, until 1990, when it was nominated for the National Book Award alongside Elena Castedo's first novel, *Paradise*. Alfau also wrote a collection of badly written poems, *Sentimental Songs/La poesía cursi*, this time in Spanish, which appeared in 1992. Altogether, his poetic voice is very much his own: sarcastic, baroque, and theatrical. The characters and scenes that permeate the volume are easily recognizable: the unmerciful scientist and collector of butterflies (which Alfau called "The Naturalist"), youth as a vanishing state of happiness, a train as a metaphor for the passage of time, the wish of the individual to be integrated into the whole, and death as an irrevocable event. A couple of poems have explosive themes, like the one titled "Afro-Ideal Evocation," a call for blacks to return to Africa. A segment:

Negrito seudo urbano,
fatuo, cursi, aspirante.
Tu mano jamás sale del guante
y el bastón jamás deja tu mano.
Pero no obstante
¿no sientes a ratos
nostalgia? ¿Será que ya no quieres
que te sirvan, sumisas, tus mujeres,
el amor en sus labios como platos?

Olvidas en tu cosmopolitanismo
tus dominios salvajes;
tierras de fetichismo,
misterioso exorcismo,
que hacían pensar al hombre blanco en viajes.
Una catedral verde
donde el explorador entra y su alma pierde
en ritos que consagran la creación del vudú;
frustrado en sus afanes,
derrotado en su empeño
por el clima, el hechizo y la mosca del sueño
y por la algarabía de loros charlatanes
en mil lenguas bantú.
Donde se sintió aturdido
por el hondo, imperioso rugido
del rey de la selva . . . y el rey, en verdad, eras tú.

Black city slicker,
conceited, pretentious, aspiring.
Your hand never leaves the glove,
the cane never leaves your hand.
But nevertheless,
don't you feel nostalgic at times?
Is it that you no longer want
your submissive women to serve you
their love on disliked lips?

In your cosmopolitanism you forget
the savage domains;
lands of fetishism,
mysterious exorcism,
that made the white man think of voyages.
A green cathedral
where the explorer enters and loses his soul
in rites celebrating the creation of voodoo;
frustrated in his enterprises,
his goal defeated by the weather,
the bewitchment, the fly that brings sleep
and the gibberish of charlatan parrots
in a thousand Bantu languages.
He feels bewildered in the place inhabited by the deep,
imperious uproar of the king of the jungle. . . . And truthfully,
that king was you.*

Racist, antiblack, and undemocratic, Alfau's feelings and images are a
result of his childhood education. He was taught that Africans were dirty and
unhealthy and that whites were superior because Western civilization was
built upon the wisdom of the Greek and Roman empires. He supported
tyranny, rather than democracy, thinking that it is far better to be ruled by a
capricious one than by the malleable many. Purity of blood and purity of
spirit, were, in his eyes, fundamental for maintaining social continuity. Alfau
believed that New York City, with its influx of "underdeveloped" Caribbeans,

*See my introduction to Alfau's *Sentimental Songs* (Elmwood Park, Ill.: Dalkey Archive Press,
1992): vii–xv.

had become "a violent jungle." Although his attitude is unquestionably extreme, it denotes latent values and principles within the Latino minority. Although Alfau kept Jewish friends, he retained a degree of skepticism. Were they Christ-killers?

A paradigm, an antihero, Alfau makes us confront our psychological and ideological fears and beliefs, pushing us to understand that deep inside we Latinos are not comfortable with democratic dialogue: Democracy remains a troublesome, evasive possibility south of the Rio Grande and in the Caribbean. Coup d'états are always impending, and the region's sovereignty is forever in question. Rather than debate opinions, we mourn courageous friends who died on the battlefield. We are uncomfortable about pondering ideas and reflecting on their value and echoes. Ours are often intransigent, dictatorial regimes, repressive and torture driven. We mourn, together with the Madres of La Plaza de Mayo and many other suffering mothers who lost their children, the million *desaparecidos* in a perpetually dirty civil war.

The explanation for this lack of democratic spirit is found in our cultural history. Children of Counter Reformation movements, we never had an age of Enlightenment. Spain and Portugal were awkward, feudal societies when Columbus first arrived in the New World. Whereas other European nations—England, France, and Holland—were already submerging themselves in the dynamics of capitalism, the retrograde model in the Iberian peninsula was still Machiavelli's *The Prince*. When romanticism finally came to us at the end of the nineteenth century in the form of *modernista* poetry, the rest of Europe and the United States had already left that mood behind. The American Revolution and the French Revolution were democratic movements that breathed the fresh air of justice, liberty, and equality. Debate, popular consensus, and collective dialogue were on their agendas. In contrast, Hispanics, always derivative, imitated the constitutional systems, although not their philosophical groundwork. Our art and fiction convey a liberating image that is discordant with our politics. Hispanics, as Octavio Paz, Ezequiel Martínez Estrada, and Pedro Henríquez Ureña have argued, lack a solid critical tradition. Therefore, it is not surprising that north of the Rio Grande they began writing, composing, and painting, although not yet articulating a coherent worldview set forth by critics.

We suffer from a frightening absence of critical thinking. Whereas our fiction is nothing short of spectacular, we have lacked, from 1848 on, a critical counterpart that would analyze, dissect, and reflect on our fiction. In fact, thinking that to criticize is to accuse, to attack, and to denigrate, we fail to recognize the true role of art and literary criticism: to create a bridge between society and culture, to reflect on the zillion channels of communication between people and a work of art. Although scores of scholars regularly produce articles and volumes published by academic presses, they often use an obtuse, almost impenetrable jargon that is inhibiting to the lay reader. Where are our Edmund Wilsons? Why have we failed to develop an intellectual framework for our culture? The answer cannot be our recent arrival in the Promised Land, simply because some among us have been around since before the *Mayflower*. Why on earth are our cultural intermediaries hidden? Do we lack a critical mind? Are we too condescending?

Latino academics, on the other hand, abound. During the late 1960s and the 1970s, as the Latino population quickly increased and as huge numbers of Anglo students who were interested in discovering the exotics and politics of Latin America and in learning Spanish enrolled in specialized courses, colleges and universities across the United States were in urgent need of language and literature teachers with a bilingual background. The phenomenon coincided with the emergence of the new Latin American novel, which began to flourish in translation and captured the attention of millions. Offers of faculty appointments accelerated rapidly, and Caribbean and Central and South American political refugees and émigrés quickly became a solid academic workforce. Campuses throughout the United States became a safe heaven for Marxists and Trotskyists during the Cold War. Dictatorial regimes and political repression south of the border pushed many educated Hispanics to seek refuge first in Europe (Paris, where Julio Cortázar wrote *Hopscotch,* was Latin America's intellectual capital in the 1960s) and especially in the United States. Writers, educators, and activists found protection on traditionally liberal campuses across the nation, and their politics were immediately possessed by a self-evident contradiction: While they were in their homelands, they vociferously accused the United States of imperialism in newspapers and radio broadcasts, but in their new homes in the United States, they remained silent, while they kept fighting for freedom in Argentina, Peru, and Chile—a display of chutzpah, not to say hypocrisy and sanctimoniousness. Mario Vargas Llosa discussed in detail the odyssey of a handful of these émigré scholars—including Julio Ortega, a Latin Americanist at Brown University, and Roberto Fernández Retamar, the Cuban critic loyal to Castro's regime— in his 1993 memoir *A Fish in the Water.* These intellectuals had quickly metamorphosed into parasites: Like Martín Ramírez, they were silent in their new milieu, although out of mediocrity, not as a symptom of mental sickness. As far as I am concerned, there's nothing wrong in criticizing the United States as long as it is productive criticism targeted to collective improvement. But to attack your bread feeder, it seems to me, is a clear sign of falseness.

As for our own tumultuous experience in colleges, it dates back to the Chicano movement. The first Mexican-American studies program in the United States was started at the University of California–Los Angeles in 1968. Others followed a year later elsewhere in the state, as well as in Arizona, Colorado, New Mexico, Texas, the Midwest, and the Pacific Northwest. But only as a result of the emergence of multiculturalism in the 1980s did Latino students—Chicanos, Cuban-Americans, mainland Puerto Ricans, and other Hispanics—about 12 percent in private colleges, acquire a global minority consciousness. For the most part, it remains a deceptive process initiated by a nervously awaited letter in the mailbox: "I am delighted to report that the Committee on Admissions and Financial Aid has voted to admit you to the Class of 1999." Suddenly, the American Dream has opened its doors: Welcome to the future! Good-bye to ghettoized barrio life! But things are never that simple. Private colleges court the select few—the bright, the athletic, the artistically talented, and those with a capacity for leadership—as if they were precious jewels. The youths' families become ecstatic with the news. Poverty, parents believe, will become a thing of the past; happily, drug trafficking has proved not to be the only path to wealth. Phone calls follow: "We just wanted to make sure the letter arrived . . ."; "We guarantee financial aid, plus a part-time campus job, access to faculty, multicultural activities"; "Have you made your decision yet?" Although thousands have applied, only a minuscule percentage is courted with promises. The pressure to excel is tremendous: Those who are chosen to enter the Promised Land become precocious heroes, role models who lack the spiritual freedom needed to experiment and to discover the reach of their intellect. Peers at home in El Barrio, less success driven, are left forgotten amid criminality and unemployment. And yet, for that privileged few, excitement soon turns into deception. After the first few weeks, life on campus becomes unbearable. Latino students quickly realize they are only tokens. The institution isn't quite ready to make them full partners and is incapable of fulfilling their needs. Promises are not kept.

Why is higher education such a disappointing experience for us nowadays, particularly in private colleges? The students' hyphenated identity still has not enough echo on campus. The combative spirit of the 1960s is still alive, but not enough changes have taken place. Is the American Dream accessible only when one denies one's own past? Once again, the young people are pushed to the margins, their journey from the barrio to the classroom marked by depression. What's wrong is a lack of genuine interest by the institutions themselves. This country's Eurocentrism excludes Spain and Portugal as pillars of Western civilization and, thus, the attention given to Latin America and the Caribbean on campus, a landscape of banana republics, is colored by paternalism and a sense of the exotic and bizarre. Protests by Chicano students at UCLA and Cornell University, with obvious echoes of the civil rights movement, are one more signal of the urgent need for change.

On the other hand, public colleges since after World War II, financially accessible to middle- and lower-middle-class families, have had a more open admission policy that has welcomed minority students. Consequently, many Latinos have gone to these schools. Given their collective background and the culture shock they experience when they submerge themselves intellectually in historical and sociological topics, these young women and men often acquire a militant edge, which pushes them to fight for more openness and acceptance of things Hispanic on campus. But the reality in private undergraduate schools is quite different. Unless the student gets some sort of financial aid, sky-high tuition makes it prohibitive for middle- and lower-income families to send their adolescents to private institutions, often in spite of their scholarly achievement and promise. And if some are accepted, they are made unwelcome by a milieu that ignores their needs and dreams. This is of course true for all ethnic groups. The same criticism can be applied to the welcome other minorities have received on campus, from the way Jewish students were treated in the 1940s and 1950s to the fashion in which Asians were approached from the 1970s on. The door to the American Dream doesn't open by uttering *hocus pocus*. The age of multiculturalism has invited each group to the banquet of American civilization, and private campuses are where the signs of such invitation ought to manifest themselves quickly and solidly.

Major universities, out of a mix of guilt and genuine curiosity, have invested considerable capital in Black Studies departments, and figures like Henry Louis Gates, Jr., and Cornel West have been turned into idols. Funds granted to the Latino curriculum, on the other hand, are for the most part applied to the study of forgotten Iberian poets and nineteenth-century revolutionary movements south of the Rio Grande that have had little impact on Latinos in the United States. Hispanic faculty members often speak poor English and have no patience for, say, Dominicans in Spanish Harlem or Cubans in Little

Havana. When I was a graduate student at Columbia University from 1987 to 1990, not a single course was offered on Puerto Ricans on the mainland, although the school, on 116th Street and Broadway in New York, is surrounded by millions of Spanish-speaking Borinquéns—evidence of the academic institution as an ivory tower, unconcerned with mundane affairs. While society is already accepting Latinos as a major economic and political force, private colleges hesitate. What is needed is the establishment of new programs focusing on Latinos and the diversification of faculty members. It isn't enough to continue to teach Iberian and Latin American courses when students are clamoring for ethnic and cultural awakening and emancipation with a new collective identity, one forged this side of the border. Furthermore, Latino courses cannot be part of ethnic studies, simply because Latinos are not an ethnic group but a sum of multiracial, multicultural backgrounds. Thus, such courses need to analyze our double-faceted past: Emerson and Borges. Enough with ambiguity. By failing to attend to the uniqueness of Latinos, the universities are deceiving the whole nation. The odyssey of Latino students from the fringes of society to center stage is permeated with fear, disillusion, and loss: loss of roots, loss of identity, loss of self-confidence. Whereas public four-year and community colleges are attended by a large number of students who are anxious to get an education but are unable to afford an expensive private school, private colleges, forced by affirmative-action programs, have embraced a minuscule elite and often reject extraordinary candidates because minority quotas are quickly filled. A reconsideration of the curriculum and a reevaluation of our national goals are essential, together with the renewal of a faculty often perceived, by students at least, as out of touch with the nation's social, linguistic, and ethnic reality.

As Richard Rodríguez and Ruben Navarrette, Jr., exemplify, the troublesome relationship between barrio and college, the way in which education turns into a journey with a sharp edge, although far from exclusive to Hispanics, is, nevertheless, painful. Does the Latino student continue to feel at home once he or she has obtained a degree? What about our most popular writers and intellectuals, from Julia Alvarez to Roberto G. Fernández, who depend on an educational institution for their daily livelihood, which generates a bookish literature invaded by sophisticated, self-referential jargon requiring the reader to have at least a small degree of acquaintance with things aesthetic to be fully understood? When writing about Nuyoricans, for example, I have been attacked for not retaining a grass-roots personal identity, for being Jewish and not Catholic; and for creating an abyss between El

Barrio and intellectual life, a familiar dilemma among U.S. ethnic writers. Readers in East Los Angeles, Little Havana, and Spanish Harlem often feel repelled by the high-brow art created by refined artisans and tricksters, preferring to satisfy their need for endless entertainment through Spanish comic strips, *fotonovelas,* and television soap operas made south of the border. Such a discrepancy between the intellectual elite and their readership is measured in economic terms. Whereas Tomás Rivera and Luis J. Rodríguez stand as rural and ghetto voices, contemporary Latino writers come, for the most part, from middle- and lower-middle class families. Bohemian models from south of the border become attractive models in a pilgrimage through ambiguity toward total assimilation and fame. Once a stable status is achieved by means of education and hard work, a sense of foreignness to grass-roots milieus emerges, and a struggle begins to retain an authentic voice, one that speaks to and about the writer's origins.

Until the late 1980s, English-speaking Latino writers had received little attention from the mainstream society. Once again, the image of the Chicano painter Martín Ramírez, forced to silence, a ghost on the periphery of culture, ought to be invoked. A plethora of autobiographical and fictional narratives, short and long, portrayed the minority group as made up of rural citizens, poor, exploited, and disliked, forced to migrate to the cities. Later came a more urban art, more humorous and lighthearted, devoted to representing its subject matter as alienated and ghettoized. The 1960s and 1970s, silently creative, were also decades of slow empowerment, activism, and social conscience, the Latino community's expedition from the fringes of society to the center. Although music by Latinos, such as Caribbean rhythms, and pictorial art had already established a reputation, literature had to wait a bit longer. Whereas natural sounds and pictures are universal languages, poetry and fiction are restricted geographically to a linguistic zone; that is, a generation of perfectly fluent English speakers had to emerge for solid novels to break into the mainstream. Our audience was reduced to college professors and students. These works almost never ignited a global debate, made it into the core curriculum, or enchanted more than a few initiated. I can think of a few exceptions to the rule: Miguel Piñero and Piri Thomas, for instance, simply because their most accessible craft, in spite of its aesthetic merit, was seen as an expression of a drug and crime culture. One can certainly talk about a sort of censorship of these works based upon limited distribution. Many writers depend on small independent, often academic, presses whose printings sometimes amount to little more than a thousand copies, houses devoted to publishing minority writers, such as the Bilingual Press at Arizona State University, in the hands of Gary Keller, nicknamed El Huitlacoche, himself a short-story writer, and Arte Público at the University of Houston, under the tutelage of Nicolás Kanellos, a scholar of Puerto Rican descent, who deserves applause for helping to shape Latino literature. Since its creation in 1980, Arte Público, while nurturing a strikingly unbalanced backlist, preferring quantity to quality, often sacrificing excellence in pursuit of fair and vocal political representation, placed on the map names like Rolando Hinojosa, a Faulknerian master responsible for the Klail City saga.

Happily, the 1990s are witnessing the birth of a narrative boom that promises to turn things upside down. After the scattered, somewhat timid voices that flourished during the Vietnam War era and afterward, a refreshing trend is now consolidating the tradition and revolutionizing the status of Hispanic letters in English by revamping the approach of those who came before. Characters see themselves as exotic citizens proud of a life in the margins, divided selves. The division between old and new, the forefathers and the renaissance group, is a response, at least in part, to two widespread developments: a growing number of ordinary Anglo readers eager to find out more about Latinos, "the strangers next door," and a higher standard of literacy inside this ethnic group. Yet, the question remains: Is there such a thing as a Hispanic readership among us? The question may sound preposterous at first. After all, numerous versions of *Don Quixote* in translation are available in inexpensive editions and are frequently used in college courses; *One Hundred Years of Solitude* has been a steady best-seller since it first appeared in the United States in 1970, wonderfully translated by Gregory Rabassa; Laura Esquivel, a Mexican writer of solid reputation who authored *Like Water for Chocolate,* has a wide following in the United States; and Jorge Luis Borges, an Argentine master and unquestionably one of the best writers of the twentieth century, remains a favorite among bookish students, high-brow intellectuals, and minimalists like Robert Coover and John Barth. (Contemporary Spanish literati, on the other hand, like the Nobel Prize winner Camilo José Cela, are still rather obscure.) The question here isn't *who* reads Hispanic writers, for after decades of neglect, books from south of the border have finally made it into the world scene. We already are, once and for all, contemporaries of the rest of the world, at least artistically speaking. The question, rather, has to do with what W. H. Auden once called "bibliophilism." The mere fact that novels and short-story collections by new Latino writers are being embraced by major publishers with huge publicity budgets is an indicator that if this often-devaluated minority is producing poets and prose stylists of such fine caliber, something in the way that young Hispanic men and women are encouraged to love literature is working quite well. Education, it seems, is promoting democracy. However, are the writings of Oscar Hijuelos and his colleagues really targeted toward a Latino audience? Or does it have an Anglo readership in mind? Are we reading our own writers? Is it that we will always be simply terrific dancers and better musicians but poor readers? Is the pilgrimage from the periphery to mainstream culture one in which the entire Latino community is embarked? Aren't many being left behind?

Let me return to the issues of modernity and culture in Latin America, particularly in Cuba. At the end of the eighteenth century, Cuba's Sociedad Patriótica was devoted to educating people. As Antonio Benítez-Rojo has pointed out, figures like José de la Luz y Caballero, an important politician, devoted their energy to the endeavor. Although many are devoted to offering a different portrait, the truth is that Cuba was always at the forefront of technology and intellectual matters. Cuba was second in Latin America to build a railway system, to increase sugar production and to unify the nation—even before Spain. And Cuba had telegraph and telephone systems rather early. The island was a rich colony, and the upper class was always keeping in touch with recent technological discoveries and scientific advances elsewhere in the world. The automatic telephone, for example, was in Cuba before it appeared in the United States or in many other countries in Europe and elsewhere in Latin America. Money and the plantation economy had forced Cubans to import technology since the beginning. In the 1830s, for instance, ice cream was already available on the island. One can see, in Boston's Old State House, a photograph in which people in Massachusetts were sending huge ice cubes to the island at that time. All this presupposes a solid educational system, at least among the aristocratic elite, who would send their children to the United States, France, and England to study, a move that made them keep in touch with advanced societies.

Culture in Cuba was always essential: There were orchestras early on, film societies, institutes of higher education. What Fidel Castro's revolution did was to continue this tradition. Under the Communist regime, people read much more than did people, say, in Spain, a European country with a strong publishing infrastructure. Even without a tradition of good libraries, bookstores, and publishing houses, the readership was always large. A small fiction book would have a first printing of 10,000 copies. The publishers would also encourage readers to send in their comments, positive or otherwise; one finds such notices on the back of every book published in the island since the 1960s. When the state-run Imprenta Nacional, founded by Alejo Carpentier, brought out its first title, *Don Quixote,* the run was 100,000 copies. And why do people read so much? One cannot argue that it was the Communist Revolution that changed reading habits because, after all, Carpentier's Imprenta Nacional appeared shortly after Castro's ascent to power, which means that people were already used to reading books. Obviously, after the revolution, the ambitious campaign to make the entire population literate, the legal obligation to finish primary school, and pressure to keep studying no matter one's age increased the need to read. Although the content of such readings is debatable, Castro's regime no doubt improved the reading habits of people on the island. His achievement stands alone in the long-standing preoccupation with educating the Hispanic masses south of the Rio Grande. From the French Revolution to the Soviet Revolution, every single attempt to use books to educate the masses has failed. Literature is only good for its own aesthetic level. Lay readers in Buenos Aires and elsewhere in the Spanish-speaking world despise Borges's art as pretentious and impenetrable. And in Mexico, from José Joaquín Fernández de Lizardi to Angeles Mastretta, sophisticated culture is produced and consumed by a small group of educated people, less than 1 percent of the total population. In spite of efforts of houses like Fondo de Cultura Económica to provide books at accessible prices and in large numbers, in spite of José Vasconcelos's dream of educating the masses to create the *raza de bronce,* the immense majority does not, and probably never will, participate in the development of the nation's literature. A typical best-seller among us will hardy sell more than 30,000. Regardless of their quality, books are still read only by a minuscule number of Hispanics, who often try to ignore the issues, but remain loyal to the art.

Whereas the old Latino guard lived anonymously, we, the members of a newer generation, thrive on book tours, lectures, and media hype. Before Terry McMillan's novel *Waiting to Exhale* came out in 1992, a similar question was pondered about blacks. Is there such thing as a black reader? critics pondered. There was a tacit agreement that Maya Angelou, Toni Morrison, and Alice Walker, although they attract a small portion of ethnic readers, are sold primarily to a largely educated white audience. McMillan, of course, has come to symbolize an emerging black middle-class eager to read "low-brow" novels about its daily anxieties and hopes.

Consequently, the current question regarding Hispanics may also suggest that something essential is changing in the texture of the Latino community. Behind the much-publicized images of poverty, drugs, and violence, upward mobility is indeed taking place. There have been improvements in household income, education, and jobs from one generation to the next. At least for the time being, the audience reading Cristina Garcia's *Dreaming in Cuban* and Victor Villaseñor's *Rain of Gold* may look as if it is mainly non-Hispanic, a white, genuinely democratic readership ready to give silence a voice, but a passionate, middle-class, English-speaking Latino readership, hidden in the shadow, is also active. The biggest Latino best-sellers are Richard Rodríguez's *Hunger of Memory*; Rudolfo Anaya's *Bless Me, Ultima,* which by 1993, more than two decades after publication, had sold some 300,000 paperback editions since its original 1972 publication; Oscar Hijuelos's *The Mambo Kings Play Songs of Love,* which sold over 220,000 copies in paperback after it received the Pulitzer Prize; and Sandra Cisneros's *Woman Hollering Creek*, which received an extraordinary critical and commercial reception in 1991 and sold more copies than did Hijuelos's book in a little over twelve months. After decades of silence, today Oscar "Zeta" Acosta, Ron Arias, José Antonio Villarreal, and others are reprinted by major publishers, their tales of discrimination, drug abuse, and economic hardship slowly reaching the core of the American Dream. Conservative critics refer to these books as "reader-in-the-box" products: stories of misery handsomely packaged for multiculturalists; that is, they claim that these books were thought of, and even designed for, non-Latinos. Perhaps these critics are right, although when asked to read them in specially designed college courses, Latino students see them as a root-awakening experience: an inspiration. True, the students often need a teacher, a mentor, to bring them to this fiesta, the literature of Latino writers, simply because as citizens of a minority they have been alienated from the mainstream culture. In any case, this new generation, already inspired, is happily aspiring to higher goals and preparing itself intellectually in ways that easily surpasses its parents, which means that a larger readership is in the making.

The assumption of an "absent" Latino readership is based on the belief that we, the Latino population, are mostly young, poor, and uneducated, which is a distortion, of course. Although the average age of non-Latinos in this country is thirty-three, the average age of Cuban-Americans (slightly over 1 million) is thirty-nine, that of Puerto Ricans (2.2 million) is twenty-seven, and that of Mexican-Americans (over 13.3 million) is twenty-four. In terms of schooling, whereas the median number of years of schooling is 12.7 for non-Hispanics, it is 10.8 for Mexican-Americans, 12 for Puerto Ricans, and 12.4 for Cuban-Americans. Close to 10 percent of native-born Mexican-Americans, 14 percent of mainland Puerto Ricans, and 26 percent of native-born Cuban-Americans have more than a high school education. These numbers are quite estimable when one realizes that only 20 percent of the Anglo (non-Latino) population has more than a high school education. Although the incomes of a large number of Latinos are sadly under the poverty level, as Richard Rodríguez, Earl Shorris, and Linda Chavez have pointed out, another important segment is rapidly emerging as newcomers to the middle class. They eat, sleep, make love, dance, vote, *and* read books. Indeed, more and more are reading books by their own native children.

So is there such a thing as a Latino readership? Certainly, the challenge for writers and editors is to find it. The reader-in-the-box phenomenon proves that soon after Anglos turn an English-language book into a best-seller, middle-class Latinos, not necessarily college educated, will follow by fully embracing one of their authors, which will result in a best-seller beyond ethnic borders. The near future, I am sure, will witness a Latino Terry McMillan. Such a development, of course, although not a promise for great literature, will at least be unquestionable proof of the existence of that evasive ghost, the Hispanic reader—one concerned with *Don Quixote* but also, and primarily, with the imagination of one of these new voices. Don't forget that soon after Langston Hughes, whose poetry was "discovered" by Vachel Lindsay, participated in the Harlem Renaissance, he wandered from the Caribbean to South America (Arnold Rampersand, in an extraordinary biography, analyzes Hughes's ties to Hispanic culture) and went on to produce an extraordinary body of literature that includes titles like *One-Way Ticket* and *The Ways of White Folks*. And the same thing goes for Richard Wright and Zora Neale Hurston. Many years later, James Baldwin, Alice Walker, Toni Morrison, and others looked back on these writers as mentors—a heroic crew who opened the door to a new beginning. The new Latino promises to produce a shelf of classics, books that will become national treasures and, at the same time, to reevaluate the long-standing tradition of Latino literature.

Which brings me back, one more time, to the issue of democracy. Latino culture is a lens through which the hardships and contradictions of our long journey from Latin America and the Caribbean ought to be pondered. We come with a set bag of archetypes, a difficult view of our collective past and a hopeful sense of the future. To become full U.S. citizens, we need more than a passport; we need to reinvent ourselves, to rewrite our history, to reformulate the paths of our imagination. Our rewriting, nevertheless, will involve a new approach to the overall national past. "All other nations had come into being among people whose families had lived for time out of mind on the same land where they were born," Theodore H. White wrote soon before he died in 1986. "Englishmen are English, Frenchmen are French, Chinese are Chinese, while their governments come and go; their national states can be torn apart and remade without losing their nationhood. But Americans are a nation born of an idea; not the place, but the idea, created the United States Government." Rather than wanting only a share of the American idea, we want to revolutionize the country's overall metabolism. Not that our goal is to dismantle democracy; we deeply cherish its sweetness and would like to join forces with Anglos to make this nation a true democracy in which everyone is included. After all, we, hundreds of thousands of Martín Ramírezes, emigrated north in search of freedom. Freedom, with a capital F: freedom and equality, freedom and justice, freedom and happiness. We do not wish to split up the United States, but to rearrange its cultural borders. Hence, our education will be completed at an expense. What we truly want is full credit for the Hispanic past that Anglo America seldom invokes in its history lessons. We want the United States to become a branch of Latin America, and vice versa, a continental village openly conscious of its Hispanic condition, one where *yo* is *you* and *tú* is *I*.

◆ ◆ ◆

Letter to My Child

Adorado Mío:

I once had a dream in which I was given a copy of an unknown work of cultural analysis, *Caliban's Utopia: or, Barbarism Reconsidered.* When I woke up, it was next to me. I carefully opened it and, quite shocked, realized its pages were totally blank. A moment later, the volume was magically gone—vanished through the invisible rabbets of reality. I never found it again. I have tried in vain to summon its content, most of which, I have come to believe, dealt with *América*—the word, the idea, the reality. Look for it! At some point in your promisingly young life, you may be the lucky one to put your fingers on it. Meanwhile, I would like to talk to you today about exile, language, democracy, and what it means for me to be a citizen of the United States, my adopted country.

I shall begin by invoking an eloquent, if disordered, writer: James Baldwin, an American in the strictest sense of the word, whose work I often read while you're asleep. Exiled as "a Negro writer" in Europe and Istanbul, where he spent two scores and some years of his life, he frequently talked about his personal plight and the hardship he underwent in coming to terms with America, the color of his skin standing between who he was and what society wanted him to be. Born and raised in Harlem, Baldwin left home because, as he put it, he doubted his "ability to survive the fury of the color problem." And he chose Europe, where that barrier was down, because "nothing is more desirable than to be released of an affliction." As an essayist and novelist, he wanted to portray blacks, his people, in their richness and diversity, and unhappy with the "protest art" Ralph Ellison and other precursors had brought forth, Baldwin wished to show, as the critic Irving Howe put it, his own people as a living culture of men and women who, even when deprived, share in the emotions and desires of common humanity.

Once he settled in the Old World (Paris, Switzerland, southern France), his views of America, her myths and traumas, acquired the type of crystalline quality that only exile can offer. In an essay published in 1959 and later collected in *Nobody Knows My Name,* he argued that "America's history, her aspirations, her peculiar triumphs, her even more peculiar defeats, and her position in the world—yesterday and today—are all so profoundly and stubbornly unique that the very word 'America' remains a new, almost completely undefined and extremely controversial proper noun."

Baldwin's odyssey, my beloved son, is helpful to me in grasping the sense of abstraction the word *America* often entreats, how elusive and shifty it really is: a set of patriotic values, an experiment in conviviality, a renewal of biblical aspirations, a desire to turn utopia into an earthly place. But utopia, as its Greek etymology points out, means *there is no such place.* At home and abroad, no one I ever talked to seems to know exactly what the word means. America: home of the brave, hell of intolerance and violence. I vividly recall, back in early 1985, while struggling to master English—a second language I felt compelled to grasp if I ever wanted to become a citizen of the United States in the intellectual sense of the word—the night I first read James Baldwin. I shared a room on 122nd Street in Manhattan, on the outskirts of Harlem, a block away from the Jewish Theological Seminary, where I was a foreign graduate student before entering Columbia University. I had come to New York City, Abraham Cahan's land of opportunity, only a few months before with the objective of finding a brand-new life, leaving forever my family and Mexico, my native country. For the first time in my life, I was dealing with blacks and other racial groups on a daily basis. What's more, I became acquainted with other Latino types: Puerto Ricans, Dominicans, Colombians, and Chicanos. Although Mexico was always a safe heaven for South American refugees, their number was always minimal. In the United States, on the other hand, I was the minority. To be honest, I simultaneously was and wasn't prepared for the experience. Like millions in the Hispanic world, I had been raised hearing nasty racial comments about blacks and *indios.* I wanted to identify with those who spoke Spanish, yet I couldn't, simply because the whiteness of my skin made me different among the bronze and brown. At the same time, as a Jew, I had always been a marginal citizen in Mexico, which means, I guess, that I knew very well my way around any alien nation. I simultaneously mistrusted the Other and was mistrusted as the Other.

I come from an intellectually sophisticated, financially unstable middle-class family in Mexico's capital, a secure, self-imposed Jewish ghetto, an autistic island where gentiles hardly existed and Hebraic symbols prevailed. Money and comfort, books, theater, and art. What made me Mexican? It's hard to know: language and the air I breathed, perhaps. Early on I was sent to Yiddish day school, Colegio Israelita de México in Colonia Narvarte, where the heroes were S. Y. Agnon, Sholem Aleichem, and Theodor Herzl, while people like Lázaro Cárdenas, José Joaquín Fernández de Lizardi, and Alfonso Reyes were our neighbors' models, not ours. Surrounded by the Other, I, together with my family and friends, inhabited a self-sufficient island, with imaginary borders built in agreement between us and the outside world, an oasis, completely uninvolved with things Mexican. In fact, when it came to knowledge of the outside world, Jewish students like me, and probably the whole middle class, were far better off talking about U.S. products (Holly-wood, syndicated shows like "Star Trek," junk food, and technology) than about Mexico—an artificial capsule, our habitat. The neighboring country across the border was for me and my schoolmates the perfect image of "paradise on earth." Money permitting, as a child and adolescent I would accompany my family on vacation trips to Texas, Florida, and California, in shopping sprees to acquire, to be part of a type of postindustrial modernity personified by the hard-to-understand English-speaking Anglo consumers in Houston's mall La Galería and by Disneyland, a microcosm where synthetic birds sing in the Tikki Tikki Room, where you take a tour through the human anatomy that begins in a microscope, eat hot dogs next to Mickey Mouse, and where, on a fake stage, the pirate Sir Francis Drake, on his ship *Golden Hind*, pillages the coasts of South America in front of your very eyes. Expansive, imperialistic, a never-ending parade of naive monolingual tourists with cameras in hand to seize the memory, the have-a-good-times of narrow-mindedness, I perceived Americans to be money driven, ready to sell Taco Bell in the land of tacos and never stop at anything to make a deal. Aside from the ubiquitous hamburger, a German import, the national cuisine, I thought, was just a sum of international palates: burritos and chili con carne, pizza and spaghetti, Caesar salad, onion soup, and crepes. Whereas the United States, where the future has already happened and history is a recent invention, was Paradise-on-Wheels, Mexico was stuck in the past, which acquires cyclic dimensions of trauma and discontent, a past incredibly heavy and intrusive, a people unable to become, in a by-then already famous sentence, "contemporary with the rest of humankind."

Everything changed at the age of twenty-five, when, as a foreign scholarship student, a counterpoint to Richard Rodríguez's vilified "scholarship boy," I was happily invited to the banquet in El Dorado and became part of the American scene. Farewell parties celebrated my early triumph. I was expected to take advantage of the exemplary academic resources across the border and become a writer and scholar. But after a few months, once I got a view from within, a deep transformation took place. Suddenly, I ceased to be Mexican and became, much to my surprise, a Latino—what's worse, a white Latino, something most people have difficulty understanding: Is every Peruvian brown skinned, every Nicaraguan short with black hair? Being from Aztecalandia, I was automatically expected to have an Emiliano Zapata mustache; carry a sombrero; hide a tequila bottle; have an accent just like Ricky Ricardo's, making no distinction between long and short vowels ("live" and "leave"); and to take a siesta every afternoon from one to three-thirty. In short, I was yet another participant in the larger-than-life mirror of stereotypes.

Obsessed with egotism, the United States points at the mirror as its favorite artifact. Mirrors everywhere—in monstrous shopping centers, airports, drugstores; mirrors in health and fitness centers; mirrors in your bedroom and mine, in our bathroom and living room; in your mother's purse; and at your school. Mirrors reflecting mirrors reflecting mirrors. Isn't the United States an overpopulated, polychromatic parade of peoples enamored with themselves? Compulsive soul-searchers and self-accusers, we Hispanics also have a constant love affair with mirrors, a passion for deciphering our labyrinthine collective self. Ours is an elusive identity—abstract, unreachable, obscure, a multifaceted monster. We look for answers to past traumas and unsolved existential dilemmas; north of the river, on the other hand, the reflection has to do with superficial appearance and the infatuation with the body: a voyage into the soul and a trip to Acapulco. I don't think I knew the meaning of the words *race* and *ethnicity* until I moved north. You see, Mexico is a multiracial society, in which Indians, Europeans, Asians, and Africans coexist more or less peacefully. But people refuse to acknowledge the mestizo heterogeneity. On the contrary, the standard perception is that we all are particles of an altogether different transatlantic race. Furthermore, I was born Mexican without really knowing what that meant, and I did not learn what it meant until I came to the United States, where people automatically began addressing me as Hispanic. *Comprende español,* eh? people would ask. *Un poquito.* Funny, you don't look Hispanic! Ever tried seafood burritos? And how do people say *fuck* in Mexican?

As you will one day find out, my dear, America, her triumphs and defeats, isn't only a nation (in Baldwin's own words, "a state of mind") but also a vast continent. From Alaska to the Argentine pampas, from Rio de Janeiro to East Los Angeles and Little Havana, the geography that the disoriented Genoese admiral Christopher Columbus mistakenly encountered in 1492 and Amerigo Vespucci baptized a few years later is also a linguistic and cultural multiplicity, a sum of parts: America the nation and America the continent. Thus, we the "Spanish-origin" people in the United States are truly twice American: as children of Thomas Jefferson and John Adams, but, also, as citizens of the so-called New World. While some persist in seeing us as the newest wave of foreigners, second-class citizens at the bottom of the social hierarchy, at least three-fifths of us were in these territories even before the Pilgrims arrived on the *Mayflower*, and only unexpectedly, unwillingly became part of the United States when the Treaty of Guadalupe Hidalgo was signed. Twice American, once in spite of ourselves: American *americanos.*

To say that in 1985 I was profoundly moved reading Baldwin's writing on the outskirts of Harlem is to translate into words what at the time seemed an inexplicable experience. Baldwin's message was a sort of revelation: I came to understand more about the United States through his perplexities than through anything I watched on television. Baldwin, a man "forced to understand so much," left me with a sense of truth unraveled. Just like him, I was undergoing a profound transformation. I was conscious of its metamorphoses and chose to experience them fully. I wanted to turn Mexico into the past, but, also and more important, I knew I would inhabit an America the black writer of *The Fire Next Time* had difficulty figuring out: America the beautiful and America the ugly.

To switch from Spanish into English was not, could not have been a personal tragedy for me. To be or *no ser*: native tongue, acquired tongue. The father tongue, I recognize, is the adopted, alternative, and illegitimate language. (Henry James preferred the term *wife tongue* because a wife, he claimed in early-twentieth-century fashion, is loyal, devoted, and nurturing— a mother substitute.) Instead, the mother tongue is genuine and authentic— a uterus: the original source. I was educated in (into) four idioms: Spanish, Yiddish, Hebrew, and a rudimentary English. Spanish was the public venue; Hebrew was a channel toward Zionism, not toward the sacredness of the synagogue; Yiddish symbolized the Holocaust and past struggles of the Eastern European labor movement; and English was the entrance to redemption: the United States. Abba Eban said it better: "Jews are like everybody else . . . except a little bit more." A polyglot, of course, has as many loyalties as homes. Spanish, I thought, was my right eye, English my left eye, Yiddish my background, and Hebrew my conscience. Or better, each could be seen as representing a different set of spectacles (near sight, bifocal, night reading) through which the universe is seen. To prefectly master the English language would be a challenge but, also, a treat.

Almost a decade later, America is in my blood: I married your mother, an adopted New Englander born in St. Louis; you came to enlighten our lives; and I am writing to you, my beloved one, in English, an acquired language I thought I would never master. Although I only recently applied to become a U.S. citizen and thus I have never voted in an election, although English isn't my native tongue, although I didn't grow up watching "The Wild, Wild West," America, I can already say, is the place I know and love best and feel a visceral attachment to. As my friend Gustavo Pérez-Firmat claims, by communicating with you in Shakespeare's tongue, I may already be falsifying what I want to say. And yes, let me confess a deep feeling of betrayal. With occasional interruptions, throughout your short life we've always talked, proudly and loudly, *en español.* Why suddenly change now when writing this letter? Against the view I've tried to promote in you, is Spanish, our vehicle, somewhat deficient, you may be asking? Is it incapable of delivering as soundly as does English the whole truth, regardless of the circumstance? Of course not. My language choice, once again, has to do with the Other. I make an exception today because strangers are listening and, as you can recognize from our past experience, when people are around, we need to open up, to share our verbal code: a sign of respect and democratic spirit. Besides, although I choose Spanish as our private tongue, English is also pretty much part of my self. Granted, I am atypical at best, a student with a multilingual past who found a room of his own in the American Dream by keeping the two languages alive. I did it, you should know, to keep straight: I am, I will always be, a Mexican in the United States. An alien—the Other.

My son, you will certainly live in an age in which the fruits of multiculturalism will be flavorful. Although some, like the Australian critic Robert Hughes, author of *Barcelona,* believe the climate has given way to a culture of complaint and the frying of America, multiculturalism, I've no doubt, is a benign weapon. It is my belief that multiculturalism will be an entrance door to a more humane world. When you become an adult, Latinos will have ceased to be marginal. Instead, we'll have become protagonists. The Rio Grande will not divide: Latin and North America will become a single unity.

And what does it mean to be Latino? What distinguishes us from our siblings across the border? Are we ever to find a unique collective identity? Our psyche is carnivalesque, introspective. And what about our agenda? In the prologue to his classic confessional autobiography, *Down These Mean Streets,* Piri Thomas said: "Yee-ah! Wanna know how many times I've stood on a rooftop and yelled out to anybody: 'Hey, World—here I am. Hallo, World. . . .'" With an inescapable echo, his words continue to resonate: Who are we? Will we ever receive the attention we deserve? Masters in the art of remembrance, we suffer from a traumatic past and refuse to inhabit the future. Could we then assimilate in the Promised Land? My impression is that neither here nor there, Latinos shall always inhabit the hyphen. My generation will prove infuriating. Others will finally realize that Spanish is here to stay, never to vanish. What's more, our stubbornness will force many non-Latinos to come to us, to adapt to our ways. You, instead, will surely share a happier future: To be Latino, to speak Spanish, will be the best asset. English alone will not suffice.

Where is Mexico, my Mexico, today? In the map of my mind, a structural column in your becoming an American. I often travel the fragile line between memory and the past. Where do facts end and my deformed recollection of incidents begin? As an adolescent, I remember what a bright high school teacher used to ask: What are the three most disastrous events in Mexican history? His answers were: (1) Moctezuma II thinking that Hernán Cortés, a bearded white man who came from the sea, was a god, and so the Aztecs didn't attack the Spanish army; (2) the European miscegenation, which resulted in the mestizo and mulatto races and inaugurated a tragic history of identity crises; and (3) Generalísimo Antonio López de Santa Ana's decision to sell only part of Mexico to the United States, not the entire country. What if the Europeans, like the Anglo-Saxon Americans, had erased the natives instead of interacting with them? The *if* is one of the Hispanic hemisphere's favorite pastimes: What if Simón Bolívar, who died in 1830, had consummated his lifelong dream of establishing *La Gran Colombia,* the United States of South America? What if Italy or France, not Spain and Portugal, had conquered Peru, Brazil, and the other countries of the region? What if, what if . . . Anglo-Saxon America, on the other hand, has seized its destiny and has little room for uncertainty and doubt. What to make, then, of Latinos in the United States, citizens of both realities, representatives of doubt in the land of certainty?

I have spent almost ten years trying to understand what it means to be a Mexican and an American, separately and together. Time and again I have returned to Baldwin's view, which I am sure you will sooner or later also share: It's indeed quite a complex thing. What *is* America? Where has it been, and where is it going? Do we, Latinos, have a fair share in its uterus? In search of answers, I have devoured various interpretations, from Abraham Cahan's *The Rise of David Levinsky* to W. E. B. DuBois's *The Souls of Black Folks,* from Robert Frost's poetry to the autobiographical verses of Allen Ginsberg, from Maxine Hong Kingston to Gay Talese. None offers a fully satisfactory response. How could they? Everybody keeps a different agenda. Everybody dreams the American Dream in a unique fashion. All are partial, elusive truths. Latinos, I believe, were, are, and will always be perpetual alien residents never fully here—strangers in a native land. We are of a different variety simply because, unlike previous immigrants, most of us didn't come to America; instead, America came to us. Ours isn't just another immigrant's story, simply because assimilation may never be fully completed. It's not my fault, mind you. Hispanics, unlike previous minorities, are about to give America the nation and the continent a big surprise. We may eat American food, buy American merchandise, and greet Americans daily with a *"Buenos días,* mister," but at the core we'll always remain untouched. We may even become fluent bilinguals, speaking and reading the American language. As Pat Mora, a native from El Paso, put it in her poem "Legal Alien": "Bi-lingual, Bi-cultural, able to slip from 'How's life?' to *'Me'stas volviendo loca.'"* Which reminds me of a joke about a cat chasing a bird that seeks refuge in a hole and won't come out. After much thought, the cat finally utters: "Plew, plew, plew . . . ," and the bird comes out. "It's nice to be bilingual," the cat exclaims after devouring its victim. Latinos, of course, are symbolized by the cat. Ours is Moctezuma's revenge: We shall infiltrate the enemy, we shall populate its urban centers, marry its daughters, and reestablish the kingdom of Aztlán. We are here to reclaim what we were deprived of, to take revenge. This isn't a political battle, a combat often stimulating to the liberal imagination, but a cosmic enterprise to set things right. We shall change and only simultaneously be changed.

Society is governed by hidden laws, unspoken but profound assumptions on the part of the people, and America, the beautiful, as well as the ugly, is no exception. It is up to the artist and critic to find out what these laws and assumptions are. "In a society much given to smashing taboos without thereby managing to be liberated from them," Baldwin remarked, "it will be no easy matter." In the book that accompanies this letter, I have done my best to map the labyrinthine ways of my own journey and that of the Hispanic people north of the Rio Grande. Mine is a personal interpretation, partial and subjective. It needs to be added to a million others found daily on any street and classroom. I suspect that the sum of them all, my son, make the content of *Caliban's Utopia*. Find the volume. Be on the alert, looking for it wherever you go. When approached with wisdom, its virginal pages will explain Baldwin's odyssey and mine. Read its invisible paragraphs, then stamp your own divided words in indelible ink.

Todo mi amor, hoy y siempre.

◆ ◆ ◆

Chronology

The development of Latino art and identity north of the Rio Grande has numerous echoes. Important events and works of art and literature are recorded here, some of which were in Spanish by Hispanic Americans, only a small fraction of which were discussed or referred to in the preceding pages.

1492   Christopher Columbus arrives in the Bahamas.

1532   Alvar Núñez Cabeza de Vaca's chronicle *Adventures in the Unknown Interior of America* is published.

1598   Gaspar Pérez de Villagrá's epic poem *History of New Mexico* is published.

1605–15 Miguel de Cervantes Saavedra's *Don Quixote of La Mancha* is published.

1822   *Los Comanches*, an allegorical drama by an anonymous author, is published.

1845   Domingo Faustino Sarmiento's *Civilación y barbarie: o, Vida de Juan Facundo Sarmiento* [*Facundo: Civilization and Barbarism*] is published.

1846   A translation of Gerónimo Boscana's *Chinigchimich*, a historical account of the San Juan Capistrano Indians of Southern California, is published.

1848   The United States and Mexico sign the Treaty of Guadalupe Hidalgo.

1855   The newspaper *El Clamor Público* is founded in Los Angeles.

1855   Juan Cortina leads a revolt to protest Anglo mistreatment of Mexicans in Texas.

1860–70   Rebels Joaquín Murrieta, Tiburcio Vásquez, and others are branded *bandidos* by the Anglo establishment in California. Eugenio María de Hostos's novel *La peregrinación de Bayoán* [*Bayoan's Peregrination*] is written. Segundo Ruiz Belvis's *Memoria sobre la esclavitud* [*Memoir of Slavery*], written with José Julián Acosta, is read in cigar factories in Puerto Rico and New York. Eugenio María de Hostos arrives in New York "sparking with rage," his soul burning with "holy fanaticism" for the independence of Puerto Rico. The Venezuelan poet Juan Antonio Pérez Bonalde settles in New York City. He will befriend other Latin American exiles: José Martí, Nicanor Bolet Peraza, Juan de Dios Uribe and Santiago Pérez Triana.

1874   The first especially Puerto Rican newspaper, *La Voz de Puerto Rico,* is published in New York. Due to poor planning, it only publishes a single issue.

1875   Mariano Vallejo writes his history of California from a Mexican perspective.

1880   José Martí, Cuban poet, essayist, and revolutionary, arrives in New York City and becomes president of the Comité Revolucionaro Cubano. During the decade, several Spanish-language journals edited by Puerto Ricans and Cubans will appear in New York: *América, El Latino-Americano, El Avisador Cubano, El Economista Americano, La Juventud, El Porvenir,* and others.

1884   Helen Hunt Jackson's novel *Ramona* appears.

1885   María Amparo Ruíz de Burton's novel *The Squatter and the Don* is published.

1888   Eugenio María de Hostos's essay on ethics and society, *Moral social* [*Social Morality*] is published.

1892   Eusebio Chacón's novel *El hijo de la tempestad* [*The Child of the Tempest*], among the first by and about Mexican Americans, appears. The first issue of *Patria*, organ of the Partido Revolucionario Cubano, is published under the editorship of José Martí.

1894	Manuel Zeno Gandía's *La charca* is published.
1895	José Martí dies in Dos Ríos, Cuba.
1897	Charles F. Lummis's collection *The Enchanted Burro: Stories from New Mexico and South America* appears. During the decade, cultural and artistic events flourish in the Spanish-speaking community of New York, many of which were centered in the Sociedad Literaria, founded by a group of intellectuals.
1898	The Spanish-American War is fought. Puerto Rico is ceded to the United States. A Cuba republic is established. Gertrude Atherton's *The Californians* is published. The border corrido flourishes, and "The Ballad of Gregorio Cortez" is published.
1900	José Enrique Rodó's philosophical essay *Ariel,* about identity south and north of the Rio Grande, appears and becomes highly influential among Latin America's youth.
1901	Frank Norris's *The Octopus* is published. Luis Muñóz Rivera, a journalist and nationalist who published the *Puerto Rico Herald* in New York City and obtained American citizenship for his country's women and men, heads the first cabinet in Puerto Rico under U.S. occupation.
1903	Mary Austin produces *The Land of Little Rain.* Spanish-speaking theater groups thrive in the Southwest.
1905	Ricardo and Enrique Flores Magón, exiled in the United States, found the magazine *Regeneración,* a syndicalist anarchist publication. They will be condemned for treason in the United States.
1910–20	Pancho Villa and Emiliano Zapata orchestrate the Mexican Revolution. Sara Estela Ramírez publishes the feminist journal *Aurora.* The newspaper *El Heraldo de México* establishes offices in Arizona, California, New Mexico, and Texas. Spanish speakers become a small yet important market. José Guadalupe Posada, the Mexican lampooner, dies. John Reed writes *Insurgent Mexico.*
1925	José Vasconcelos's groundbreaking essay *La raza cósmica* [*The Cosmic Race*] and William Carlos Williams's collection of vignettes, *In the American Grain,* are published.
1926	The newspaper *La Opinión* begins publication in Los Angeles. A substantial portion of its shares will be acquired by the *Los Angeles Times* in the late 1980s.

1927   Willa Cather's *Death Comes for the Archbishop* is published. Mexican poet José Juan Tablada writes *haiku* in New York.

1928   Daniel Venega's *Las aventuras de Don Chipote: o, Cuando los pericos mamen* [*Don Chipote's Adventures: or, When Parrots Suck*] and Pedro Henríquez Ureña's collection of essays on Hispanic identity *Seis ensayos en busca de nuestra expresión* [*Six Essays in Search of Our Expression*] are published.

1929   Artist Antonio García produces his sculpture *Aztec Advance*, based on pre-Columbian themes. Federico García Lorca writes his collection *Poeta en Nueva York* [*Poet in New York*].

1930   John Dos Passos's novel *The 42nd Parallel* and Katherine Anne Porter's *Flowering Judas* are published.

1932–33 Antonio Helú writes his drama *Los mexicanos se van* [*Mexicans Are Leaving*], about economic depression and repatriation. Mexican muralists Diego Rivera, José Clemente Orozco, and David Alfaro Siqueiros—Los Tres Grandes—paint murals in the United States. New Mexican carver Patrocinio Barela gains recognition.

1935   *My Life on the Frontier: 1864–1882*, by Miguel Antonio Otero, the first and only Hispanic governor of New Mexico, is published.

1936   Felipe Alfau's experimental novel *Locos: A Comedy of Gestures* is published, and is later praised by Mary McCarthy.

1937   Roberto Torres's stories about the Mexican Revolution are published in *Esquire,* William Carlos Williams's novel *The White Mule,* the first installment of the Steche trilogy, and John Steinbeck's *Tortilla Flat* are published.

1939   Josephina Neggli's *Sunday Costs Five Pesos* is published.

1940   Fray Angélico Chávez's *New Mexico Triptych* and Paul Horgan's *Figures in a Landscape* are published. Spanish-language radio and cinema begin to thrive in cities of the Southwest.

1942   The Sleepy Lagoon Incident occurs in Los Angeles. Alfonso Reyes's essay on America as Europe's utopia, *Ultima Thule,* is published.

1943   The Zoot Suit Riots occur in Los Angeles.

1945   Josephina Neggli's *Mexican Village* is published. Alejandro Galindo's film *Campeón sin corona* becomes a hit south of the border.

1946   KCOR in San Francisco become the first full-time Spanish-language television station in the United States.

1947–48 *Arizona Quarterly* publishes stories by Mario Suárez, among the first to use the word *Chicano* in print. John Huston's film *The Treasure of the Sierra Madre,* based on B. Traven's novel, is issued.

1949   Armando Baeza's sculpture of the Virgin Mary wins a prize in Los Angeles.

1950   Octavio Paz's *The Labyrinth of Solitude,* whose first chapter is devoted to Pachucos in Los Angeles, is published.

1951   William Carlos Williams's *Autobiography* is published. René Marqués's drama *La carreta* [*The Oxcart*], about an immigrant *jíbaro* family traveling from Puerto Rico to New York, is produced. The first of 179 half-hour episodes of "I Love Lucy," with Desi Arnaz and Lucille Ball, airs on CBS Television Network. Spanish-language television and variety shows begin to acquire popularity as forms of entertainment.

1952   Edna Ferber's *Giant* is published. The Commonwealth of Puerto Rico is proclaimed.

1953   Herbert Biberman's film *The Salt of the Earth* and Alejandro Galindo's film *Espaldas mojadas* [*Wet Backs*], about undocumented immigrants from the Hispanic world in the United States are shown.

1956   Pedro Juan Soto's collection of stories and miniatures, *Spiks,* later praised by William Kennedy, appears.

1957   Ritchie Valens (aka Richard Valenzuela), who recorded "La Bamba" and "Donna," dies in a plane crash.

1958   Américo Paredes's influential folklore study *With His Pistol in His Hand: A Border Ballad and Its Hero* and Edmundo O'Gorman's collection of interconnected essays, *La invención de América* [*The Invention of America*], about the Old World and the New, are published.

1959   Fidel Castro stages a Communist revolution in Cuba. José Antonio Villarreal's *Pocho,* considered the first Chicano novel in English, is published.

1960   Bilingual education originates in Dade County, Florida.

1961 U.S. troops invade Cuba in the Bay of Pigs incident. Jesús Colón's *A Puerto Rican in New York and Other Sketches* and Oscar Lewis's anthropological narrative *The Children of Sanchez* are published. Robert Wise's film *West Side Story,* with music by Leonard Bernstein, is released. SIN, the first Spanish-language television network in the United States, is created.

1962 René Marqués's essay "The Docile Puerto Rican" is published. The Cuban missile crisis occurs.

1963 John Rechy's *City of Night,* about gay life, is published.

1964 *El Malcriado,* a newspaper of the National Farm Worker's Association, begins publication.

1965 *El Teatro Campesino* is founded by Luis Valdez in California. Peter Matthiessen's novel *At Play in the Fields of the Lord* is published.

1966 Oscar Lewis's *La Vida,* an ethnological study of Puerto Ricans in New York, is published. César Chávez and Dolores Huerta lead farm workers in a march from Delano to Sacramento, California.

1967 Numerous Latin American fiction writers—including Julio Cortázar, José Donoso, Carlos Fuentes, and Mario Vargas Llosa—capture world attention. Gabriel García Márquez's novel *One Hundred Years of Solitude*; Piri Thomas's *Down These Mean Streets*; and Rodolfo "Corky" Gonzáles's poem "Yo Soy Joaquín," inspired by the life of Joaquín Murrieta, are published. The magazine *El Grito: Journal of Contemporary Mexican American Thought* begins publication. Quinto Sol, an independent Chicano press, is created.

1968 José Iglesias's *An Ordinary Life*; Singer Joan Baez's memoir *Daybreak*; and Carlos Castaneda's anthropological study *The Teachings of Don Juan,* which inaugurates a long list of sequels, are published. Chicano murals inspired by Rivera, Orozco, and Siqueiros, as well as by the Cuban Revolution, are painted in Los Angeles, Houston, El Paso, Denver, and other major cities.

1969 Raymond Barrio's rural novel *The Plum Plum Pickers*; *Espejo,* edited by Octavio I. Romano-V, one of the first anthologies of Chicano literature; and Victor Hernández Cruz's collection of poems *Snaps* are published. *El plan espiritual de Aztlán* [*Aztlán's Spiritual Plan*] is produced by Rodolfo "Corky" Gonzáles and the National Chicano

Youth Liberation Conference. Luis Valdez's film *Yo Soy Joaquín/I Am Joaquin,* based on Rodolfo "Corky" Gonzáles's text, is shown.

1970   Richard Vásquez's novel *Chicano* and Luis Omar Salinas's book of poetry *Crazy Gypsy* are published. Rubén Salazar, a *Los Angeles Times* reporter, is killed by the police and immediately becomes a mythical figure. *Aztlán: Chicano Journal of the Social Sciences and Arts* is founded. A leader of the Young Lords, an organization of young Puerto Rican activists (they call themselves "revolutionary nationalists"), is arrested for robbery, assault, and possession of a dangerous weapon. The arrest leads to rioting in East Harlem.

1971   Tomás Rivera's *. . . y no se lo tragó la tierra* [*And the Earth Did Not Part*], which becomes the most influential work of fiction by a Chicano; Sabine R. Ulibarrí's *Tierra Amarilla: Stories of New Mexico*; Ernesto Galarza's ethnographic autobiography *Barrio Boy*; and Alurista's poetry *Floricanto de Aztlán* are published. David Garcia's documentary *Requiem 29* is shown.

1972   Oscar "Zeta" Acosta's autobiographical narrative, *The Autobiography of a Brown Buffalo,* based on his relationship with Hunter S. Thompson; Rudolfo A. Anaya's prize-winning novel *Bless Me, Ultima,* about a *curandera* in New Mexico; actor Anthony Quinn's autobiography, *The Original Sin: A Self-Portrait*; and Rodolfo Acuña's history *Occupied America: The Chicano's Struggle Toward Liberation* are published. Jesús Salvador Treviño's film *Yo Soy Chicano* [*I Am Chicano*] is issued.

1973   Oscar "Zeta" Acosta's *The Revolt of the Cockroach People,* a sequel to *The Autobiography of a Brown Buffalo*; Rolando Hinojosa-Smith's *Sketches of the Valley and Other Works*; Thomas Sanchez's *Rabbit Boss*; Nicholasa Mohr's *Nilda*; Pedro Pietri's *Puerto Rican Obituary*; and Victor Hernández Cruz's poems *Tropicalization* are published. The *Revista Chicano-Riqueña,* precursor of *The Americas Review,* is created. Bilingual Press starts publication. Pepito Romay's Mexican film *De sangre chicana* [*Of Chicano Blood*] is shown.

1974   Tony Castro's *Chicano Power*; James Baldwin's *If Beale Street Could Talk*; John Nichols's *The Milagro Beanfield War,* first installment of his Nirvana trilogy; and Miguel Méndez's polyphonic novel *Peregrinos de Aztlán* [*Pilgrims in Aztlán*] are published. Miguel Piñero's play *Short Eyes* is produced.

1975 Ron Arias's magic-realist novel *The Road to Tamazunchale*;
Nicholasa Mohr's memoir *El Bronx Remembered*; Edwin Torres's
Carlito's Way; Angela de Hoyos's poetry *Arise Chicanos and Other
Poems*; and Miguel Algarín and Miguel Piñero's *Nuyorican Poetry:
An Anthology of Puerto Rican Words and Feelings* are published.

1976 Aristeo Brito's *El diablo en Texas* [*The Devil in Texas*], influenced by
William Faulkner and Juan Rulfo; Luis Rafael Sánchez's *La
guaracha del Macho Camacho* [*Macho Camacho's Beat*]; and Isaac
Goldemberg's *La vida a plazos de Don Jacobo Lerner* [*The
Fragmented Life of Don Jacobo Lerner*] are published. Les Blank's
film *Chulas Fronteras* is issued.

1977 Juan Gómez-Quiñones's influential essay "On Culture" and
Nash Candelaria's *Memories of the Alhambra* are published.
Jesús Salvador Treviño's film *Raíces de sangre* [*Blood Roots*] is
issued.

1978 Miguel Algarín's *Mongo Affair* is published. Alfonso Arau's film
The Promised Dream is shown.

1979 Amado Muro's (aka Chester L. Seltzer) *The Collected Stories of
Amado Muro* is published. Sylvia Morales's film *Chicana*, Robert
Young's film *Alambrista: The Illegal*, and Alfonso Arau's film
Mojado Power are released.

1980 The Mariel boat lift brings thousands of refugees from Cuba to
Florida, including writer Reinaldo Arenas, author of the novel *The
Palace of White Skunks* and the memoir *Before Night Falls,* who,
after suffering from AIDS, would commit suicide in Manhattan in
1990. Arte Público Press begins publication.

1981 Cherríe Moraga and Gloria Anzaldúa's *This Bridge Called My Back:
Writings by Radical Women of Color* and Lorna Dee Cervantes's
poetry *Emplumada* are published. CALIFAS, a conference on
Chicano art, is held at the University of California at Santa Cruz.
Luis Valdez's film *Zoot Suit* is released.

1982 Richard Rodríguez's *Hunger of Memory: The Education of Richard
Rodriguez,* Edward Rivera's fictional autobiography *Family
Installments,* Ariel Dorfman's *The Last Song of Manuel Sendero,* and
Eugene Mohr's *The Nuyorican Experience: Literature of the Puerto
Rican Minority* are published.

1983   Cherríe Moraga's *Loving in the War Years: Lo que nunca pasó por sus labios*; Danny Santiago's (aka Daniel L. James) novel *Famous All Over Town*; and Dell Shannon's (aka Elizabeth Linington) *Exploit of Death*, inaugurating a long list of detective novels with a Chicano detective as protagonist; and Ricardo Pau-Llosa's poetry *Sorting Metaphors* are published. Robert Young's film *The Ballad of Gregorio Cortez*, based on Américo Paredes's ethnological study; Brian DePalma's film *Scarface*, about Cuban exiles; and John Huston's film *Under the Volcano*, based on the novel by Malcolm Lowry, are released.

1984   Sandra Cisneros's novel *The House on Mango Street*; Arturo Islas' novel *The Rain God*; Harriet Doerr's novel *Stones for Ibarra*, about an American couple in a small Mexican village; Tino Villanueva's collection of poetry *Shaking Off the Dark*; Tato Laviera's collection of poems *AmeRícan*; and Paul Horgan's *Great River: The Rio Grande in North American History* are published. Bernardo Vega's memoir about his Puerto Rican activist adulthood, *Memorias de Bernardo Vega* [*Memoirs of Bernardo Vega*], appears in an English translation edited by César Andreu Iglesias. Gregory Nava's film *El Norte*, about Guatemalan wetbacks, is released.

1985   Ed Vega's *The Comeback* is published. Leon Ichazo's film *Crossover Dreams*, with Rubén Blades, is issued.

1986   Ana Castillo's epistolary novel *The Maxquiahuala Letters*, Denise Chávez's collection of stories *The Last of the Menu Girls*, Victor Perera's memoir *Rites: A Guatemalan Boyhood*, and Carlos Fuentes's *The Old Gringo* are published. Hector Babenco's film *Kiss of the Spider Woman*, based on a novel by Manuel Puig, is released. Telemundo is consolidated.

1987   Gloria Anzaldúa's *Borderlands/La Frontera: The New Mestiza*, Judith Ortíz Cofer's *Terms of Survival*, Jimmy Santiago Baca's collection of poems *Martín & Meditations on the South Valley*, and Gustavo Pérez-Firmat's poems *Carolina Cuban* are published. Luis Valdez's film *La Bamba*; Nestor Almendros and Jorge Ulla's documentary *Nobody Listened*, about censorship, homosexuality, and repression in Cuba; Luis Puenzo's film *The Old Gringo*, based on the novel by Carlos Fuentes; and Cheech Marin's film *Born in East L.A.* are released. A major exhibit of Cuban American painters travels from New Jersey to Georgia.

1988   Alejandro Morales's fiction *The Brick People,* Alma Villanueva's novel *The Ultraviolet Sky,* Roberto G. Fernández's polyphonic novel *Raining Backwards,* and Elías Miguel Muñoz's *Crazy Love* are published. Ramon Menendez's film *Stand and Deliver,* about mathematician and educator Jaime Escalante; Lourdes Portillo's documentary *La Ofrenda: The Days of the Dead;* and Robert Redford's film *The Milagro Beanfield War* are issued.

1989   Oscar Hijuelos's novel *The Mambo Kings Play Songs of Love* and Virgil Suarez's *Latin Jazz* are published.

1990   Felipe Alfau's second novel, *Chromos: A Parody,* written in the 1940s; Alberto Alvaro Ríos's poetry *Teodoro Luna's Two Kisses;* Elena Castedo's novel *Paradise;* Oswald Rivera's *Fire and Rain: A Novel of Vietnam;* Pablo Medina's autobiography *Exiled Memories;* John Bruce Novoa's collection of essays *Retrospace;* and Martín Espada's poetry *Rebellion is the Circle of a Lover's Hands/Rebelión es el giro de manos del amante* are published. Beverly Sánchez Padilla's video *The Corrido of Juan Chacón* is issued.

1991   Julia Alvarez's novel *How the García Girls Lost Their Accents,* Sandra Cisneros's *Woman Hollering Creek and Other Stories,* Victor Villaseñor's epic narrative *Rain of Gold,* and Yvonne V. Sapia's novel *Valentino's Hair* are published.

1992   Celebrations of the Quincentennial create an international controversy, as the so-called heroism of Columbus is called into question. Intellectuals and artists join forces to try to stop the festivities in Mexico, Latin America, and the United States. They call 1492 the year of an "encounter," not a "discovery." Cristina Garcia's novel *Dreaming in Cuban;* Alfau's poetry *Sentimental Songs;* Michael Nava's *The Hidden Law;* Floyd Salas's autobiographical fiction *Buffalo Nickel;* Jaime Manrique's *Latin Moon in Manhattan,* about gays in New York; Francisco Goldman's *The Long Night of White Chickens;* and Carlos Fuentes's *The Buried Mirror,* essays on Spain and the Americas, are published. Sydney Pollack's film *Havana* is released.

1993   Abraham Rodríguez, Jr.'s, novel *Spidertown*; Harold Augenbraum and Ilan Stavans's anthology *Growing Up Latino,* which traces the development of Latino fiction in English; Luis Rodríguez's autobiography *Always Running: La Vida Loca: Gang Days in LA*; and Juan Flores's *Divided Borders: Essays on Puerto Rican Identity* are published. Mario Moreno (aka Cantinflas) dies in Mexico. The English translation of Reinaldo Arenas's *Before Night Falls,* about underground gay life in Fidel Castro's Cuba and in Miami after the Mariel boatlift, is published.

◆ ◆ ◆

Selected Sources

A book such as this, attempting to analyze my entire culture, is obviously the result of many years of reading. It is impossible to give an inclusive list of all the volumes and works of art that have contributed to its pages. Take Jewish and Latin American literature as two examples: Kafka, Maimonides, Walter Benjamin, Gershom Scholem, Borges, Octavio Paz, Gabriel García Márquez, and Mario Vargas Llosa alone have provided a huge shelf that has occupied many of my days and nights and will surely continue to do so. Without them, my understanding of Hispanic civilization in general, and of Latinos in the United States in particular, would be essentially different—or would simply not exist. What I then offer, for the purpose of bibliographical reference, is a selected list of those books and films I frequently consulted, was inspired by, or thought about while writing *The Hispanic Condition*. They are crucial to the development of what I have called "the newest Hispanic diaspora as a community of Latin Americans in a sort of exile." My hope is that they serve as a map of our collective psyche. In a sense, this list is a bibliography of myself: who I am, where I came from, and what I've become.

Filmography

Almodóvar, Pedro. *Matador* (1978).
Almendros, Nestor, and Jorge Ulla. *Nobody Listened* (1987).
————, and Orlando Jiménez-Leal. *Improper Conduct* (1983).
Arau, Alfonso. *The Promised Dream* (Mexico, 1978).

————. *Mojado Power* (Mexico, 1979).

Babenco, Hector. *Kiss of the Spider Woman* (1986).

Barreto, Bruno. *Doña Flor and Her Two Husbands* (Brazil, 1977).

Biberman, Herbert. *The Salt of the Earth* (1953).

Blank, Les. *Chulas Fronteras* (1976).

Camus, Marcel. *Black Orpheus* (Brazil, 1958).

Costa-Gavras, Constantin. *Missing* (1983).

De Palma, Brian. *Scarface* (1983).

————. *Carlito's Way* (1993).

Dulgan, John. *Romero* (1989).

Franqui, Carlos, and Valerio Rivas. *The Other Cuba* (Italy, video, 1983).

Galindo, Alejandro. *Campeón sin corona* (Mexico, 1945).

————. *Espaldas mojadas* (Mexico, 1953).

Glimcher, Arne. *The Mambo Kings* (1992).

Gomez, Don. *The Situation* (United States/El Salvador, 1986).

Gutiérrez Alea, Tomás. *Death of a Bureaucrat* (Cuba, 1966).

————. *Memories of Underdevelopment* (Cuba, 1968).

————. *La ultima cena* (Cuba, 1976).

Huston, John. *Juarez* (1939).

————. *The Treasure of the Sierra Madre* (1948).

————. *Under the Volcano* (1983).

Ichazo, León. *Crossover Dreams* (1985).

————, and Orlando Jiménez-Leal. *El Super* (1979).

Leduc, Paul. *Frida* (Mexico, 1984).

Lester, Richard. *Cuba* (1979).

Lillenthal, Peter. *The Uprising* (Germany/Nicaragua, 1981).

Littín, Miguel. *Alcino and the Condor* (1983).

Martin, Cheech. *Born in East L.A.* (1987).

Menendez, Ramon. *Stand and Deliver* (1988).

Morales, Sylvia. *Chicana* (1979).

Nava, Gregory. *El Norte* (1984).

Olmos, Edward James. *American Me* (1992).

Palcy, Euzhan. *Sugar Cane Alley* (France, 1984).

Pollack, Sydney. *Havana* (1990).

Portillo, Lourdes. *La Ofrenda: The Days of the Dead* (1988).

Puenzo, Luis. *The Old Gringo* (1987).

Redford, Robert. *The Milagro Beanfield War* (1988).

Romay, Pepito. *De sangre chicana* (Mexico, 1973).

Sánchez Padilla, Beverly. *The Corrido of Juan Chacón* (video, 1990).

Shaffer, Deborah. *Dance of Hope* (1989).

Shlame, Tom. *Mambo Mouth* (1991).

Stone, Oliver. *Salvador* (1985).

————. *JFK* (1991).

Treviño, Jesús Salvador. *Requiem 29* (1971).

————. *Yo Soy Chicano* (1972).

————. *Raíces de sangre* (1977).

Valdez, Luis. *Yo Soy Joaquín* (1969).

———. *Zoot Suit* (1981).
———. *La Bamba* (1987).
Wexler, Haskell. *Latino* (1985).
Wise, Robert. *West Side Story* (1961).
Young, Robert. *Alambrista: The Illegal* (1979).
———. *The Ballad of Gregorio Cortez* (1983).

Bibliography

Acosta, Oscar "Zeta." *The Autobiography of a Brown Buffalo.* San Francisco: Straight Arrow Books, 1972.
———. *The Revolt of the Cockroach People.* San Francisco: Straight Arrow Books, 1973.
Acosta-Belen, Edna. *The Puerto Rican Woman.* New York: Praeger, 1979.
Acuña, Rudolfo. *A Mexican American Chronicle.* New York: American Book Co., 1971.
———. *Occupied America: The Chicano's Struggle Toward Liberation.* San Francisco: Harper & Row, 1972.
———. *Occupied America: A History of Chicanos.* Rev. ed. New York: Harper & Row, 1981.
Aguilar, John, with Shifra Goldman and Tomás Ybarra-Frausto. *Chicano Aesthetics: Rasquachismo.* Phoenix: MARS, 1989.
Alfau, Felipe. *Locos: A Comedy of Gestures.* Naperville, Ill.: Dalkey Archive, 1988.
———. *Chromos: A Parody.* Naperville, Ill.: Dalkey Archive Press, 1990.
———. *Sentimental Songs/La poesía cursi.* Trans. with an Introduction by Ilan Stavans. Naperville, Ill.: Dalkey Archive Press, 1992.
Algarín, Miguel. *Mongo Affair.* New York: Nuyorican Press Book, 1978.
———. *On Call.* Houston: Arte Público Press, 1980.
Algarín, Miguel, with Miguel Piñero. *Nuyorican Poetry: An Anthology of Puerto Rican Words and Feelings.* New York: William Morrow, 1975.
Alurista (aka Alberto Baltazar Urista). *Floricanto de Aztlán.* Los Angeles: University of California Chicano Studies Center, 1971.
Alvarez, Julia. *How the García Girls Lost Their Accents.* Chapel Hill, N.C.: Algonquin Books of Chapel Hill, 1991.
Anaya, Rudolfo A. *Bless Me, Ultima.* Berkeley: Tonatiuh/Quinto Sol International, 1972.
———. *Heart of Aztlán.* Berkeley: Editorial Justa Publications, 1976.
———. *Tortuga.* Berkeley: Editorial Justa Publications, 1979.
———. *Alburquerque.* Albuquerque: University of New Mexico Press, 1992.
Andrews, Bart. *Lucy & Ricky & Fred & Ethel: The Story of "I Love Lucy."* New York: Dutton, 1976.
Anzaldúa, Gloria, ed. *Borderlands/La Frontera: The New Mestiza.* San Francisco: Spinsters/Aunt Lute Foundation, 1987.
———. *Making Faces, Making Soul/Haciendo Caras: Creative and Critical Perspectives by Women of Color.* San Francisco: Aunt Lute Foundation, 1990.

Arenas, Reinaldo. *Hallucinations*, trans. Gordon Brotherston. New York: Harper & Row, 1971; retrans. as *The Ill-Fated Peregrinations of Fray Servando*. New York: Anchor, 1973.

———. *Farewell to the Sea*. Trans. by Andrew Hurley. New York: Viking Press, 1974.

———. *Before Night Falls*. Trans. by Dolores M. Koch. New York: Viking Press, 1993.

Arias, Ron. *The Road to Tamazunchale*. New York: Anchor Books, 1992.

Arnaz, Desi. *A Book*. New York: William Morrow, 1976.

Arnold, Eliot. *The Time of the Gringo*. New York: Alfred A. Knopf, 1953.

Atherton, Gertrude. *The Californians*. London: J. Lane, 1898.

Augenbraum, Harold, and Ilan Stavans, eds. *Latinos in English. A Bibliography*. Introduction by Ilan Stavans. New York: Mercantile Library Press, 1992.

———. *Growing Up Latino: Memoirs and Stories*. Boston: Houghton Mifflin, 1993.

Baca, Jimmy Santiago. *Martín & Meditations on the South Valley*. New York: New Directions, 1987.

———. *Black Mesa Poems*. New York: New Directions, 1989.

———. *Immigrants in Our Own Land & Early Selected Poems*. New York: New Directions, 1990.

Baldwin, James. *If Beale Street Could Talk*. New York: Dial Press, 1974.

Barrio, Raymond. *The Plum Plum Pickers*. Sunnyvale, Calif.: Ventura Press, 1969.

———. *Mexico's Art and Chicano Artists*. Guerneville, Calif.: Ventura Press, 1984.

Behar, Ruth. *Translating Woman: Crossing the Border with Esperanza's Story*. Boston: Beacon Press, 1993.

Benítez-Rojo, Antonio. *The Repeating Island: The Caribbean and the Postmodern Perspective*. Trans. by James Marannis. Durham, N.C.: Duke University Press, 1992.

Bingham, Hiram. *Across South America*. Boston: Houghton Mifflin, 1911.

———. *Lost City of the Incas*. New York: Duell, Sloan & Pearce, 1948.

Borges, Jorge Luis. "Autobiographical Essay," in *The Aleph and Other Stories*. Trans. by Norman Thomas Di Giovanni. New York: E. P. Dutton, 1974.

———. *Borges: A Reader*. Emir Rodríguez Monegal and Alastair Reid, eds. New York: E. P. Dutton, 1981.

Boscana, Gerónimo. *Chinigchimich: Life in California During a Residence of Several Years in That Territory, Compromising a Description of the Country and the Missionary Establishments*. New York: Da Capo Press, 1969.

Brito, Aristeo. *The Devil in Texas*. Trans. by David William Foster. New York: Anchor Books, 1992. Original: *El diablo en Texas*. Tucson: Editorial Peregrinos, 1976.

Bruce-Novoa, John. *Chicano Authors: Inquiry by Interview*. Austin: University of Texas Press, 1980.

———. *Retrospace: Collected Essays on Chicano Literature*. Houston: Arte Público Press, 1990.

Burgos, Julia de. *Obra poética*. San Juan: Instituto de Cultura Puertorriqueña, 1954.

Cabeza de Vaca, Alvar Núñez. *Adventures in the Unknown Interior of America*. Trans. and ed. by Cyclone Covey. New York: Collier Books, 1961; Albuquerque: University of New Mexico Press, 1983. Also published as *Castaways*, trans. by Frances M. Lopez-Morillas. Edited with an introduction by Enrique Pupo-Walker. Berkeley: University of California Press, 1993.

Cabrera, Lydia. *Cuentos negros de Cuba*. Havana: Imprenta La Verónica, 1940.
———. *Yemayá y Ochún*. Madrid: Ediciones R, 1974.
Cabrera Infante, Guillermo. *Holy Smoke*. New York: Harper & Row, 1985.
———. *Mea Cuba*. Barcelona: Plaza & Janés-Cambio 16, 1992.
Calderón, Héctor, with José David Saldívar, eds. *Chicano Criticism in a Social Context*. Durham, N.C.: Duke University Press, 1989.
———. *Criticism in the Borderlands: Studies in Chicano Literature, Culture, and Ideology*. Durham, N.C.: Duke University Press, 1991.
Camarillo, Albert. *Chicanos in a Changing Society*. Cambridge, Mass.: Harvard University Press, 1979.
Canclini, Néstor García. *Transforming Modernity: Popular Culture in Mexico*. Trans. by Lidia Lozano. Austin: University of Texas Press, 1993.
Cardinal, Roger. "El mensaje de Martín Ramírez," *Vuelta* 112 (March 1986):56–58.
Carpentier, Alejo. *The Kingdom of This World*. Trans. by Harriet de Onis. New York: A. A. Knopf, 1957. Original: *El reino de este mundo,* 1949.
Carrero, Jaime. *Jet neorriqueño/Neo-Rican Jetliner Poems*. San Germain: Inter-American University, 1964.
———. *El hombre que no sudaba*. Houston: Arte Público Press, 1982.
Castaneda, Carlos. *The Teachings of Don Juan*. Berkeley: University of California Press, 1968.
———. *A Separate Reality: Further Conversations with Don Juan*. New York: Simon & Schuster, 1971.
———. *Journey to Ixtlán: The Lessons of Don Juan*. New York: Simon & Schuster, 1972.
———. *Tales of Power*. New York: Simon & Schuster, 1974.
———. *The Second Ring of Power*. New York: Simon & Schuster, 1977.
———. *The Eagle's Gift*. New York: Simon & Schuster, 1981.
———. *The Fire from Within*. New York: Simon & Schuster, 1984.
———. *The Power of Silence*. New York: Simon & Schuster, 1987.
Castañeda, Jorge G. *Utopia Unarmed: The Latin American Left After the Cold War*. New York: Alfred A. Knopf, 1993.
Castedo, Elena. *Paradise*. New York: Grove Weidenfeld, 1990.
Castillo, Ana. *The Mixquiahuala Letters*. Binghamton, N.Y.: Bilingual Review Press, 1986.
———. *Sapaogonia: An Anti-Romance in 3/8 Meter*. Tempe, Ariz.: Bilingual Review Press, 1989.
———. *So Far From God*. New York: W. W. Norton, 1993.
Castro, Tony. *Chicano Power*. New York: E. P. Dutton, 1974.
Cather, Willa. *The Song of the Lark*. Boston: Houghton Mifflin, 1915.
———. *The Professor's House*. New York: Alfred A. Knopf, 1925.
———. *Death Comes for the Archbishop*. New York: Alfred A. Knopf, 1927.
Chacón, Eusebio. *El hijo de la tempestad: Tras la tormenta la calma: Dos novelistas originales*. Santa Fe, N.M.: Tipografía de El Boletín Popular, 1892.
Chavez, Linda. *Out of the Barrio: Toward a New Politics of Hispanic Assimilation*. New York: Basic Books, 1991.
Cisneros, Sandra. *The House on Mango Street*. Houston: Arte Público Press, 1984.
———. *Woman Hollering Creek and Other Stories*. New York: Random House, 1991.
———. *Loose Woman*. New York: Alfred A. Knopf, 1994.

Colón, Jesús. *A Puerto Rican in New York and Other Sketches*. New York: International Publishers, 1982.

———. *The Way It Was and Other Writings*. Edna Acosta-Belén and Virginia Sánchez Korrol, eds. Houston: Arte Público Press, 1993.

Conrad, Joseph. *Nostromo: Tale of the Seaboard*. Garden City, N.Y.: Doubleday, 1919.

———. *A Set of Six*. Garden City, N.Y.: Doubleday, 1924.

Corpi, Lucha. *Eulogy for a Brown Angel*. Houston: Arte Público Press, 1992.

Cortázar, Julio, "Axolotl," in *End of the Game and Other Stories*. Trans. by Paul Blackburn. New York: Pantheon, 1963.

Crawford, James. *Hold Your Tongue: Bilingualism and the Politics of "English Only."* Reading, Mass.: Addison-Wesley, 1992.

Da Cunha, Euclides. *Rebellion in the Backlands*. Trans. by Samuel Putnam. Chicago: University of Chicago Press, 1944.

Day, Douglas. *The Prison Notebooks of Ricardo Flores Magón*. San Diego: Harcourt Brace Jovanovich, 1991.

Dealy, Glen Caudill. *The Latin Americans: Spirit & Ethos*. Boulder, Colo.: Westview Press, 1992.

Dee Cervantes, Lorna. *Emplumada*. Pittsburgh, Penn.: University of Pittsburgh Press, 1981.

Delgado, Abelardo. *Chicano: 25 Pieces of a Chicano Mind*. Denver, Colo.: Barrio Publications, 1969.

Didion, Joan. *Salvador*. New York: Simon & Schuster, 1983.

———. *Miami*. New York: Simon & Schuster, 1987.

Doerr, Harriet. *Stones for Ibarra*. New York: Viking Press, 1984.

———. *Consider This, Señora*. San Diego: Harcourt Brace, 1993.

Doob, Penelope Reed. *The Idea of the Labyrinth*. Ithaca, N.Y.: Cornell University Press, 1990.

Dorfman, Ariel. *Death & the Maiden*. New York: Penguin, 1991.

Dos Passos, John. *The 42nd Parallel*. New York: Harper, 1930.

———. *The Big Money*. New York: New American Library, 1979.

Du Bois, W. E. B. *The Souls of Black Folk*. Introduction by Henry Louis Gates, Jr. New York: Bantam Books, 1989.

Espada, Martín. *Rebellion Is the Circle of a Lover's Hands/Rebelión es el giro de manos del amante*. Willimantic, Conn.: Curbstone Press, 1990.

———. *City of Coughing and Dead Radiators*. New York: W. W. Norton, 1993.

Ferber, Edna. *Giant*. New York: Grosset, 1952.

Fernández, Roberto. *Raining Backwards*. Houston: Arte Público Press, 1988.

Fernández Retamar, Roberto. "Caliban: Notes Toward a Discussion of Culture in Our America," *Massachusetts Review* 15, nos. 1–2 (Winter–Spring 1974):7–72.

Ferré, Rosario. *Fabulas de la garza Lesangrada*. Mexico City: Joaquín Mortiz, 1982.

Figueroa, José Angel. *East 110th Street*. Detroit: Broadside Press, 1973.

Fitz, Earl E. *Rediscovering the New World: Inter-American Literature in a Comparative Context*. Iowa City: University of Iowa Press, 1991.

Flores, Juan. *Divided Borders: Essays on Puerto Rican Identity*. Houston: Arte Público Press, 1991.

Frank, Waldo. *America Hispana: Portrait & Prospect*. New York: Charles Scribner's Sons, 1931.

Fuentes, Carlos. *Old Gringo*. Trans. by Margaret Sayers Peden with the author. New York: Farrar, Straus & Giroux, 1985.

———. *Myself with Others*. New York: Farrar, Straus & Giroux, 1988.

———. *The Buried Mirror: Reflections on Spain and the New World*. Boston: Houghton Mifflin, 1992.

Fuentes-Pérez, Ileana, with Graciella Cruz-Taura and Ricardo Pau-Llosa. *Outside Cuba: Contemporary Cuban Artists*. New Brunswick, N.J. and Miami, Fla.: Rutgers University Press–University of Miami Press, 1989.

Galarza, Ernesto. *Merchants of Labor: The Mexican Bracero Story*. Santa Barbara: McNally & Loftin, 1964.

———. *Barrio Boy: The Story of a Boy's Acculturation*. Notre Dame, Ind.: University of Notre Dame Press, 1971.

Gann, L. H., with Peter J. Duigan. *The Hispanics in the United States: A History*. Boulder, Colo.: Westview Press, 1986.

Garcia, Cristina. *Dreaming in Cuban*. New York: Alfred A. Knopf, 1992.

Garcia, Guy. *Skin Deep*. New York: Farrar, Straus & Giroux, 1988.

Garcia, Mario. *Mexican Americans*. New Haven, Conn.: Yale University Press, 1989.

García Lorca, Federico. *Poet in New York*. New York: Grove Press, 1983.

García Márquez, Gabriel. *One Hundred Years of Solitude*. Trans. by Gregory Rabassa. New York: Harper & Row, 1970.

———. *The General in His Labyrinth*. Trans. by Edith Grossman. New York: Alfred A. Knopf, 1989.

Garza, Rodolfo O. de la, et al. *The Mexican American Experience*. Austin: University of Texas Press, 1985.

Goldemberg, Isaac. *La vida a plazos de Don Jacobo Lerner*. Hanover, N.H.: Ediciones del Norte, 1974.

———. *The Fragmented Life of Don Jacobo Lerner*. Trans. by Roberto Piccioto. New York: Persea, 1976.

Gómez-Peña, Guillermo. "Documented/Undocumented," *Graywolf Annual Five: Multi-Cultural Literacy,* edited by Rick Simonson and Scott Walker. St. Paul, Minn: Graywolf Press, 1988.

Gómez-Quiñones, Juan. *Las ideas políticas de Ricardo Flores Magón*. Trans. by Roberto Gómez Ciriza. Mexico City: Era, 1977.

———. "On Culture," *Revista Chicano-Riqueña* 5, no. 2 (1977):29–42; reprinted by Los Angeles: UCLA-Chicano Studies Center, 1977; reprinted in *Modern Chicano Writers: A Collection of Critical Essays,* Joseph Sommers with Tomás Ybarra-Frausto, eds. Englewood Cliffs, N.J.: Prentice Hall, 1979.

———. *Mexican Students of La Raza: The Chicano Student Movement in Southern California, 1967–1977*. Santa Barbara: Editorial La Causa, 1978.

———. *Chicano Politics: Reality & Promise, 1940–1990*. Albuquerque: University of New Mexico Press, 1990.

Gonzáles, Rudolfo. *I Am Joaquín/Yo Soy Joaquín: An Epic Poem*. New York: Bantam Books, 1972.

González, José Luis. *En Nueva York y otras desgracias*. Río Piedras, P.R.: Ediciones Huracán, 1981.

———. *Puerto Rico: The Four-Storeyed Country*. Trans. by Gerald Guinness. New York: Markus Wiener Publishing, 1993.

Gonzalez-Wippler, Migene. *Santería*. New York: Crown, 1973.

Greene, Graham. *Our Man in Havana*. New York: Viking Press, 1958.

———. *The Lawless Roads*. New York: Viking Press, 1982.

———. *The Power and the Glory*. New York: Viking Press, 1982.

———. *Getting to Know the General*. New York: Simon & Schuster, 1984.

Griswold del Castillo, Richard, with Teresa McKenna and Yvonne Yarbro-Bejarano. *Chicano Art: Resistance and Affirmation, 1965–1985*. Los Angeles: Wright Art Gallery and University of California–Los Angeles, 1991.

Helú, Antonio. *Los mexicanos se van*. Mexico City: Editorial Nacional, S.A., 1947.

Hemingway, Ernest. *The Old Man and the Sea*. New York: Charles Scribner's Sons, 1952.

Henríquez Ureña, Pedro. *A Concise History of Latin American Culture*. Trans. by Gilbert Chase. New York: Praeger, 1966.

———. *Ensayos en busca de nuestra expresión*. Buenos Aires: Editorial Raigal, 1952.

———. *Literary Currents in Hispanic America*. Cambridge, Mass.: Harvard University Press, 1945.

Herrera, Hayden. *Frida: A Biography of Frida Kahlo*. New York: Harper & Row, 1983.

———. *Frida Kahlo: The Paintings*. New York: HarperCollins, 1991.

Hijuelos, Oscar. *Our House in the Last World*. New York: Persea, 1983.

———. *The Mambo Kings Play Songs of Love*. New York: Farrar, Straus & Giroux, 1989.

———. *The Fourteen Sisters of Emilio Montez O'Brien*. New York: Farrar, Straus & Giroux, 1993.

Hinojosa, Rolando. *Sketches of the Valley and Other Works*. Berkeley: Quinto Sol International, 1973.

——— *Klail City*. Houston: Arte Público Press, 1987.

Horgan, Paul. *Great River: The Rio Grande in North American History*. Middletown, Conn.: Wesleyan University Press, 1984.

Hospital, Carolina, ed. *Los Atrevidos: Cuban American Writers*. Princeton, N.J.: Linden Lane Press, 1988.

Hostos, Eugenio María de. *La peregrinación de Bayoán*. Río Piedras, P.R.: Editorial Edil, 1970.

Hudson, W. H. *Idle Days in Patagonia*. New York: E. P. Dutton, 1923.

Huerta, Alberto. "Joaquin Murieta: California's Literary Archetype," *Californians* 5, no. 6 (November–December, 1987):46–50.

———. "Daniel Lewis James (1911–1988): Socrates and Santiago in California," *Californians* 6, no. 6 (November–December 1988):48–53.

Hughes, Robert. *Culture of Complaint: The Frying of America*. New York: Oxford University Press/New York Public Library, 1993.

Humboldt, Alexander von. *Political Essays on the Kingdom of New Spain*. Introduction by Mary Maples Dunn. New York: Alfred A. Knopf, 1972.

Hurlburt, Laurence P. *The Mexican Muralists in the United States*. Albuquerque: University of New Mexico Press, 1989.

Huxley, Aldous. *Beyond the Mexique Bay*. New York: Harper & Row, 1934.

Isherwood, Christopher. *The Condor and the Cows*. New York: Random House, 1954.

Islas, Arturo. *The Rain God: A Desert Tale*. Stanford: Alexandrian Press, 1984.

———. *Migrant Souls*. New York: William Morrow, 1990.

Jackson, Helen Hunt. *Ramona*. Boston: Roberts Bros., 1884.

Kanellos, Nicolás. *Understanding the Chicano Experience Through Literature*. Houston: University of Texas Press, 1981.

Kazin, Alfred. "In Puerto Rico," *Commentary* (February 1960), pp. 108–14.

Kellman, Steven G. "Translingualism and the Literary Imagination," *Criticism* 33, no. 4 (Fall 1991):527–41.

Kipling, Rudyard. *Brazilian Sketches*. New York: Doubleday, 1927.

Laviera, Tato. *AmeRícan*. Houston: Arte Público Press, 1985.

———. *Enclave*. Houston: Arte Público Press, 1985.

———. *Mainstream Ethics*. Houston: Arte Público Press, 1988.

Lawrence, D. H. *Mornings in Mexico*. New York: Alfred A. Knopf, 1927.

Leaf, Munro. *The Story of Ferdinand*. Drawings by Robert Lawson. New York: Viking Press, 1936.

Leonard, Irving A. *Colonial Travelers in Latin America*. New York: Alfred A. Knopf, 1972.

Lewis, Oscar. *The Children of Sanchez*. New York: Random House, 1961.

———. *La Vida*. New York: Harper & Row, 1966.

Lezama Lima, José. *Paradiso*. Trans. by Gregory Rabassa. New York: Farrar, Straus & Giroux, 1974.

Limón, Graciela. *In Search of Bernabé*. Houston: Arte Público Press, 1993.

Locke, Alain, ed. *The New Negro: Voices of the Harlem Renaissance*. Introduction by Arnold Rampersand. New York: Atheneum, 1992.

Lowry, Malcolm. *Under the Volcano*. New York: New American Library, 1971.

Loza, Steven. *Barrio Rhythm: Mexican American Music in Los Angeles*. Urbana: University of Illinois Press, 1993.

Maciel, David R. *El Norte: The U.S.–Mexican Border in Contemporary Cinema*. San Diego: Institute of Regional Studies of the Californias, San Diego State University, 1990.

MacShane, Frank, ed. *Impressions of Latin America: Five Centuries of Travel and Adventure by English and North American Writers*. New York: William Morrow, 1963.

Manrique, Jaime. *Latin Moon in Manhattan*. New York: Delacorte Press, 1992.

Mariátegui, José Carlos, *Seven Interpretative Essays on Peruvian Reality*. Trans. by Marjorie Urquidi. Austin: University of Texas Press, 1971.

Marqués, René. *The Oxcart*. Trans. by Charles Pildritch. New York: Charles Scribner's Sons, 1969.

———. *Los soles truncos*. Rio Piedras, P.R.: Editorial Cultural, 1970.

———. *The Docile Puerto Rican: Essays*. Trans. by Barbara Bockus Aponte. Philadelphia: Temple University Press, 1976.

Martí, José. *Selected Writings of José Martí*. New York: Noonday Press, 1954.

Martin, Gerald. *Journeys Through the Labyrinth*. London and New York: Verso, 1989.

Martínez, Rubén. *The Other Side: Notes from the New L.A.* (London: Verso, 1992).

Matthiessen, Peter. *The Cloud Forest*. New York: Viking Press, 1961.

———. *At Play in the Fields of the Lord*. New York: Vintage Books, 1967.

———. *Sal Si Puedes: César Chávez and the New American Revolution*. New York: Random House, 1969.

Mazón, Mauricio. *The Zoot-Suit Riots: The Psychology of Symbolic Annihilation*. Austin: University of Texas Press, 1984.

McWilliams, Carey. *North from Mexico: The Spanish-Speaking People of the United States.* Rev. ed. New York: Greenwood Press, 1968.

Medina, Pablo. *Exiled Memories: A Cuban Childhood.* Austin: University of Texas Press, 1990.

Meier, Matt S., with Feliciano Rivera. *The Chicanos: A History of Mexican Americans.* New York: Hill, 1972.

Meléndez, Edwin, with Edgardo Meléndez, eds. *Colonial Dilemma: Critical Perspectives on Contemporary Puerto Rico.* Boston: South End Press, 1993.

Méndez, Miguel. *Pilgrims of Aztlán.* Trans. by David William Foster. Tempe, Ariz.: Bilingual Review Press, 1992.

Mohr, Eugene. *The Nuyorican Experience: Literature of the Puerto Rican Minority.* Westport, Conn.: Greenwood Press, 1982.

Mohr, Nicholasa. *Nilda.* New York: Harper & Row, 1973.

———. *The Bronx Remembered: A Novella and Stories.* New York: Harper & Row, 1975.

———. *Rituals of Survival: A Woman's Portfolio.* Houston: Arte Público Press, 1985.

Montaigne, Michael Eyquem. "On Cannibals," *Complete Essays.* Trans by Donald M. Frame. Stanford: Stanford University Press, 1958.

Moore, Joan V.., with Harry Pachon. *Hispanics in the United States.* Englewood Cliffs, N.J.: Prentice Hall, 1985.

Moraga, Cherríe. *The Last Generation.* Boston: South End Press, 1993.

Moraga, Cherríe, with Gloria Anzaldúa, eds. *This Bridge Called My Back: Writings by Radical Women of Color.* Watertown, Mass.: Persephone, 1981.

Morales, Alejandro. *The Brick People.* Houston: Arte Público Press, 1988.

Morgan, Thomas B. "The Latinization of America," *Esquire* (May 1983), pp. 47–56.

Morton, Carlos. *The Many Deaths of Danny Rosales.* Houston: Arte Público Press, 1983.

Muñoz, Jr., Carlos. *Youth, Identity, Power: The Chicano Movement.* London and New York: Verso, 1989.

Muñoz, Elias Miguel. *Crazy Love.* Houston: Arte Público Press, 1988.

———. *The Greatest Performance.* Houston: Arte Público Press, 1991.

Nava, Julian. *Mexican-Americans: Past, Present, and Future.* Millbrae, Calif.: American Book Co., 1969.

Navarrette, Jr., Ruben. *A Darker Shade of Crimson: Odyssey of a Harvard Chicano.* New York: Bantam Books, 1993.

Neruda, Pablo. "Fulgor y muerte de Joaquín Murieta," *Obras Completas* 3. Buenos Aires: Aguilar, 1973.

Nichols, John. *The Milagro Beanfield War.* New York: Holt, Rinehart & Winston, 1974.

———. *The Magic Journey.* New York: Holt, Rinehart & Winston, 1978.

———. *The Nirvana Blues.* New York: Holt, Rinehart & Winston, 1981.

Niggli, Josephina. *Mexican Folk Plays.* Chapel Hill, N.C.: University of North Carolina Press, 1938.

———. *Soldadera.* New York: Dodd, 1938.

———. *This Is Villa.* New York: Dodd, 1939.

———. *Step Down, Elder Brother.* New York: Rinehart & Co., 1947.

———. *Mexican Village.* Chapel Hill, N.C.: University of North Carolina Press, 1945. Reprinted with an introduction by María Herrera-Sobek. Albuquerque: University of New Mexico Press, 1994.

Noriega, Chon A. *Chicanos and Film: Essays on Chicano Representation and Resistance.* Minneapolis: University of Minnesota Press, 1992.

O'Gorman, Edmundo. *The Invention of America.* Bloomington, Ind.: Indiana University Press, 1961.

Ortega y Gasset, José. *Revolt of the Masses.* London: Allen & Unwin, 1932.

Ortíz, Fernando. *La reconquista de América. Reflexiones sobre el panhispanismo.* Paris: Paul Ollendorff, 1910.

———. *Cuban Counterpoint: Tobacco and Sugar.* Trans. by Harriet de Onís. New York: Alfred A. Knopf, 1947.

Ortíz Cofer, Judith. *The Line of the Sun.* Athens: University of Georgia Press, 1989.

———. *Silent Dancing: A Partial Remembrance of a Puerto Rican Childhood.* Houston: Arte Público Press, 1990.

———. *The Latin Deli.* Athens: University of Georgia Press, 1993.

Otero, Miguel Antonio. *My Life on the Frontier 1865–1882.* New York: Pioneers, 1935.

———. *My Life on the Frontier 1882–1897.* Albuquerque: University of New Mexico Press, 1939.

———. *My Nine Years as Governor of the Territory of New Mexico 1897–1906.* Albuquerque: University of New Mexico Press, 1940.

Padilla, Heberto. *Self-Portrait of the Other.* Trans. by Alexander Coleman. New York: Farrar, Straus & Giroux, 1988.

Paredes, Américo. *With His Pistol in His Hand: A Border Ballad and Its Hero.* Austin: University of Texas Press, 1958.

———. *Folktales of Mexico.* Chicago: University of Chicago Press, 1970.

———. *A Texas-Mexican "Cancionero": Folksongs of the Lower Border.* Urbana, Ill.: University of Illinois Press, 1976.

———. *George Washington Gómez.* Houston: Arte Público Press, 1990.

Paz, Octavio. *The Labyrinth of Solitude.* Trans. by Lysander Kempt. New York: Grove Press, 1961.

———. "Reflections: Mexico and the United States," *New Yorker* (September 17, 1979), pp. 136–53.

———. "William Carlos Williams: The Saxifrage Flower," *On Poets and Others.* New York: Arcade, 1985.

———. *Convergences: Essays on Art and Literature.* San Diego: Harcourt, Brace, Jovanovich, 1987.

———. "Arte e identidad: Los hispanos en los Estados Unidos," *Convergencias.* Barcelona: Seix Barral, 1991.

———. "Literatura de y en los Estados Unidos," *Al paso.* Barcelona: Seix Barral, 1992.

Perera, Victor. *Rites: A Guatemalan Boyhood.* San Diego: Harcourt Brace Jovanovich, 1986.

Pérez de Villagrá, Gaspar. *History of New Mexico.* Albuquerque: University of New Mexico Press, 1992.

Pérez-Firmat, Gustavo. *The Cuban Condition: Translation and Identity in Modern Cuban Literature.* Cambridge, England: Cambridge University Press, 1989.

———. *Do the Americas Have a Common Literature?* Durham, N.C.: Duke University Press, 1990.

———. *Life on the Hyphen: The Cuban-American Way.* Austin: University of Texas Press, 1994.

Pietri, Pedro. *Puerto Rican Obituary.* New York: Monthly Review Press, 1973.

Piñero, Miguel. *Short Eyes.* New York: Hill & Wang, 1975.

————. *The Sun Always Shines for the Cool/A Midnight Moon at the Greasy Spoon/Eulogy for a Small Time Thief.* Houston: Arte Público Press, 1984.

Porter, Katherine Anne. *Flowering Judas and Other Stories.* New York: Modern Library, 1940.

Prescott, William Hickling. *The Conquest of Mexico.* New York: Henry Holt, 1922.

————. *The Conquest of Peru.* New York: Washington Square Press, 1966.

Puig, Manuel. *Kiss of the Spider Woman.* Trans. by Thomas Colchie. New York: Alfred A. Knopt, 1979.

————. *Eternal Curse on the Reader of These Pages.* New York: Random House, 1982.

Quinn, Anthony. *The Original Sin: Self-Portrait.* Boston: Little, Brown, 1972.

Quirarte, Jacinto. *Mexican American Artists.* Austin: University of Texas Press, 1973.

————. *A History and Appreciation of Chicano Art.* San Antonio: Research Center for the Arts and Humanities, 1984.

Ramos, Samuel. *Profile of Man and Culture in Mexico.* Trans. by Peter Earle. Introduction by Thomas B. Irving. Austin: University of Texas Press, 1962.

Rechy, John. *City of Night.* New York: Grove Press, 1963.

————. *The Fourth Angel.* New York: Viking Press, 1973.

————. *Bodies and Soul.* New York: Carroll & Graf, 1983.

Reed, John. *Insurgent Mexico.* New York: International Publishers, 1969.

Renan, Ernest. *Caliban, Suite de La Tempête: Drame Philosophique.* Paris: 1878.

Reyes, Alfonso. *Ultima Thule,* in *Obras Completas,* vol. 11. Mexico City: Fondo de Cultura Económica, 1982.

Rieff, David. *Going to Miami: Exiles, Tourists, and Refugees in the New America.* Boston: Little, Brown, 1987.

————. *Los Angeles: Capital of the Third World.* New York: Simon & Schuster, 1992.

————. *The Exile: Cuban in the Heart of Miami.* New York: Simon & Schuster, 1993.

Rivera, Edward. *Family Installments: Memories of Growing Up Hispanic.* New York: William Morrow, 1982.

Rivera, Oswald. *Fire and Rain.* New York: Four Walls Eight Windows, 1990.

Rivera, Tomás. . . . *y no se lo tragó la tierra/And the Earth Did Not Part.* Trans. by Evangelina Vigil-Piñón. Houston: Arte Público Press, 1987.

Rodó, José Enrique. *Ariel.* Trans. by Margaret Sayers Peden. Foreword by James W. Symington, Prologue by Carlos Fuentes. Austin: University of Texas Press, 1988.

Rodríguez, Abraham, Jr. *The Boy Without a Flag and Other Stories from the South Bronx.* Minneapolis, Minn.: Milkweed Editions, 1992.

————. *Spidertown.* New York: Hyperion, 1993.

Rodríguez Monegal, Emir, ed. *The Borzoi Anthology of Latin American Literature.* 2 vols. New York: Alfred A. Knopf, 1984.

Rodríguez, Luis J. *Always Running: La Vida Loca: Gang Days in L.A.* Willimantic, Conn.: Curbstone Press, 1993.

Rodríguez, Richard. *Hunger of Memory: The Education of Richard Rodriguez.* Boston: David R. Godine, 1982.

————. *Days of Obligation: An Argument with My Mexican Father.* New York: Viking Press, 1992.

Romano-V., Octavio I, with Herminio Ríos C. *El Espejo/The Mirror.* Berkeley: Quinto Sol Publications, 1969.

Romo, Ricardo. *East Los Angeles: History of a Barrio.* Austin: University of Texas Press, 1983.

Rowe, William, with Vivian Schelling. *Memory and Modernity: Popular Culture in Latin America.* London and New York: Verso, 1991.

Ruíz de Burton, María Amparo. *The Squatter and the Don.* Introduction and edited by Rosaura Sánchez and Beatrice Pita. Houston: Arte Público Press, 1992.

Rulfo, Juan. *El llano en llamas.* Mexico: Fondo de Cultura Económica, 1953; *The Burning Bush.* Trans. by George D. Schade. Austin: University of Texas Press, 1967.

———. *Pedro Páramo.* Mexico: Fondo de Cultura Económica, 1955; *Pedro Páramo,* trans. Lysander Kemp. New York: Grove, 1959.

Said, Edward W. *Orientalism.* New York: Vintage Books, 1978.

———. *Culture and Imperialism.* New York: Alfred A. Knopf, 1992.

Salas, Floyd. *Buffalo Nickel.* Houston: Arte Público Press, 1992.

Salazar, Rubén. "Who Is a Chicano? And What Is It the Chicanos Want?" *Los Angeles Times,* February 4 and 6, 1970.

Saldívar, José David. *The Dialectics of Our America: Genealogy, Cultural Critique, and Literary History.* Durham, N.C.: Duke University Press, 1991.

Sánchez, George J. *Becoming Mexican American. Ethnicity, Culture and Identity in Chicano Los Angeles, 1900–1945.* New York: Oxford University Press, 1993.

Sánchez, Luis Alberto, *¿Existe América Latina?* Mexico City: Editorial Nacional, 1945.

Sánchez, Luis Rafael. *Macho Camacho's Beat.* Trans. by Gregory Rabassa. New York: Pantheon, 1981.

———. *La importancia de llamarse Daniel Santos.* Hanover, N.H.: Ediciones del Norte, 1987.

Sánchez, Thomas. *Rabbit Boss.* New York: Alfred A. Knopf, 1973.

———. *Zoot-Suit Murders.* New York: E. P. Dutton, 1978.

———. *Mile Zero.* New York: Alfred A. Knopf, 1989.

Santiago, Danny [Daniel L. James]. *Famous All Over Town.* New York: Simon & Schuster, 1983.

Sarmiento, Domingo Faustino, Facundo. *Life in the Argentine Republic in the Days of the Tyrants; or, Civilization and Barbarism.* Trans. by Horace Mann. New York: Collier, 1966.

Sayles, John. *Los Gusanos.* New York: HarperCollins, 1991.

Shorris, Earl. *Latinos: A Biography of the People.* New York: W. W. Norton, 1992.

Simmen, Edward. *North of the Rio Grande: The Mexican-American Experience in Short Fiction.* New York: Mentor, 1992.

Sinnette, Elinor DesVerney. *Arthur Alfonso Schomburg: Black Bibliophile & Collector.* New York and Detroit: New York Public Library–Wayne State University Press, 1989.

Skerry, Peter. *Mexican Americans: The Ambivalent Minority.* New York: Free Press, 1993.

Sondheim, Stephen. *West Side Story.* Introduction by Norris Houghton. New York: Dell, 1965.

Soto, Gary. *The Elements of San Joaquín.* Pittsburgh: University of Pittsburgh Press, 1978.

———. *Small Faces.* Houston: Arte Público Press, 1982.

———. *Living up the Street.* San Francisco: Strawberry Hill Press, 1985.

———. *Lesser Evils: Ten Quartets.* Houston: Arte Público Press, 1988.

———. *Baseball in April.* San Diego: Harcourt Brace Jovanovich, 1990.

Soto, Pedro Juan. *Spiks.* Río Piedras, P.R.: Editorial Cultural, 1956.

Steinbeck, John. *The Pastures of Heaven.* New York: Viking Press, 1932.

———. *Tortilla Flat.* New York: Modern Library, 1937.

———. *The Long Valley.* New York: Viking Press, 1938.

———. *The Grapes of Wrath.* New York: Viking Press, 1939.

———. *The Wayward Bus.* New York: Viking Press, 1947.

Steiner, Stan. *La Raza: The Mexican Americans.* New York: Harper & Row, 1969.

Suárez, Mario. "El Hoyo," *Arizona Quarterly* 3 (Summer 1947):112–15.

———. "Kid Zopilote," *Arizona Quarterly* 3 (Summer 1947):130–37.

———. "Señor Garza," *Arizona Quarterly* 3 (Summer 1947):115–21.

———. "Maestría," *Arizona Quarterly* 4 (Winter 1948):368–73.

Suarez, Virgil, with Delia Poey. *Latin Jazz.* New York: William Morrow, 1989.

———. *The Cutter.* New York: Ballantine, 1991.

———. *Iguana Dreams: New Latino Writing.* New York: HarperCollins, 1992.

Takaki, Ronald. *A Different Mirror: A History of Multicultural America.* Boston: Little, Brown, 1993.

Thomas, Piri. *Down These Mean Streets.* New York: Alfred A. Knopf, 1967.

———. *Savior, Savior, Hold My Hand.* New York: Doubleday, 1972.

———. *Seven Long Times.* New York: Praeger, 1974.

———. *Stories from El Barrio.* Houston: Arte Público Press, 1985.

Torres, Robert Herman. "Mutiny in Jalisco," *Esquire* (March 1935), pp. 37ff.

———. "The Brothers Jimenez," *Esquire* (June 1936), pp. 90ff.

Turner, Faythe. *Puerto Ricans at Home in the USA: An Anthology.* Seattle: Open Hand Publishing, 1991.

Ulibarrí, Sabine. *Tierra Amarilla: Stories of New Mexico.* Trans. by Thelma Campbell. Albuquerque: University of New Mexico Press, 1971.

Valdez, Luis. *Actos.* San Juan Bautista, Calif.: El Centro Campesino Cultural, 1971.

———. *The Shrunken Head of Pancho Villa: West Coast Plays* 11–12 (Winter–Spring 1982):1–61.

———. *Zoot Suit and Other Plays.* Houston: Arte Público Press, 1992.

Valdez, Luis, with Stan Steiner. *Aztlán: An Anthology of Mexican American Literature.* New York: Alfred A. Knopf, 1965.

Vargas Llosa, Mario. *Conversation in the Cathedral.* Trans. by Gregory Rabassa. New York: Harper & Row, 1975.

———. "The Miami Model," trans. Mark Falkcoff, *Commentary* (April 1992), pp. 34–41.

———. *The Fish in the Water: A Memoir.* Trans. by Helen Lane. New York: Farrar, Straus & Giroux, 1994.

Vásquez, Richard. *Chicano.* Garden City, N.Y.: Doubleday, 1970.

———. *Another Land.* New York: Avon Books, 1982.

Vega, Bernardo. *Memoirs of Bernardo Vega.* Trans. by Juan Flores, edited by César Andreu Iglesias. New York: Monthly Review Press, 1984; *Memorias de Bernardo Vega.* Río Piedras, P.R.: Ediciones Huracán, 1977.

Vega, Ed. *The Comeback.* Houston: Arte Público Press, 1985.

———. *Mendoza's Dreams.* Houston: Arte Público Press, 1987.

———. *Casualty Report.* Houston: Arte Público Press, 1991.

Venegas, Daniel. *Las aventuras de Don Chipote: o, Cuando los pericos mamen.* Mexico City: Frontera-Secretaría de Educación Pública, 1984.

Villanueva, Tino. *Scene from the Movie "Giant."* Willimantic, Conn.: Curbstone Press, 1993.

———, ed. *Chicanos: Antología histórica y crítica.* Mexico City: Fondo de Cultura Económica, 1980.

Villarreal, José Antonio. *Pocho.* New York: Doubleday, 1959.

———. *The Fifth Horseman: A Novel of the Mexican Revolution.* New York: Doubleday, 1974.

———. *Clemente Chacón.* Binghamton, N.Y.: Bilingual Review Press, 1984.

Villaseñor, Victor. *Macho!* New York: Bantam Books, 1973.

———. *Jury: The People vs. Juan Corona.* Boston: Little, Brown, 1977.

———. *Rain of Gold.* Houston: Arte Público Press, 1991.

Wachtel, Nathan. *The Vision of the Vanquished: The Spanish Conquest of Peru Through Indian Eyes, 1530–1570.* Trans. by Ben and Sian Reynolds. New York: Barnes & Noble, 1977.

Wagenheim, Karl, with Olga Jimenez. *The Puerto Ricans.* New York: Praeger, 1973.

Wakefield, Dan. *Island in the City: The World of Spanish Harlem.* Boston: Houghton Mifflin, 1959.

West, John O. *Mexican-American Folklore.* Little Rock: August House, 1988.

Weyr, Thomas. *Hispanic U.S.A.: Breaking the Melting Pot.* New York: Harper & Row, 1988.

Williams, Eric. *From Columbus to Castro.* London: Deutsch, 1970.

Williams, William Carlos. *In the American Grain.* New York: New Directions, 1956.

———. *The Autobiography of William Carlos Williams.* New York: New Directions, 1967.

Wilson, Edmund. *Red, Black, Blond and Olive.* New York: Oxford University Press, 1936.

Wollen, Peter. *Posada: Messenger of Mortality.* Julian Rothenstein, ed. London: Redstone Press, 1989.

Zeno Gandía, Manuel. *La charca.* San Juan: Instituto de Cultura Puertorriqueña, 1970.

Zimmerman, Marc. *U.S. Latino Literature: An Essay and Annotated Bibliography.* Chicago: Marcha/Abrazo, 1992.

Index

Federación Libre de Trabajadores, 44
Feliciano, José, 25, 85
Félix, María, 150
Ferber, Edna, 76.
Fernández, Emilio "El Indio," 150
Fernández, Enrique, 130
Fernandez, Joseph, 25
Fernández, Roberto G., 184
Fernández de Lizardi, José Joaquín, 151,
    171, 188, 195
Fernández de Oviedo, Gonzalo, 149
Fernández Retamar, Roberto, 148, 156, 181
Ferré, Rosario, 47, 132
Ferrer, Fernando, 25
Fielding, Henry, 170
Fierro de Bright, Josefina, 125–26
Figueroa, José-Angel, 42
Flores, Francisca, 79
Flores, Juan, 41–42, 64
Flores, Pedro, 25
Flores Magón, Enrique, 77–78
Flores Magón, Ricardo, 12, 19, 77–78
Florit, Eugenio, 132
Fondo de Cultura Económica, 188
Foster, David William, 73
Francia, Doctor, 110
Francis Ferdinand, Archduke of Austro-
    Hungarian Empire, 23
Francisco, Don, 165
Franco, Francisco, 175
Frank, Waldo, 149
Franklin, Benjamin, 92, 152
French Caribbeans, 32
    see also Haiti and Haitians
Freud, Sigmund, 155
Frost, Robert, 200
Fuentes, Carlos, 8, 25, 70, 101, 107, 133,
    172

Gaddis, William, 74
Galarza, Ernesto, 160
Galindo, Alejandro, 85, 129
Gandhi, Mohandas K., 79, 81
Gandía, Manuel Zeno, 48
Gann, L. H., 31
Garcia, Andy, 169
García, Antonio, 82
Garcia, Cristina, 55, 93, 189

García Canclini, Néstor, 100
García Lorca, Federico, 177
García Márquez, Gabriel, 15, 72, 93, 102,
    117, 125, 172
Garvey, Marcus, 105
Gass, William H., 21
Gates, Henry Louis, Jr., 183
Gaugin, Paul, 84
Gerchunoff, Alberto, 175–77
Gilbert, Humphrey, 147
Giles, Herbert A., 147
Ginsberg, Allen, 200
Girard, René, 100
Gironella, Alberto, 88
Gold, Michael, 149
Goldemberg, Isaac, 133
Gomez, Magda, 169
Gómez, Sebastián, 105
Gómez de Avellaneda, Gertrudis, 171
Gómez-Peña, Guillermo, 18
Gómez Quiñones, Juan, 11–13, 156–57,
    159, 165
Góngora, Luis de, 14
González, José Luis, 19, 35, 43, 48
González, Rodolfo "Corky," 12, 67–69, 79,
    87, 90
González Prada, Manuel, 154
Goodman, Benny, 109
Good Neighbor Policy, 26, 54, 78
Gorbachev, Mikhail, 58–59
Gorras Blancas, Las, 75–76
Goya y Lucientes, Francisco José, 150
Grau San Martín, Ramón, 53
Great Depression, 75, 80, 130, 159
Greenblatt, Stephen, 147–48
Greene, Graham, 149
Grito de Aztlán, El, 86
Guadalupe Hidalgo, Treaty of, 18, 62, 72,
    75, 129, 130, 197
Guantánamo Naval Base, 37
Guatemalans, 34, 39, 123, 132, 133
Guayanans, 32
Guerrero, Julio, 155
Guevara, Ernesto "Che," 8, 53, 54, 86, 95
Guillén, Nicholás, 99
Gumilla, José, 149
Gutiérrez, José Angel, 79
Gutiérrez Nájera, Manuel, 72